D1129102

Madame Lalaurie, Mistress of the Haunted House

UNIVERSITY PRESS OF FLORIDA

Florida A&M University, Tallahassee
Florida Atlantic University, Boca Raton
Florida Gulf Coast University, Ft. Myers
Florida International University, Miami
Florida State University, Tallahassee
New College of Florida, Sarasota
University of Central Florida, Orlando
University of Florida, Gainesville
University of North Florida, Jacksonville
University of South Florida, Tampa
University of West Florida, Pensacola

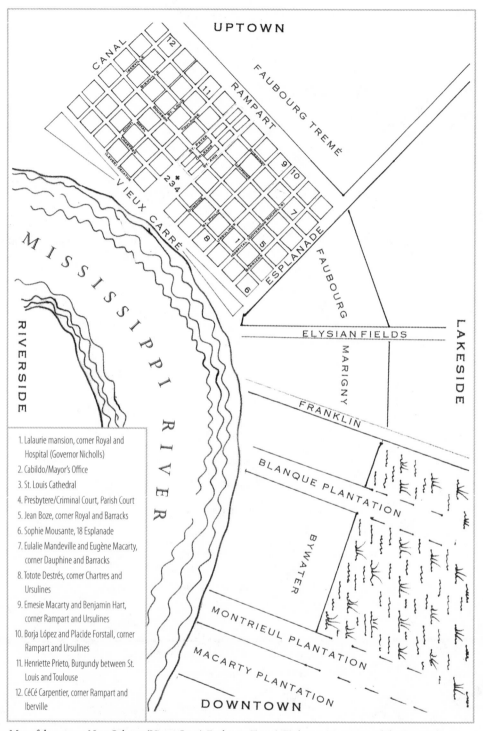

UPTOWN

CANAL

FAUBOURG TREMÉ

RAMPART

VIEUX CARRÉ

ESPLANADE

FAUBOURG

ELYSIAN FIELDS

LAKESIDE

MARIGNY

FRANKLIN

M I S S I S S I P P I   R I V E R

RIVERSIDE

BLANQUE PLANTATION

BYWATER

MONTRIEUL PLANTATION

MACARTY PLANTATION

DOWNTOWN

1. Lalaurie mansion, corner Royal and Hospital (Governor Nicholls)
2. Cabildo/Mayor's Office
3. St. Louis Cathedral
4. Presbytere/Criminal Court, Parish Court
5. Jean Boze, corner Royal and Barracks
6. Sophie Mousante, 18 Esplanade
7. Eulalie Mandeville and Eugène Macarty, corner Dauphine and Barracks
8. Totote Destrés, corner Chartres and Ursulines
9. Emesie Macarty and Benjamin Hart, corner Rampart and Ursulines
10. Borja López and Placide Forstall, corner Rampart and Ursulines
11. Henriette Prieto, Burgundy between St. Louis and Toulouse
12. CéCé Carpentier, corner Rampart and Iberville

Map of downtown New Orleans (Vieux Carré, Faubourg Tremé, Faubourg Marigny, and the Bywater)

MADAME LALAURIE

Mistress of the Haunted House

Carolyn Morrow Long

University Press of Florida
Gainesville/Tallahassee/Tampa/Boca Raton
Pensacola/Orlando/Miami/Jacksonville/Ft. Myers/Sarasota

The cloth edition of this book has been made possible in part through a grant
from the Louisiana Endowment for the Humanities, a state affiliate
of the National Endowment for the Humanities.

Copyright 2012 by Carolyn Morrow Long
All rights reserved
Printed in the United States of America on acid-free paper

First cloth printing, 2012
First paperback printing, 2015

22 21 20 19 18   7 6 5 4 3 2

Library of Congress Cataloging-in-Publication Data
Long, Carolyn Morrow.
Madame Lalaurie, mistress of the haunted house / Carolyn Morrow Long.
p. cm.
Includes bibliographical references and index.
ISBN 978-0-8130-3806-3 (cloth: alk. paper)
ISBN 978-0-8130-6183-2 (pbk.)
1. Lalaurie, Delphine 2. Women murderers—Louisiana—New Orleans—Biography.
3. Slaveholders—Louisiana—New Orleans—Biography. 4. Socialites—Louisiana—New
Orleans—Biography. 5. Slaves—Abuse of—Louisiana—New Orleans—19th century. 6. Torture—
Louisiana—New Orleans—History—19th century. 7. New Orleans (La.)—Biography. I. Title.
HV6248.L1825L66 2012
364.152'3092—dc23   [B]   2011037545

The University Press of Florida is the scholarly publishing agency for the State University System
of Florida, comprising Florida A&M University, Florida Atlantic University, Florida Gulf Coast
University, Florida International University, Florida State University, New College of Florida,
University of Central Florida, University of Florida, University of North Florida, University
of South Florida, and University of West Florida.

University Press of Florida
15 Northwest 15th Street
Gainesville, FL 32611-2079
http://upress.ufl.edu

CONTENTS

PREFACE

New Orleans is famous for its vivid and bizarre characters, around whom a complex tangle of legend, romance, and controversy has evolved. Most notable among these personalities are the gentleman pirate Jean Laffite, the Voudou Queen Marie Laveau, and Madame Delphine Macarty Lalaurie, "Mistress of the Haunted House," an accused slave torturer whose misdeeds were exposed by a fire at her home in 1834.

My purpose in writing this book has been to discover the truth about the stories surrounding Madame Lalaurie. While earlier authors have relied on published sources and their own inventions, I am the first to make extensive use of the archival record to reconstruct the lives of Delphine Macarty Lalaurie and her extended family.[1] I have devoted particular attention to identifying all of her human property, and I have attempted to name the enslaved men, women, and children who were the subjects of her cruelty and to trace the fate of those who survived the fire.

This narrative, like the Mississippi River, meanders at a leisurely pace through twists and bends, and sometimes wanders away from the central plot when an intriguing archival discovery leads into less-traveled tributaries and bayous. It is not only the story of Delphine Macarty Lalaurie, but of her ancestors, her three husbands, her six children, and the whole sprawling and rambunctious Macarty family, white and non-white. These people provide a glimpse into issues and events that affected their lives during the eighteenth and nineteenth centuries: slavery, yellow fever epidemics, interracial cohabitation, intrigues at the Spanish court, the Louisiana Purchase and the ensuing conflict between Creoles and Americans, piracy and smuggling, medicine, Freemasonry, theater and opera, Louisiana civil law, the controversy over integrated public schools, and the rise of racism and segregation during and after Reconstruction. Through Delphine and her family we meet notable personalities who played major or minor roles in this story: the planter Joseph Xavier Delfau de Pontalba, the free colored entrepreneur Eulalie Mandeville de Marigny, Louisiana governor William C. C. Claiborne, the Spanish monk and pastor of St. Louis Cathedral Antonio de Sedella, the pirates Jean and Pierre Laffite, composer and concert pianist Louis Moreau Gottschalk, the brilliant and flashy American attorney John Randolph Grymes, the poet William Cullen Bryant, and the curmudgeonly philanthropist John McDonogh.

Owing to Louisiana's Roman Catholic and civil law heritage, the archival repositories of New Orleans are a treasure unlike any other in the United States. Many valuable resources are available to the researcher of New Orleans history: French and Spanish colonial documents, family papers, nineteenth-century newspapers, city directories, and the United States Decennial Census, but most important are the sacramental registers of the Catholic Church, the acts of the city's notaries, and the records of the lower courts and the state supreme court.

Beginning in 1720, the Church kept meticulous documentation of baptisms, marriages, and funerals that were often very specific about an individual's ancestry, racial mixture, place of birth, legitimacy, and occupation. The Church recorded these sacramental acts not only for white persons but also for free persons of color and slaves. It is therefore possible to find documentation of the rites of passage for Delphine Macarty Lalaurie and her white family, for her relatives who were of mixed African and European ancestry, and—most remarkable of all—for her slaves. Most of the records pertaining to this story will be found in the sacramental registers of St. Louis Cathedral. Sacramental acts for all parishioners, regardless of race, were at first recorded in the same volume, but by 1777 the Church began keeping separate registers for white persons and for free persons of color and slaves. The sacramental registers and the burial books for the St. Louis Cemeteries are now housed at the Archives of the Archdiocese of New Orleans.

French and Spanish civil law required that every important transaction, especially those involving property, be enacted before a notary, and this was continued under the American administration. The Louisiana notary was more like a family lawyer than the notary public with which the average American is familiar. Most eighteenth- and nineteenth-century notarial acts deal with the buying and selling of land and slaves, but the notary also enacted slave manumissions, marriage contracts, acknowledgment of children born outside of marriage, powers of attorney, wills, matters relating to the settlement of a deceased person's estate (called the succession in Louisiana), and various other business agreements. The Notarial Archives Research Center is the repository for millions of acts dating from 1733 to 1970.

Some of New Orleans' early court records have been lost, but those that exist, including civil suits for debts, married women's separation petitions, probate matters, and criminal prosecutions, are available in the City Archives, Louisiana Division, New Orleans Public Library. Cases that went on to the Louisiana Supreme Court are housed in the Louisiana and Special Collections Division at the Earl K. Long Library, University of New Orleans. The cases pertaining to Madame Lalaurie and her kin offer an amazingly intimate glimpse into their private lives.

I searched every available source in New Orleans and elsewhere. In addition to ecclesiastical and civil records, I found unpublished business and personal letters written by Delphine Macarty Lalaurie, her adult children, her husband Dr. Louis Lalaurie, and Lalaurie's father and siblings in the DeLassus–St. Vrain Collection at the Missouri History Museum. I also discovered letters and recollections by other New Orleanians, some published and some not, that shed light on events surrounding the accusations of torture and the fire at the Lalaurie home. The most significant of these are the letters from Jean Boze to his employer Henri de Ste-Gême, now in the Ste-Gême Family Papers at the Historic New Orleans Collection.

Thanks to a grant from the Louisiana Endowment for the Humanities, I was able to hire Jérôme Malhache, a professional researcher and genealogist in Paris, to mine the French archives and send me digital photographs of the records. The information discovered by M. Malhache allowed me to tell, for the first time, what happened to Madame Lalaurie and her family when they fled New Orleans after her offenses were revealed.

Tales of the infamous Madame Lalaurie have become increasingly fanciful and grotesque in the years following the 1834 fire. This book will clarify, confirm, or refute aspects of the legend already in circulation and incorporate significant new information found in archival sources and family letters. But the facts unearthed in church and civil records, and even the personal information gleaned from letters and court cases, can only tell us so much. Some mysteries remain unsolved. My task has been to interpret the evidence, to read between the lines, to pose questions that cannot be answered, to intuit the emotions, motivations, and indeed the sanity of the characters in this account—in other words, to make an educated guess about what *might* have happened. Some readers will wish I had been more imaginative in reconstructing the story, and others will think I have been too speculative. My occasional conjectures are always identified as such, and are never presented as fact.

Following an introduction to the legend of Madame Lalaurie and the Haunted House, the first eight chapters are arranged chronologically, from the arrival of Delphine's ancestors in the Louisiana colony to the fate of her descendants. "The Macartys" discusses Delphine's forebears and her kin. "López y Ángulo" and "Blanque" deal with her first and second marriages and her transformation from a giddy young girl reared on her parents' country plantation into a wealthy and powerful New Orleans socialite. "Lalaurie" looks at Delphine's stormy relationship with her much younger, third husband. "Passive Beings" is devoted to the accusations of cruelty against her and identifies the enslaved men and women who were her property. "The Fire" examines the events of that catastrophic day, using newspaper reports of the time and the narratives of other eyewitnesses. "Exile" uncovers the particulars of Delphine's life in Paris and clarifies the circumstances of her death and burial. In "Denouement" we learn what became of her six children, her grandchildren, and her other relatives. The final chapter, "The Haunted House," traces the actual chain of ownership of her mansion on Royal Street and explores the legends associated with it. In the conclusion, I reiterate the substantial evidence regarding the slave abuse that occurred within the Lalaurie household, and present my own deductions about the cultural and personal factors that enabled and motivated Delphine Macarty Lalaurie to commit this crime. The epilogue, describing the visit of three psychics to the Lalaurie mansion on the 175th anniversary of the fire, is what New Orleanians call *lagniappe*, meaning "a little something extra."

DEFINITION OF TERMS

The word *Creole* has engendered a great deal of confusion. In colonial and antebellum New Orleans, anyone born in the city and its environs (excepting indigenous people) was called a Creole. This was not a racial designation; Creoles could be white, brown, black, or any shade in between. With the rise of virulent racism after the Civil War and Reconstruction, white Creoles feared that outsiders perceived all Creoles to be people of mixed race. They therefore appropriated the designation for themselves, claiming that only native Louisianians of pure white blood, descended from French and Spanish colonists who came directly from Europe, were entitled to call themselves Creoles. Today, most people who identify as Creoles are the biracial descendants of French-speaking, Roman Catholic antebellum free people of color.[1]

In nineteenth-century Louisiana, an individual referred to in English as black or negro was a person of pure African descent and was assumed to be enslaved. A free black or free negro was a free person of unmixed African descent. A free man or woman of color meant a free person of mixed race. Collectively, they were colored or free people of color. These men and women were further classified as free mulatto, of half African and half European ancestry, or free quadroon, of one-quarter African and three-quarters European ancestry. These words were simply descriptors, and were not capitalized. In official documents one finds the abbreviations f.m.c./f.w.c. for free man/woman of color.

Those who are unfamiliar with New Orleans will be confused by the fact that the directions north, south, east, and west have little relevance there. The city's streets follow the twists and bends of the Mississippi River; the only thoroughfare that runs true north-south is Elysian Fields Avenue. Directions are expressed as downtown (down the river), uptown (up the river), riverside (toward the river), and lakeside (toward Lake Pontchartrain). The original settlement, called the Vieux Carré (Old Square) or French Quarter, faces the river's "beautiful crescent" and is bounded by Canal Street on the uptown side, Esplanade Avenue on the downtown side, and Rampart Street on the lakeside. Anything above Canal Street is uptown, and anything below is downtown. During the early decades of the nineteenth century, uptown was mostly the domain of the Americans, and most Creoles and immigrants from France, Spain, and the Caribbean lived downtown. Because the characters in this story were Creoles, they lived downtown. The Macarty plantation was downriver from the Vieux Carré, in the neighborhood now called the Bywater. The "Haunted House" was in the heart of the Vieux Carré, and other Macarty family members and associates also lived in the Vieux Carré or in the neighborhood immediately down the river, the Faubourg Marigny.

INTRODUCTION

Delphine Macarty Lalaurie's precipitous fall from grace occurred on the morning of April 10, 1834, when a fire at her luxurious Royal Street home revealed seven slaves—starved, tortured, and chained—in the upper part of an outbuilding. The nearly helpless bondspeople were carried to the Cabildo (city hall), where they received medical treatment, food, and drink; two thousand citizens came to view the victims. Appalled by what they had seen, the people began to gather around the Lalaurie mansion, expecting the sheriff to arrest the guilty party at any moment. But all remained quiet within the house, and as the day passed and the officers of the law failed to appear, the crowd became increasingly angry. When Madame Lalaurie escaped without punishment, the enraged throng attacked the empty residence. They stripped the interior of its elegant contents and continued their operations on the roof and walls. By the next morning, they had nearly demolished the house. Details of the fire and its aftermath, as reported by eyewitnesses, emerged in the local newspapers during the following week. The account was soon picked up by journals with a national circulation. Madame Lalaurie was reviled as a "monster," a "demon in the shape of a woman," and a "fury escaped from hell."[1]

In 1836, two years after the fire, the English writer Harriet Martineau spent ten days in New Orleans. On a walk through the Vieux Carré,

Undated oil portrait of Delphine Macarty Lalaurie by an unidentified artist, courtesy of John Ellis. For a lady said to have been fond of luxury, her plain hair style, modest dress, and absence of jewelry are surprising. In 1936, the original painting belonged to Corrine and Rathbone DeBuys; its present location is unknown.

Martineau came upon what was left of the Lalaurie mansion. She later wrote in her two-volume memoir, *Retrospect of Western Travel*, that the building "stands, and is meant to stand, in its ruined state. It was the strange sight of its gaping windows and empty walls, in the midst of such a busy street, which excited my wonder, and was the cause of my being first told the story" by friends who were familiar with the catastrophe. Martineau introduced the account of a little enslaved girl, pursued by Madame Lalaurie with whip in hand, from the courtyard, through the house, and out onto the roof, where the child fell to her death. This incident supposedly resulted in a criminal investigation and the confiscation of nine of the Lalaurie slaves. Martineau was also the first to give an account of Madame Lalaurie's escape on the afternoon of the fire. According to *Retrospect of Western Travel*, the lady's enslaved coachman arrived at the door with her carriage, she stepped in, and they flew at a gallop along the road to Lake Pontchartrain, where she boarded a schooner. She eventually escaped to France and "took up her abode in Paris."[2]

In 1851, another foreign visitor, the Swedish writer Fredrika Bremer, visited New Orleans and heard additional recollections of the infamous Madame Lalaurie from local informants. Bremer wrote that the lady's viciousness had "roused her neighbors in arms against her," and brought her to the attention of the authorities. The Lalaurie incident was included in Bremer's travel account, *Homes of the New World*.[3]

The 1834 New Orleans newspaper articles and even the later accounts given to Martineau and Bremer were provided by eyewitnesses. By the late nineteenth century, few people were left alive who had actually experienced the dramatic events at the time of the fire. The popular New Orleans author George Washington Cable included a chapter titled "The Haunted House in Royal Street" in his 1889 collection *Strange True Stories of Louisiana*. Cable drew upon published sources and added some new information provided by his research assistants, New Orleanians J. W. Guthrie and Dora Richards Miller.[4]

After the publication of Cable's *Strange True Stories*, the narrative of Madame Lalaurie and the "Haunted House" passed into the realm of New Orleans legend, growing more fantastic with each retelling. The story was periodically rehashed in newspaper articles of the 1890s, bearing headlines such as "The Haunted House—Its Interesting History and Strange Romance."[5] The local historian Henry Castellanos included a chapter called "A Tale of Slavery Times" in his 1895 collection of vignettes, *New Orleans as It Was*.[6] The "Haunted House" was touted as a tourist attraction in *The Picayune's Guide to New Orleans* for 1897.[7]

During the 1920s, 1930s, and 1940s a movement to rehabilitate the reputation of Delphine Macarty Lalaurie was launched by her descendants and their friends, all members of New Orleans' elite society. The impetus behind this effort came from Corinne Von Maysenburg, wife of the eminent architect Rathbone DeBuys, and Miriam Duggan, wife of the respected pediatrician Dr. Lawrence Richard DeBuys. The DeBuys brothers were great-great-grandsons of Madame Lalaurie.[8]

On November 2, 1924, journalist John P. Coleman contributed to the *New Orleans States* a long and highly inaccurate article titled "Historic New Orleans Mansions—The Famous Haunted House in Royal Street—Tragedy Led to Its Reputation." Relying on information furnished by William Warrington, a friend of the DeBuys family and director of a social service agency that occupied the Lalaurie house at the time, Coleman attempted to justify Madame Lalaurie's actions. He postulated that Delphine's mother had been killed by her own slaves, and that "the crime and its circumstances so preyed upon [the daughter] that she brought to her Royal Street home three suspects—a man, a woman, and a girl. Crazed with grief, she . . . tortured these slaves in the hope of making them confess."[9]

Other New Orleans journalists, influenced by the DeBuys ladies, attempted to refute the legend altogether by portraying Madame Lalaurie as the innocent victim of jealousy and gossip. Meigs Frost's article, "Was Madame Lalaurie of Haunted House Victim of Foul Plot?" appeared in the Sunday magazine section of the *New Orleans Times-Picayune* on February 4, 1934, almost a hundred years after the fire. The whole "smear campaign" against Madame Lalaurie, he opined, resulted from the spite of one man, her neighbor and kinsman Monsieur Montreuil. In reality, wrote Frost, Delphine was the kindest and most gracious of ladies: "Her indulgence of her slaves was told by friends. She would hand her half-empty wine glass at dinner to the slave who waited behind her chair, bidding him graciously to drink it. Her black coachman was fed to sleekness." Frost protested that "the little negress who 'leaped from the roof' fleeing Delphine's whip" was actually "sliding down a curving bannister in play, fell three stories, and was killed on the marble hall-floor."[10]

On August 10, 1936, Corinne DeBuys told Charles Richards of the *New Orleans Morning Tribune* that the reports of Madame Lalaurie's cruelty to her slaves were nothing but "fiction," and claimed that the "false rumors" originated with the lady's husband and were "given momentum by a spurned suitor who lived next door."[11]

Bob Brown, writing for the *New Orleans States* on January 27, 1941, quoted Miriam DeBuys and other family friends who advanced the opinion that Madame Lalaurie "has been unjustly accused and mercilessly victimized." Mrs. DeBuys objected that George Washington Cable had written "The Haunted House in Royal Street" "purely from what he had been told, without attempting to authenticate facts." Cable, she sniffed, "was a novelist, not a historian."[12] The descendants of Madame Lalaurie may have been responsible for the rumor that she had refused to receive Cable owing to his "colored blood," and that he was motivated by spite to publish the story. Cable actually was born in 1844, ten years after Madame Lalaurie fled New Orleans, and was a man of unmixed Caucasian ancestry.[13]

In addition to local newspaper men, popular historians and local-color writers joined the discussion without offering any documentation for their opinions. Grace King, Herman de Bachellé Seebold, and Stanley Clisby Arthur allied themselves with the defenders of Madame Lalaurie, particularly with Miriam DeBuys, who furnished illustrations for their published works. King, author of *Creole Families of New Orleans* (1921), and Seebold, author of *Old Louisiana Plantation Homes and Family Trees* (1941), extolled the outstanding qualities and aristocratic lineage of Delphine Macarty Lalaurie without ever alluding to the fire and the mutilated slaves. In his book *Old New Orleans: A History of the Vieux Carré, its Ancient and Historical Buildings* (1936), Stanley Arthur did give a bare outline of the incident, but went on to say that "like all such tales, [it] has grown in ferocity through its countless retellings and the probabilities are that even the original story of a century ago was a gross exaggeration." Arthur claimed that Madame Lalaurie was a "victim of yellow journalism."[14]

Taking the opposite viewpoint, Lyle Saxon, in *Fabulous New Orleans* (1928), and Herbert Asbury, in *The French Quarter: An Informal History of the New Orleans Underworld* (1936), portrayed Madame Lalaurie as a sadistic monster while embellishing the story of the fire and the tortured slaves.[15]

The newspaper articles of April 1834, the additional details provided by Harriet Martineau and Fredrika Bremer, and the subsequent retelling of the story by George Washington Cable, Henry Castellanos, Lyle Saxon, and Herbert Asbury are grim enough to shock any reader. But Jeanne Delavigne surpassed them all with "The Haunted House of the Rue Royale" in her 1946 *Ghost Stories of Old New Orleans*, adding disgusting details that are obviously the product of her perverted imagination. Delavigne, claiming to have gleaned the information from "old newspaper accounts, interviews, and neighborhood hearsay," described the discovery by those who rushed into the house to fight the fire:

> The men who smashed the garret door saw powerful male slaves, stark naked, chained to the wall, their eyes gouged out, their fingernails pulled off by the roots; others had their joints skinned and festering, great holes in their buttocks where the flesh had been sliced away, their ears hanging by shreds, their lips sewed together, their tongues drawn out and sewed to their chins, severed hands stitched to bellies, legs pulled joint from joint. Female slaves there were, their mouths and ears crammed with ashes and chicken offal and bound tightly; others had been smeared with honey and were a mass of black ants. Intestines were pulled out and knotted around naked waists. There were holes in skulls, where a rough stick had been inserted to stir the brains. Some of the poor creatures were dead, some were unconscious; and a few were still breathing, suffering agonies beyond any power to describe.[16]

Delavigne went on to declare that after Madame Lalaurie fled to France and the house was sold, "workmen . . . began digging up human skeletons from under the house. . . . They were found in all sorts of positions, helter-skelter, barely covered with soil, shreds of fabric still adhering to the bones. . . . Some of the skulls had great holes in them." The new owner of the property, in "an attempt to down the mansion's gruesome reputation," made excuses that the house was built over an earlier burial ground, or that the remains were those of yellow fever victims. The authorities, however, concluded that "they were bodies of the Lalaurie slaves, buried thus in order that their manner of death should not become known."[17] Jeanne Delavigne's sensationalistic fantasy has been repeated almost verbatim—and sometimes made even more shocking—by tour guides, the creators of Web sites, and the writers of books on the paranormal.

Today one of the most popular features of New Orleans tourism is the "ghost" or "haunted history" tour. Tour groups gather day and night before the Lalaurie house at the corner of Royal and Governor Nicholls, listening raptly to the spooky yarns spun by their fantastically costumed leaders. When I took such a tour in March 2008, our guide related that the fire had started during one of the Lalauries' lavish evening parties: "Guests, tables and chairs, the elegant dinner, and the musicians were simply moved out into the street, and the celebration continued. Meanwhile, Madame Lalaurie had slipped away in her carriage. When the fire brigade arrived," said the tour guide, "they found the cook chained to the stove,

"Haunted History" tour guide Paul Chasse in front of the Lalaurie mansion, March 20, 2008. Chasse died in his sleep six months later. (Photograph by the author.)

and thirteen slaves in the attic, of which five were already dead and seven barely alive." The sight caused the firefighters to "run into the street and vomit." The guide continued that "when a local doctor bought and renovated the Lalaurie mansion in the later twentieth century, many skeletons were found under the floorboards, which had fingernail scratches on the underside, indicating that the people had been buried alive."[18]

Variations on the Lalaurie legend have appeared in numerous publications in the late twentieth and early twenty-first centuries. "Madame Delphine Lalaurie, Murderer" is among the "female poisoners, kidnappers, thieves, extortionists, terrorists, swindlers, and spies" discussed in J. R. Nash's *Look for the Woman* (1981). A chapter in Randall Floyd's *More Great Southern Mysteries* (1990) is titled "The Cruel Mistress of Royal Street." *The Book of Secrets* by Lloyd Bradley (2005) includes a short entry on "New Orleans's Secret Burial Pit."[19]

The graphic novel *Nightmares and Fairytales: 1140 Rue Royale* (2007), written by Serena Valentino and illustrated by "Crab Scrambly," offers an interesting twist on the story of the "Haunted House." In the late nineteenth century a young girl called Rebecca and her elderly Aunt Victoria return from France to occupy the mansion that the aunt has recently purchased. Soon the ghosts of the tortured slaves begin to attack the older lady, but Rebecca is protected by a benign spirit. In a surprise ending, Aunt Victoria turns out to be Delphine Macarty Lalaurie, and her victims at last have their revenge.[20]

A Web search for "Madame Lalaurie" yields nearly 17,000 hits. Sites such as "Ghost Source," "Haunted New Orleans," and "Mistress of Death" adhere to the lurid story concocted by Jeanne Delavigne in 1946, while adding even more nauseating details about victims "strapped to makeshift operating tables" and "confined in cages" surrounded by buckets full of "human heads, body parts, and organs." Some theorize that Delphine's husband, Dr. Lalaurie, was conducting medical experiments on the slaves.[21] On the Web site "Madame Delphine Lalaurie—Crucible of Horror on Royal Street," one finds the suggestion that Delphine had an intimate friendship with the "infamous Voodoo Queen, Marie Laveau. . . . It is said that under Laveau's tutelage, Madame Lalaurie began to act upon her latent interest in the occult, learning the secrets of voodoo and witchcraft at the hands of a mighty mistress of the craft."[22] Another Web site claims that Madame Lalaurie's "abusive actions were [carried out] in retaliation against the black servant who had molested one of her daughters."[23]

"What Do You Want of Me?" In Serena Valentino's 2007 graphic novel *Nightmares and Fairytales: 1140 Rue Royale*, Madame Lalaurie returns from France to reclaim her home in New Orleans and is attacked by the ghosts of the tortured slaves. (Collection of the author.)

Several sensationalistic videos about Madame Lalaurie and the "Haunted House," including a tour guide's spiel, have been posted on YouTube.[24]

Delphine Macarty Lalaurie is probably best known to present-day readers as a character in Barbara Hambly's 1998 historical mystery novel, *Fever Season*. In contrast to the overblown productions quoted above, *Fever Season* is written with skill and subtlety. The story, with some variations, follows the accounts from the 1834 newspapers and the works of Harriet Martineau, Fredrika Bremer, George Washington Cable, and Henry Castellanos. Hambly's book is particularly notable for the author's depiction of Madame Lalaurie's physical appearance and her character. Delphine is "glowing with energy, with intelligence, with strength . . . a tall woman, imperially straight. . . . Her voice was a lovely mezzo-soprano . . . her eyes were large, coffee dark, and brilliant," but her face was "gouged with fine lines . . . more than simple weariness could account for." Her dress was always impeccable, severe but fashionable. In the novel, we first glimpse Madame Lalaurie's tyrannical nature when she bullies and humiliates her daughters during their piano lesson. We see a far more complex side when she volunteers as a nurse during a yellow fever and cholera epidemic. Holding a dying man who is befouled by his own bodily fluids, her face takes on "a look of holy ecstasy . . . an expression of deep, intense pity . . . an inward look, yearning, longing . . . as if she knelt in meditation at the Stations of the Cross." She remains detached from the filth and stink around her, "a woman whom no disarray or dishevelment could touch." She also has no sense of wrongdoing. Even during the fire, as the starved and tortured slaves are being carried out of the building and the crowd reacts with shock and horror, Madame Lalaurie stands by, "calm as always, perfect as always, as if none of this had anything to do with her."[25]

In the chapters that follow, we will investigate how closely the real Delphine Macarty Lalaurie adheres to the legend created by journalists, popular historians, and writers of fiction.

1

THE MACARTYS

The woman who has become infamous as the "Mistress of the Haunted House" was born Marie Delphine Macarty. Thanks to the European civil law by which Louisiana was, and still is, governed, her legal surname remained Macarty. She never lost her personal identity, as was the case for married women in the colonies/states governed by English common law. With each of her three marriages, she was designated in official documents as Delphine Macarty, first as wife of López y Ángulo; then as wife of Blanque; and finally as wife of Lalaurie. After becoming Madame Lalaurie, she signed her name "Lalaurie née Macarty."

Delphine was a member of the large, wealthy, and socially powerful Macarty clan, which included military officers, planters, and merchants. Both male and female relatives owned and managed extensive real estate and numerous slaves, and were connected by marriage to other influential families. As their surname indicates, the Macartys originated in Ireland. Legend says that the family patriarch, Maccarthey-Mactaig, fled to France to escape the political and religious tyranny imposed by England's monarchs. He is believed to have settled in the French province of Languedoc, where he entered the military service of the French king. Two of his descendants, Jean Jacques and Barthélémy Daniel (Delphine's grandfather), immigrated to Louisiana in the early years of the colony.[1] During their time in France the family name had become gallicized as "de Macarty" or "de Macarti," pronounced "Ma-car-TEE." By the nineteenth century the family name was simply rendered as "Macarty."

The French settlement of La Nouvelle Orléans was in its infancy when Jean Jacques and Barthélémy Daniel de Macarty settled there. In 1718, the Canadian explorers Pierre Le Moyne, Sieur de Iberville, and his younger brother Jean Baptiste Le Moyne, Sieur de Bienville, had selected a location about one hundred miles from the mouth of the Mississippi, where a sharp bend in the river comes within five miles of the vast lake the French called Pontchartrain. There, on the slender crescent of high ground along the river, they established the capitol of the Louisiana colony. French military engineers laid out the squares of the original Vieux Carré in a perfect grid pattern, with the parish church of St. Louis and the public square and military parade ground front and center facing the river.

New Orleans in those early years was little more than a collection of shacks surrounded by rough wooden ramparts, and outside this barrier lay a dense, swampy wilderness. When the Macartys arrived, the town and surrounding area had a population of around 4,800, consisting of a small number of French government functionaries and members of religious orders, 200 soldiers and military officers, approximately 900 white settlers and indentured servants, 3,659 enslaved Africans, and some indigenous Indians and free blacks.[2]

Jean Jacques and Barthélémy Daniel de Macarty were both distinguished officers in the French navy, and both were accorded the title of Chevalier of the Royal and Military Order of St. Louis. Barthélémy Daniel held the rank of major of engineers, and most of his career was spent in various leadership positions in the French-controlled Illinois Territory.[3] Despite his long absences from home, Barthélémy Daniel de Macarty and his wife Françoise Hélène Pellerin produced eleven children, one of whom was Delphine's father, Louis Barthélémy.

In 1763 the Louisiana colony was transferred from French to Spanish rule. The newly appointed Spanish governor, Antonio de Ulloa, lacked the will and the resources to assume leadership, and French merchants, planters, and officials finally banished him from the colony. In 1769, the Spanish crown sent the Irish mercenary Alejandro O'Reilly to New Orleans with a contingent of 2,100 troops to impose control. Upon arrival O'Reilly assumed the position of captain-general and governor of Louisiana. The rebel leaders were executed by firing squad, and their co-conspirators were imprisoned for eighteen months and permanently exiled.[4]

The Macartys were not involved in the coup against the Spanish, and in fact they flourished under the Spanish regime while retaining their French language and culture. Barthélémy Daniel de Macarty returned from the Illinois Territory and established a plantation on the Mississippi River below New Orleans. The Spanish censuses of 1763 and 1770 show that he lived with his wife, children, slaves, and livestock on a plantation of 205 French arpents, or 172 acres.[5] Barthélémy Daniel died suddenly on February 14, 1781, without leaving a will. As required by Spanish civil law, his estate was divided equally among his surviving children.[6]

As a young man, Delphine's father, Louis Barthélémy de Macarty, also pursued a military career and was knighted a Chevalier of the Royal and Military Order of St. Louis. In 1776 he married Marie Jeanne Lerable, the widow of Charles Lecomte, a French merchant and ship captain. Although Louis Barthélémy and Marie Jeanne enacted their marriage contract before a notary, the record of their wedding is missing from the church's sacramental register.[7]

The first child of Louis Barthélémy de Macarty and Marie Jeanne Lerable was also named Louis Barthélémy, born in 1783. In later years the elder Macarty signed his name "Louis Chevalier Macarty" to distinguish himself from his son. Marie Delphine was born on March 19, 1787. Her baptismal record, which was not entered into the sacramental register until December 26, 1793, states that she had been baptized privately at an earlier date, a common practice when an infant was considered to be in danger of death.[8]

Delphine's mother, a wealthy widow, had brought a significant fortune to her marriage with the Chevalier Louis Barthélémy de Macarty: cash, furniture, horses and mules, slaves, and an indigo plantation fronting the Mississippi River below New Orleans. In the 1780s and 1790s, Macarty began adding to his wife's landholdings. In 1785 he bought a another plantation on the river, including a large house with galleries, a garden with ornamental trees, a hospital, a fully equipped sawmill, four cabins, a chicken coop, twenty-four slaves with various skills, eight oxen, twelve cows, and two bulls. In 1794, Macarty bought two adjacent parcels of land with buildings.[9] Altogether the Macartys now possessed a plantation of about 1,344 acres roughly between today's Bartholomew and Independence Streets backed by what is now St. Claude Avenue. By this time the Chevalier de Macarty, like other Louisiana planters, would have taken up the cultivation of sugar and cotton after indigo was attacked by an infestation of worms.

Later maps created by the surveyors Jacques Tanesse (1815) and Barthélémy Lafon (1816) show the Macarty plantation, with a cluster of buildings
near the river, extending back into the cypress swamp. Just upriver toward
the town was the plantation of the Montreuil family, a name that will
prove significant to the story of Madame Lalaurie.[10] The Macartys' main
residence would have been a typical Louisiana French colonial manor
house. Such dwellings usually had a raised basement meant to survive

"Plan of the City and Suburbs of New Orleans from an actual survey made in 1815 by
Jacques Tanesse." The "Habitation Makarty" is seen in the lower right corner, just below the
"Habitation Montreuil" and the "Fortification Montreuil, ordounce par le General Jackson,"
that was erected during the Battle of New Orleans. Further up the river is the plantation of
Mr J^n Blanque, Delphine's second husband. (New Orleans 1817, accession no. 1971.4, courtesy
of The Historic New Orleans Collection.)

floods; the family lived on a main floor with living and sleeping rooms that opened onto breezy galleries, and a half story with dormer windows was located under the ample hipped roof. The kitchen and quarters for the domestic servants would have been in an attached service wing or a separate building, and other functional outbuildings and cabins for the field hands would have been further from the house.[11]

·

No personal letters of the Chevalier de Macarty or Madame Marie Jeanne Lerable de Macarty have come to light. Some idea of the milieu in which they lived and their daughter Delphine grew up can be gleaned from the 1796 letters of Macarty family friend and kinsman-by-marriage Joseph Xavier Delfau de Pontalba.[12]

During that year, Pontalba kept a daily letter journal addressed to his wife Jeanne Louise, Delphine's older cousin.[13] Jeanne Louise, with their young son Célestin, had traveled to Spain to assist her aunt Céleste Elénore de Macarty, the widow of former Louisiana governor Estebán Miró. During Jeanne Louise's absence the unhappy husband devoted considerable space to moaning over his loneliness and fretting about the safety of his wife and son, but he also included news of the Macartys, with whom he socialized frequently.

Pontalba often mentioned Delphine's parents, particularly her vivacious and frolicsome mother. He was invited to several summertime parties at the Macarty plantation, at which all present comported themselves in a decidedly indecorous manner. One such event was characterized by "much noise, many kisses, races, romping" and a quarrel over who would control the card tables. At a bathing party, Madame de Macarty and the other women went swimming in a canal attached to the plantation sawmill, into which they would "plunge, head and all." In late July, there was another large bathing party at the Macartys.' This, observed Pontalba, would be the last of the season because the water in the canal was so low that "the ladies must have bathed in the mud." He noted the participation of the "master of the house," the Chevalier Louis Barthélémy de Macarty, on this occasion.[14] In none of his letters does Pontalba mention the two Macarty children, Delphine, age nine, and Louis Barthélémy, age thirteen, but one supposes that they were somewhere in the background at these gatherings of family and friends.

Life in late eighteenth-century New Orleans was not all frivolity. The populace was gripped by the fear of slave insurrection, and these concerns must have been especially real to Pontalba and his wife. In 1771 Jeanne Louise's father, Jean Baptiste Césaire le Breton (Delphine's uncle by marriage), was murdered by slaves on his upriver plantation in what is now the Carrollton neighborhood. Awakened by a blaze in the shed adjacent to the kitchen, le Breton stepped out onto the gallery to direct the men who were extinguishing the fire, and was shot dead. The next day the Spanish governor conducted an inquiry. Two slaves, Temba and Mirliton, confessed after being tortured on the rack. They were sentenced "to be dragged from the tail of a pack-horse with a . . . halter tied to the neck, feet, and hands, the town crier to go before announcing the crime they have committed. They must pass through the accustomed streets to the gallows where they will be hanged until dead." A further indignity was reserved for Temba, whose body was "to remain on the gibbet . . . until consumed." His hands were "to be cut off and nailed up on the public road." Three other slaves, including Temba's woman Mariana, were convicted as accomplices to the le Breton murder. They received 100 to 200 lashes, their ears were cut off, and one man was "tarred and feathered and mounted on a pack-beast."[15]

A massive slave revolt in the French colony of Saint-Domingue began in 1791, when Delphine Macarty was four years old, and was still ongoing in 1796, at the time of Pontalba's letters. What had begun as an isolated outbreak on the sugar plantations near Cap Français, in the northern part of the country, had escalated into a full-scale war. An associate of Pontalba's, newly arrived from the island, wrote that "the negroes are absolute masters there; all the principal positions are held by them, and there are at Cap Français only twenty to forty whites, who are treated in a worse manner than the negroes had been at any time during slavery. It seems that they aspire to be independent of white people, even of the French Republic." Pontalba commented that there was "no market at all for slaves" in Louisiana because of the "sense of uncertainty" and fear that prevailed at the time.[16]

The fighting and political turmoil in Saint-Domingue lasted for thirteen years as slaves and free mulattos fought for the abolition of slavery and the equality of all people, regardless of color or former status. Although slavery had been outlawed by the French Republic in 1794, Napoleon Bonaparte, pressured by those who had formerly profited from it, resolved to reinstate slave labor in the French colonies. He sent his brother-in-law, General Charles Victor Emmanuel Leclerc, along with

20,000 troops, to put down the rebellion once and for all. "Rid us of these gilded Africans," wrote Napoleon to Leclerc, "and we shall have nothing more to wish." Leclerc's expedition arrived at Cap Français in early 1802; it was ultimately defeated by the skill and ferocity of the black and mulatto insurgents, by lack of money and supplies, by the mountainous terrain of the island, and by yellow fever. This realization of every slaveholder's nightmare lasted until 1804, resulting in the creation of the Republic of Haiti.[17]

Joseph de Pontalba, the Macartys, and their neighbors had good reason to be nervous. In July 1791, an abortive uprising involving Africans of the Mina nation had occurred at Pointe Coupée, 150 miles upriver from New Orleans. Pontalba referred to this incident in a letter to his wife, recalling the time "when our situation in this colony was so critical [that] we did not go to bed without being armed to the teeth; often then I would go to sleep in the midst of the most sinister reflections, thinking of the baleful calamities of Saint-Domingue and the germ of insurrection which had only too well spread among our own slaves. I often reflected then . . . on the . . . means that I should employ to save you and our son if we should be attacked."[18]

In 1795, a new threat arose as slaves at Pointe Coupée again plotted an insurrection, this time to begin at the plantation of Julian Poydras. A large number of slaves and a few white sympathizers drew inspiration from the revolution that was raging in Saint-Domingue. Spanish governor Carondelet was informed of the plot by an anonymous letter and the conspirators were apprehended. When the would-be rebels were eventually tried, fifty-seven slaves and three local whites were convicted. In the end, thirty-one of the enslaved conspirators were flogged and sentenced to hard labor, the three white men were deported and sentenced to hard labor, and twenty-three slaves were hung and their severed heads displayed on pikes along the Mississippi River from Pointe Coupée to New Orleans.[19]

The Spanish Codigo Negro (Black Code) was more liberal than the Code Noir in effect during the French colonial period. Enslaved persons had more autonomy under Spanish law, and skilled men and women could hire themselves out for wages or market their crafts or produce, using their earnings to purchase their own liberty. Many slave owners objected to these humane provisions, and the Cabildo, composed of twelve prominent citizens who served as city councilmen and judges, protested to the governor that implementation of the new law would be impractical.

Considerable time was spent discussing the maroons or "savage negroes" who had escaped to the cypress swamps and the "insubordination of the . . . slaves and the crimes committed by them daily, without any fear of punishment."[20]

In his 1796 letters to his wife, Joseph de Pontalba revealed his ambivalence toward his own slaves. His attitude of paternalism coupled with petty tyranny was probably shared by his relatives and neighbors, including the Macartys. He did not particularly fear his bondspeople, but he complained of their illnesses and malingering and spoke of them as troublesome children for whom he was responsible. He worked alongside the men in the vegetable garden and employed the women as domestics or sent them out to sell produce and milk in New Orleans. He could at times be cruel. He casually mentioned that he had his manservant Augustin whipped because he was repeatedly late in bringing his breakfast, and complained of the inconvenience when Augustin subsequently ran away. The slave Jeannete lost or spent some of the money collected from her vending duties; she also ran away, and was consigned to the stocks when she was returned by a neighbor. Lucille, another vendor, was put in the stocks because she failed to sell the expected quantity of milk.[21]

In addition to the pervasive anxiety about slave rebellion, another threat that constantly hovered over the population was lingering sickness or sudden death from the many tropical fevers that plagued the region. During the summer and fall of 1796, New Orleans was experiencing its first serious yellow fever epidemic. The symptoms were a yellow or bronze discoloration of the skin and regurgitation of blackened, partially digested blood caused by internal hemorrhaging—thus the nicknames "Yellow Jack," "Bronze John," and "the black vomit." Professional medical men treated sufferers with extreme measures involving blood-letting, sweating, and administration of harsh drugs. Ipecac (Ipecacuanha root from Brazil) induced vomiting; jalap (Ipomoea jalapa root from Mexico) and calomel (mercurous chloride) purged the bowels. These "cures" probably killed as many people as the fever.[22]

Pontalba wrote at length of the ravages of the disease among his friends and relatives. But even under these dire circumstances, members of the elite, including the governor, slept over at each other's country plantations, diverting themselves with parties, pranks, horse races, and card games such as bourré and coq. Delphine's mother, Marie Jeanne Lerable de Macarty, continued in her role as hostess while keeping close watch over her children. Pontalba noted that he had spent the night at the Macarty plantation, and that the ladies had stolen the clothes and shoes of all the male guests, forcing them to go home barefoot in their nightshirts. That evening one of Pontalba's closest friends died of the fever.[23] The epidemic finally ended with the onset of cold weather.

·

In his letters, Joseph de Pontalba never mentioned the practice, common among his white male associates, of cohabitation with women of color. The development of a population of biracial free people of color (*gens de couleur libres*) began in the earliest days of the Louisiana colony. Although both Jean Jacques and Barthélémy Daniel de Macarty succeeded in finding wives, Louisiana suffered from a severe shortage of marriageable white women during its early years. As a result, there were frequent sexual encounters and long-term domestic partnerships between white men and enslaved or free women of color, and many children of mixed race were born of these unions. The practice continued even when the ratio of white women to white men became more equal, and it was still ongoing after Louisiana became part of the United States.[24] Legally, a women involved in such a relationship was called a concubine, but the French-speaking Creoles often used the term *ménagère* (housekeeper) or *plaçée* (from the French verb *placer*—meaning to place under a man's protection). A search of the archival record turns up numerous persons of mixed race who were the concubines and natural children of Delphine Macarty's kinsmen.

Delphine's uncle Eugène Théodore de Macarty, her cousins Jean Baptiste Barthélémy and Augustin de Macarty, and her father, the Chevalier Louis Barthélémy de Macarty, all openly cohabited with one or more free women of color. An exception is Delphine's brother, Louis Barthélémy Macarty, who never married but had a domestic relationship and fathered a child with a white woman. In almost every case, the Macarty men acknowledged the offspring of these liaisons by allowing their names to be included in the baptismal record or signing the register, by going before a notary to claim paternity, or by remembering their concubines and children in their wills. Both scholarly and non-scholarly writers have theorized that Delphine's anger and mortification over this situation motivated her to torture her slaves.[25] This justifies a closer look at the non-white branch of the Macarty family.

Delphine's uncle Eugène de Macarty had a fifty-four-year relationship with the free woman of color Eulalie Mandeville de Marigny. Eulalie was the natural daughter of an enslaved woman named Jeanne Louise with "that magnificent and courtly citizen," Count Pierre Philippe Mandeville de Marigny.[26] The Mandeville de Marignys, like the Macartys, were major property owners and were considered to be among the most distinguished families in Louisiana. The Faubourg Marigny, an early nineteenth-century neighborhood just below the Vieux Carré, was subdivided from the Marigny plantation. In 1779, five-year-old Eulalie, referred to as "a little mulatto girl" (una mulatita), was freed by her paternal grandfather for the "good services received from her mother" and for "the love and affection I have for one born in my household."[27] Eulalie was raised as a member of the family in her grandparents' home, and was treated as a sister by her father's legitimate children, Bernard and Céleste de Marigny.[28]

Eulalie Mandeville received from her father several thousand dollars, slaves, cattle, and a tract of land in St. Bernard Parish, and with these resources she established a dairy. Eulalie allowed Eugène de Macarty to lease her land for cutting timber and raising vegetables, which he sold in New Orleans. By at least 1793 Eulalie and Eugène had formed what proved to be a loving and highly successful partnership.[29] Their seven quadroon children were born between 1794 and 1815.[30]

In 1808 the couple moved from St. Bernard Parish to a large cottage on the corner of Dauphine and Barracks Streets in the Vieux Carré.[31] From this home Eulalie conducted a lucrative retail dry goods business, using her own female slaves and hiring free women of color as door-to-door vendors to sell fabrics, Madras kerchiefs, ribbons, and such. She was reputed to be a person of extraordinary energy and business acumen, described as "remarkably industrious," and "well looked upon by many ladies." Eulalie turned over the profits from her mercantile efforts to Eugène de Macarty, a professional broker, who managed her business and loaned the money to other New Orleanians at high interest. Eugène used his own funds to finance the education of their children and establish the sons in commerce.[32]

Despite his lifelong conjugal and business partnership with Eulalie Mandeville, Eugène de Macarty also had children with two other free women of color. Between 1810 and 1823 he fathered five children with Marie Jeanne "Totote" Destrés (also spelled Detré, Destryes, Detree, and Destreez), a free quadroon from Croix-des-Bouquets on the island of Saint-Domingue.[33] He also had a son, born around 1817, with the free woman of color Helöise Croy, a native of Cap Français, Saint-Domingue.[34]

Delphine's cousin Jean Baptiste Barthélémy de Macarty was the father of five children, born between 1797 and 1807, with the free quadroon Henriette Prieto.[35] He later formed a relationship with another free quadroon, Magdeleine "CéCé" Carpentier, a native of Port-au-Prince. Macarty had two sons with CéCé, born in 1813 and 1815.[36]

Delphine's cousin Augustin François de Macarty, mayor of New Orleans from 1815 to 1820, also cohabited with several free women of color. He fathered three children with two earlier partners, and by 1799 he had entered into a long-term relationship with Céleste Perrault, with whom he had a son. Delphine Macarty stood as godmother at this child's baptism.[37] Unlike the other Macarty men, Augustin never publicly acknowledged his children.

After—or perhaps before—the death of his wife in 1807, Delphine's father formed a liaison with the free quadroon Sophie Mousante. In 1815 Sophie gave birth to a daughter named Delphine Emesie Macarty. Emesie's St. Louis Cathedral baptismal record describes the child as "a free girl of mixed race" (*una niña mestiva libre*), natural daughter of Sophie Mousante. The baptismal entry originally specified the father as "unknown," but this was crossed out and "Dⁿ Luis Chevalier Macarty" inserted above. The godparents were Macarty's legitimate children, Delphine and Louis Barthélémy.[38]

.

The historian Charles Gayarré (born in 1805) had actually known Delphine's father and brother. In 1890 Gayarré contributed a recollection of Macarty *père* and *fils* to Harper's New Monthly Magazine. The Chevalier de Macarty, wrote Gayarré, "continued to wear, until the last day of his existence, a powdered head and a queue of the old regime." Gayarré went on to relate that every afternoon "this aged gentleman" arrived in his carriage at Hewlett's Exchange at Chartres and St. Louis Streets, where he "appropriated for his special use the same corner and the same arm-chair, holding converse with a few friends of congenial habits and thoughts, passing with them in successive review all the visitors of the establishment as they went in or out, and commenting on each one of those who were of sufficient importance to be noticed."

Gayarré also included a description of the Macarty plantation house, which the elderly Chevalier de Macarty shared with his son Louis Barthélémy: it was "a spacious two-story dwelling, after the fashion of the old

Table 1. The Macarty family in Louisiana

First generation (Delphine's grandfather and great-uncle)

Barthélémy Daniel de Macarty married Françoise Hélène Pellerin

Legitimate children: Jeanne Françoise, Jean Baptiste, Louis Barthélémy, Françoise Brigitte, Marie Françoise, Marie Catherine Adelaide, Céleste Elénore, Louise, Marie Marthé called Manette, Eugène Théodore, and Nicolas Théodore

Jean Jacques de Macarty married Françoise Barbe de Trépagnier

Legitimate children: Elizabeth, Catherine Ursule, Jeanne, Jean Baptiste, and Augustin Guillaume

Second generation (Delphine's father, aunts, and uncles)

Jeanne Françoise de Macarty married Jean Baptiste Césaire le Breton

Legitimate daughter: Jeanne Louise, wife of Joseph Xavier Delfau de Pontalba

Jean Baptiste de Macarty married Charlotte Fazende

Legitimate children: Jean Baptiste Barthélémy and Céleste, wife of Paul Lanusse
Natural son: Théophile with his concubine Rosette Beaulieu, f.w.c.

Céleste Elénore de Macarty married Governor Esteban Miró

The Chevalier Louis Barthélémy de Macarty married Marie Jeanne Lerable, Widow Leconte

Legitimate children: Louis Barthélémy and Marie Delphine
Natural daughter: Delphine Emesie Macarty with his concubine Sophie Mousante, f.w.c.

Marie Marthé, called Manette, married François Robert Gauthier Montreuil

Legitimate children: Barthélémy, Théodule, Desirée, and Elmire

Eugène Théodore Macarty, never married

Natural children: Emelitte, Théophile, Isidore Barthélémy, Eulalie, Pierre Villarceaux, Bernard, and Eugène Jr. with his concubine Eulalie Mandeville, f.w.c.
Natural children: Theodore, Marie, Françoise, Eugène, and Rose Eugènia with his concubine Totote Destrés, f.w.c.
Natural son: Eugène Victor with his concubine Helöise Croy, f.w.c.

Augustin Guillaume Macarty married Marie Jeanne Chauvin Delery

Legitimate son: Augustin François Macarty

Third generation (Delphine, her brother, and her cousins)

Jean Baptiste Barthélémy Macarty, never married

Natural children: Céleste, Dorsin, Lucine, Drauzin, and Adele with his concubine Henriette Prieto, f.w.c.
Natural children: Armand and Gustave with his concubine Madeleine "CéCé" Carpentier, f.w.c.

Louis Barthélémy Macarty, never married

Natural daughter: Louise with his white concubine Adelaide Eugenie Gomez

Marie Delphine Macarty, married Ramon López y Ángulo (1800), Jean Blanque (1807), and Louis Lalaurie (1828)

> *Legitimate children: Marie Delphine Francisca Borja López y Ángulo; Pauline, Laure, Jeanne, and Paulin Blanque; and Jean Louis Lalaurie*

Augustin François Macarty, never married

> *Natural daughter: Philonise with his concubine Sanitté Rivére, f.w.c.*
> *Natural daughters: Josephine and Bridgette with his concubine Victoria Wiltz, f.w.c.*
> *Natural son: Patrice with his concubine Céleste Perrault, f.w.c.*

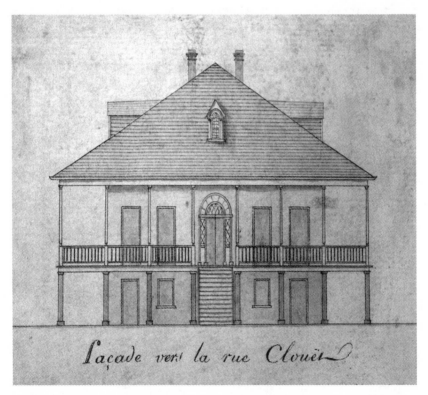

Detail of manor house on Clouet Street between Burgundy and Dauphine. This dwelling, located near the Macarty plantation, was probably similar to the Macarty house. Both have now been demolished. (*Façade vers la rue Clouët*, Plan de 8 lots de terre situés au Faubourg Washington, Municipalité no. 3, May 24, 1845, J. A. d'Hemecourt, Plan Book 21, folio 28. Courtesy of the Notarial Archives Research Center.)

colonial or creole homes, with large open . . . galleries running along every side of the edifice, and supported by massive brick pillars. It was divided in the centre by a broad hall. On the left of this hall the apartments were exclusively occupied by the father, and on the right by the son. . . . When so disposed, they reciprocally invited each other in turn to breakfast or dinner. They continued to live with the same formality until the senior Macarty departed this life [in 1824]."[39] Gayarré, of course, neglected to mention that both men had concubines, and that both father and son had produced children with their respective partners.

·

The Macartys were people of their times—a numerous, acquisitive, and far from straight-laced clan. Although life had become somewhat more stable by the later eighteenth century than it was in the early years when Jean Jacques and Barthélémy Daniel de Macarty first arrived, a frontier mentality still prevailed. Lives and fortunes were uncertain owing to the vagaries of plantation agriculture, the constant fear of slave insurrections, and the recurring epidemics for which there was no known cause or cure. Despite these obstacles, Delphine's parents and other relatives amassed land and slaves and numbered among the aristocracy of what would become Orleans Parish. Several of the Macarty men unashamedly broke the law and crossed racial boundaries to produce a line of prosperous free people of color. This is the family and the community in which Marie Delphine Macarty grew up and became a young woman.

2

LÓPEZ Y ÁNGULO

In 1800, when Louisiana was still a Spanish colony, Delphine Macarty married Ramon López y Ángulo de la Candelaria. She was barely fourteen years old and he was a thirty-five-year-old widower. López y Ángulo, a native of the Galician port city of La Coruña, Spain, had arrived in Louisiana in 1799 to take the position of intendant. This officer of the Spanish Crown, who was second in command to the governor, served as the representative of the royal treasury and had jurisdiction in matters of police, justice, and war. Five years later, López died under peculiar circumstances and Delphine gave birth to the couple's only child.

Grace King and Stanley Clisby Arthur spun romantic yarns about the events that left Delphine a young widow. These stories, like much of the material used by King, Arthur, and other writers who sought to defend Delphine's reputation in the 1920s and 1930s, might have originated with family members such as Corinne and Miriam DeBuys.

Grace King wrote, in *Creole Families of New Orleans*, that Ramon López y Ángulo had fallen into disfavor with the Spanish government for unexplained reasons and had been sentenced to an unspecified punishment. Delphine had sailed for Spain "to solicit the protection of the Queen of Spain [Maria Luisa] for her husband." The queen allegedly saw the young woman kneeling in the garden where she took her morning walk: "Her long black hair was unbound and hanging about her shoulders, her lovely eyes raised in supplication. The queen stopped at sight of her, so young and so beautiful, and approached her with the words: 'Your petition, whatever it is, is granted.'"[1]

Stanley Arthur told a similar tale in *Old Families of Louisiana*: Delphine had been "returning from Spain, where she had gone to successfully plead with the king to save her husband from military punishment." Her daughter, according to this account, was born on shipboard, but López had died in Havana before she was able to rejoin him. A different version appeared in Arthur's later book *Old New Orleans*. Here he declared that Ramon López y Ángulo had been "recalled to the court of Spain . . . [where] the young Spanish officer was to take his place . . . as befitting his new position. . . . While in Havana, en route to Madrid, Don Ramon suddenly died and a few days later his daughter was born in the Cuban city."[2]

John S. Kendall, in his 1934 *Louisiana Historical Quarterly* article "Old New Orleans Houses," related that "as a consequence of having married without permission from the king," López y Ángulo was recalled to Spain to "give an accounting of himself." Kendall scoffed at this "curious story" from an unnamed source. "What," he asked sarcastically, "do you suppose the king cared about [López y Ángulo's] marriage?"[3]

The facts regarding Delphine's first husband emerge from the records of the Spanish colonial government, the Archivo General de Indias, which includes the Papeles Procedentes de la Isla de Cuba and the Audiencia de Santo Domingo. Here we learn that what Kendall dismissed as a "curious story" was actually true.[4]

Before coming to Louisiana, López y Ángulo had served for eight years in the Spanish diplomatic service at Copenhagen and the Hague, and for another six years as undersecretary in the Ministry of Foreign Affairs at Madrid. Evidently his performance was considered satisfactory, since he was inducted into the prestigious Royal Order of Carlos III. During this stage of his career he was married to Francisca Borja Enderis. In 1799 López was appointed to the intendancy of Louisiana and West Florida, replacing Juan Ventura Morales. Far from considering this a promotion, López felt that he was being sent into exile.[5]

Don Mariano Luis de Urquijo, chief minister to King Carlos IV, wrote to López y Ángulo on May 3, 1799, ordering the newly appointed intendant to travel from Madrid to the port of La Coruña. From there he was scheduled to depart for Louisiana on the mail boat *El Rey*. Several months and many letters were devoted to haggling about the travel arrangements. A dispatch from Miguel Cayetano Soler, secretary of state, licensed López y Ángulo, his wife, and four servants, plus their "equipage," to embark for his new post, and they set sail on July 7, 1799.[6]

The voyage, undertaken at what López called "the worst season of the year," was a disaster. As he wrote to Soler, by the time they reached Havana his entire party was sick owing to "a trip made so precipitously and with so many harassments and misfortunes." In late October, López, overwhelmed with grief, confided to Soler that his wife Borja had died: "burning with fever and fatigued by the journey . . . her life was ended by cruel pains." His personal valet had also died, and his other servants were in danger. Presenting himself as a martyr to duty, López pointed out that "all of this could have been avoided, if we had left La Coruña a month later to avoid the heat," but, he sighed, he had "acted out of blind obedience to his Royal Highness and respect for his determinations."[7]

In late 1799, Ramon López y Ángulo arrived in New Orleans a shattered man. He complained of the ill fortune that was "the cause of the bitterness that I suffer, and of the madness [that has affected] my constitution." Not only had he been forced into what he considered an objectionable situation in Louisiana, on the voyage to this wretched place he had lost his beloved wife, to whom he referred as "my soul."[8]

López, as the new intendant, was no doubt welcomed and entertained by the leading planters and merchants of the area, including the Macartys. Before long he had become romantically involved with young Delphine Macarty. Had López seduced an innocent girl? Had the impetuous adolescent thrown herself at one whom she perceived as a glamorous older man? Or was this a matchmaking attempt on the part of her family? We cannot know the exact nature of the relationship between the couple, but it was such that López felt compelled to marry Delphine without delay in order to avert a scandal.

Although the marriage of a fourteen-year-old seems shocking to present-day sensibilities, both civil and canon law at the time of Delphine's marriage to López allowed females above the age of twelve to marry with parental consent. By age twelve, girls were thought to possess "sufficient discretion" to make the decision to marry and, with puberty, to have attained the "capability of procreating."[9]

Spanish policy required high-ranking government and military personnel, such as Ramon López y Ángulo, to obtain royal permission to wed local women. The Crown wanted to ensure that representatives of Spain did not become overly intimate with the colonists in order to keep themselves free from social or commercial influence.[10] In actuality, many government officials and military officers in Spanish Louisiana married New Orleans women, with and without permission. Governor Luis de Unzaga y Armezaga married a daughter of the planter Gilbert Antoine de St. Maxent in 1770, and in 1777 Governor Bernardo de Gálvez married another of St. Maxent's daughters. In 1779 Governor Estebán Miró married Delphine's aunt, Céleste Elénore de Macarty.[11]

Ramon López y Ángulo had applied for royal permission on April 25, 1800, citing the position and wealth of Delphine's family and noting their connection with a former Spanish governor of Louisiana.[12] But the slowness and uncertainty of correspondence with Spain prompted López to marry first and trust that the license would eventually arrive. To this end he solicited the help of Luis Peñalver y Cardenas, Bishop of Louisiana and the Floridas.

In early June 1800, López approached the bishop, asking him to perform the wedding ceremony. He not only cited reasons of "honor and conscience" but pointed out that the relationship between himself and Delphine had caused an unseemly dispute between Delphine's parents, who were involved in a "noisy feud" that could lead to a separation. This marriage would presumably cause the Macartys to resolve their differences and "thus end the possible ruination of their community property; more importantly [it would] avoid offending God, which is a bitter result of these disputes." Delaying the wedding, he argued, would cause irreparable harm. He hoped that "the marriage will be kept secret until the necessary license is received, or at least with the discretion that decorum dictates that I should keep for the memory of my dead wife."[13]

Bishop Peñalver was at first reluctant to comply, saying that "I have always abstained from considering similar requests," but given the compelling circumstances, he agreed to perform the ritual and dispense with the usual publication of the banns. The bishop's secretary recorded López y Ángulo's statement of his age, parentage, and legitimacy, and accepted testimony that he was a widower and free to marry. Delphine's father gave his approval. The document confirmed that the bride would receive no dowry, and that López was not marrying for financial gain.[14] After the couple had made their confession and received communion, they were united by the bishop in a private ceremony at the Macarty plantation on

June 11, 1800. The marriage was recorded in the sacramental register of St. Louis Cathedral by the pastor, Fray Antonio de Sedella, popularly known as Père Antoine.[15]

A few days after the wedding, Bishop Peñalver wrote an official report justifying this act, which he claimed to have performed in order to "end a disturbance within an honorable family." He went on to describe "The scandalous parting of Don Luis Macarty and Doña Maria Juana Lerable, the parents of Doña Maria Delfina; the divorce suit that they initiated, the hidden division of their community property, criminal claims that they filed against each other in royal court, even public assaults, that are well known by all." The bishop added that he and the previous governor, Manuel Gayoso de Lemos, had tried without success to mediate this dispute, and that he was "convinced that this marriage [between Delphine and Ramon] will persuade these parents to their duties."[16]

In reality, Delphine's father and mother were already feuding when López y Ángulo arrived in Louisiana in November or December of 1799, and their difficulties did not begin with their daughter's involvement with the new intendant. Given what we know of the Chevalier de Macarty's liaison with at least one woman of color, one suspects that the dispute had more to do with his infidelities than with Delphine's love affair. The bishop's statement that he and Gayoso had tried mediation is borne out by a May 9, 1799, letter from Gayoso informing him that Macarty, "repentant, under counseling, and upon better reflection," wanted to renew the marriage vows between himself and his wife. Gayoso asked the bishop to "be so kind as to trouble yourself to be present" at the ceremony on May 18, "as proof of the interest that we hold in reuniting this couple."[17] Whatever the conflict between Delphine's parents, no documentation of the "divorce suit, criminal claims, and public assaults" described by Bishop Peñalver could be discovered in archival sources.

We know nothing of the subsequent domestic life of Ramon López y Ángulo and Delphine Macarty, or whether or not their marriage was a happy one. Since the Spanish government did not provide an official residence for the intendant, the couple would have found their own housing or lived with the bride's family. While the great urgency to wed leads one to assume that Delphine was pregnant, there is no indication that she gave birth to a child during the first year of their marriage. Perhaps she miscarried or the infant did not survive.

On November 13, 1801, Delphine was confirmed in the Roman Catholic faith at St. Louis Cathedral by Bishop Peñalver y Cardenas. At the same confirmation ceremony, she served as sponsor for Ana Maria de Rueda, daughter of a Spanish official, and for Josefa, daughter of her father's slave Constanza.[18] It is intriguing to imagine that the Chevalier de Macarty had an intimate relationship with Constanza, and that Josefa was his child, but there is no evidence to substantiate this.

On February 2, 1802, Ramon López y Ángulo, described in the sacramental record as "knight of the royal and distinguished order of Carlos III," was a witness at the marriage of Delphine's cousin Céleste to the Frenchman Paul Lanusse.[19] Céleste Macarty Lanusse, like Delphine, would later acquire a reputation as a cruel slave mistress.

López y Ángulo's term as intendant of Louisiana and West Florida was generally unexceptional; his only appearance in the history books deals with his reopening of the African slave trade in 1800. The importation of African captives had been banned in 1796. Slaves had come to outnumber the white population, and the revolts in Louisiana, Saint-Domingue, and elsewhere in the Caribbean bred widespread paranoia. In addition, the cultivation of indigo had failed, and the colony had no need for more workers. The Cabildo petitioned the Spanish king to "prohibit the importation of Negroes or Mulattoes of any class whatever from the Guinea Coast [of Africa] or from the Americas, until such time as circumstances less critical and more peaceful will permit."[20] But by 1799 cotton and sugarcane had proven successful as cash crops and there was a renewed demand for plantation labor. A group of planters petitioned the government to reopen the African slave trade. The proposal was defeated by the Cabildo, who cited the recent uprisings as reason not to import more slaves.[21] In December 1800, Ramon López y Ángulo nevertheless issued a proclamation permitting the importation of captives directly from Africa. Not only did he defy the decision of the Cabildo, but he took this action without obtaining the governor's approval.[22]

López y Ángulo had expected, or at least hoped, that his unauthorized nuptials with Delphine would be overlooked. Instead, seven months later he received a notice, dated January 7, 1801, in which he was reprimanded, relieved of his duties as intendant, and ordered to return to Spain.[23] It seems obvious that López was being singled out for discipline for something other than the rather minor infraction of marrying without permission. He was unpopular with local officials, and he was engaged in a power struggle with the previous intendant, Juan Ventura Morales, referred to by one historian as "contentious," "insufferable," and "a scandalmonger who never had a good word for anyone."[24] A letter from López y Ángulo to Morales reveals the enmity between the two men. López wrote, concerning the affairs of the trading company of Panton and Leslie in Pensacola: "Even if I had formed an opinion of Panton, I would not tell you, so that you might tarnish it as you have done with all that I have been able to do during my administration."[25] As López later discovered, his downfall was at least partially orchestrated by the machinations of the wily Morales.

The governor, the intendant, and other officials of the Louisiana colony were under the authority of the captain-general of Cuba, Louisiana, and the Floridas, located in Havana. The captain-general answered directly to the king, his Catholic Majesty Carlos IV. López y Ángulo had apparently ignored the king's command that he relinquish his position and return to Spain in January 1801. Correspondence between López and various officials indicates that at least until the following September he continued his duties as intendant as though nothing had happened.[26] On September 22, 1801, the captain-general wrote to the Ministry of Finance for the Indies concerning "the royal order of last January 7 in regard to the departure for Spain of Don Ramon López y Ángulo, Intendant of this province." The captain-general stated that the king had learned of "the matrimony of Don Ramon López y Ángulo with Doña Maria Delfina Macarti, native of New Orleans," for which he had not obtained the "corresponding license." He declared that because López had broken the law that prohibits marrying without royal permission, he was to be "removed from the intendancy and that His Majesty has ordered he be sent to Spain by registered vessel."[27]

López finally left New Orleans for Havana on the schooner *El Volador* in the spring of 1802. Although the presence of his wife is never mentioned in official correspondence, one assumes that Delphine was also on board. By mid-April 1802, López was writing to his superiors from Havana, and in late July a missive from the captain-general directed that López was to travel to Barcelona on the merchant frigate *Dolores*.[28] In late October, López had arrived in the Bay of Barcelona and wrote to the Spanish secretary of state, Miguel Cayetano Soler, from on board the *Dolores*, asking what he was supposed to do next. The unwelcome answer came soon enough, when López was exiled to the Atlantic coastal town of San Sebastian, near the French border, and assigned to a low-level clerical position. From there he wrote a flood of impassioned letters to Spanish officials in which he attempted to elicit sympathy for his plight.

One such plea was addressed to Prime Minister Manuel Godoy, known as the "Prince of Peace," who was the lover of Queen Maria Luisa of Spain. In this letter, which runs to fourteen pages, López y Ángulo complained self-righteously of "the slander that . . . was raised . . . against my unfortunate Borja [his first wife] and her respectable father, in order to set against me powerful enemies to facilitate the means to effect my total destruction." He identified the "perpetrator of all the misfortunes and concerns that I have suffered for the last four years" as the king's chief minister, Mariano Luis de Urquijo. Urquijo, according to López y Ángulo, "gravely offended me by [attempting to] seduce my virtuous wife" and then spread rumors that Borja had offered sexual favors to an unidentified government official in order to obtain preferential treatment for her father. López believed that Urquijo had hustled him off to Louisiana "in order to cover up his evil deeds."[29] One would imagine from López's description that Mariano Luis de Urquijo was a disgusting old lecher. He was actually a few years younger than López, described as a handsome and charming intellectual who translated the works of Voltaire, was a friend of the painter Francisco Goya, and worked to limit the power of the Spanish Inquisition.[30]

In June 1803, López y Ángulo wrote to Secretary of State Soler, begging him to "use your powerful influence so that His Majesty will concede to my just request . . . and get me out of the shameful and threatening state . . . in which I have been for the last two years." He particularly wished to "return to my former diplomatic career" in New Orleans in order to be near his wife's family. López asked Soler to disregard "any accusations or slanders" directed against him from Louisiana as a result of the "ambition, greed and perversity of . . . my predecessor and successor, Don Juan Ventura Morales." This statement confirms the suspicion that it was Morales, the former intendant, who engineered López's removal from office.[31]

Morales had been reappointed as intendant after López y Ángulo's departure, and he served in that capacity until the end of the Spanish colonial administration in November 1803. It was he who, on his own initiative and without orders from the king of Spain, rescinded the treaty between the United States and Spain that allowed American traders to warehouse their goods at the port of New Orleans while awaiting shipment overseas. The loss of this "right of deposit" stiffened American determination to control New Orleans and eventually led to the Louisiana Purchase of 1803.[32]

Despite Grace King's often-repeated tale (from *Creole Families of New*

Orleans) of Delphine's touching intercession with Queen Maria Luisa of Spain on behalf of her husband, it is more likely that López y Ángulo's fervent letter-writing campaign finally paid off. By late 1804 he had been pardoned and appointed Spanish consul to New Orleans under the American administration. As he was proceeding to his new post on the American ship *Ulysses* from Bordeaux, the vessel ran upon a sandbar and capsized near Havana. A despatch from Havana dated January 11, 1805, reported that López y Ángulo had died "as a result of the running aground of the ship." He may have drowned, he may have sustained injuries that resulted in his death or, as one historian has suggested, he may have died of heart failure from the shock. The Widow López desired "to preserve the corpse in salt so that she could give it a holy burial."[33]

At the time of her husband's death, Delphine was far advanced in pregnancy. According to the January 11 despatch, "the widow is staying at the home of the Postal Administrator [of Havana] awaiting her eminent delivery."[34] Sometime in early 1805 Delphine gave birth to a daughter, Marie Delphine Francisca Borja López y Ángulo de Candelaria, named in part for her husband's deceased wife, Francisca Borja Enderis. This may seem macabre to present-day readers, but such naming practices were not unusual at the time.[35] Legend has it that the girl was known to family members as "Borquita" because she was "born on shipboard."[36] Borquita is actually the diminutive of Borja, and has no reference to being born on a ship. In official records she was sometimes called Borja and sometimes Delphine; she was always identified as a "native of Havana on the Island of Cuba."

Delphine Macarty López apparently remained in Havana long enough to bury her husband and arrange for the baptism of her infant daughter. According to Delphine's later testimony, López y Ángulo died intestate without leaving any property, and there is no indication that she received a pension as the widow of a Spanish government official. Having no financial assets of her own, she probably lived with her parents on the Macarty plantation. Her father was appointed as legal tutor to young Borja, meaning that he served as a guardian who oversaw the child's financial interests.[37]

By the time Delphine returned to New Orleans sometime in 1805, Louisiana had become an American possession. The colony had been secretly ceded by Spain to the French Republic on July 30, 1802, but this did not become official until November 30, 1803.[38] In less than a month Napoleon Bonaparte had sold to the United States not only the port of New Orleans but the entire area from the Gulf Coast to the Canadian border between the Mississippi River and the Rocky Mountains. Louisiana was formally transferred to American rule on December 20, 1803, in a ceremony at the Cabildo in New Orleans. Lower Louisiana, including the city of New Orleans, became the Territory of Orleans. President Thomas Jefferson appointed William C. C. Claiborne, a twenty-eight-year-old Tennessean who at the time was governor of the Mississippi Territory, as governor of the Territory of Orleans.[39]

The first few years of American ownership were a time of great confusion. Governor Claiborne made numerous complaints to Secretary of State James Madison about the continued presence of the former Spanish governor, the Marquis de Casa Calvo, along with other Spanish officials and the Spanish militia, who encouraged the notion that Louisiana would "shortly return under the dominion of Spain." Claiborne especially desired the departure of López y Ángulo's old nemesis, the conniving Juan Ventura Morales. In one of his many letters to Madison, Claiborne described Morales as "an unprincipled, intriguing man [whose] views are hostile to the interest of the United States."[40] Casa Calvo and his entourage were finally ejected in early 1806.[41] Even then Claiborne was not rid of Morales, who subsequently became the intendant of Spanish West Florida and continued to declare that Spain had voided the treaty that ceded Louisiana to France.[42]

The former French colonial prefect Pierre Clément de Laussat, his assistants, and the French military remaining in New Orleans were also a source of concern to the American authorities. As Claiborne wrote to Madison, Laussat was still interfering in affairs of government, and some of the French military officers were "mischievous, riotous, disorderly characters, and have contributed greatly to interrupt the harmony of this City."[43]

While Spanish and French officials were still hoping to regain control of the Territory, American planters and merchants from the mid-Atlantic states and New England poured into New Orleans. As one historian has so aptly described those early years, the newly arrived Americans were "derived from a democratic republic, children of English common law and the language of Shakespeare, heirs of the Protestant Reformation. In almost every conceivable way they represented a tradition utterly unknown to the indigenous population. . . . They came in ever-increasing numbers, vigorous, assertive, demanding, often boisterous and domineering."[44]

From the beginning, there was conflict and animosity between Louisiana Creoles and the American newcomers. The Americans viewed the Creoles as childlike, lacking in business sense, addicted to frivolous pleasures, woefully uneducated, and devoted to a practice of Roman Catholicism that bordered on idolatry. To his credit, Governor Claiborne tried to be even-handed in his administration, but privately he wrote to President Jefferson that the Creoles were "illy fitted to be useful citizens of a Republic."[45]

Everything that the Creoles held dear—their cultural practices, their French language, their Roman Catholic religion, and their system of civil law—was under attack during Louisiana's territorial period. It was to this rapidly changing world that eighteen-year-old Delphine Macarty, now the Widow López, returned with her daughter, Borja.

3

BLANQUE

Delphine Macarty López y Ángulo did not remain a widow for long. On her twentieth birthday, March 19, 1807, she married Jean Paul Blanque, a native of the French province of Nay-Bourdettes, Department of Pyrénées-Atlantiques. As was the case with her first marriage, Delphine's new husband, at forty-three, was a widower more than twice her age. Once again the ceremony was entered into the sacramental register by the pastor of St. Louis Cathedral, Fray Antonio de Sedella.[1]

While Ramon López y Ángulo appears to have been a weak, sycophantic whiner, Jean Blanque was every bit Delphine's match: a ruthless wheeler-dealer who was a merchant, slave trader, lawyer, banker, state legislator, political intriguer, and associate of the pirates Jean and Pierre Laffite.[2] Blanque had come to New Orleans with Pierre Clément de Laussat in 1803, when the colonial prefect arrived to govern Louisiana under the terms of the retrocession from Spain. Instead of returning to France after the Louisiana Purchase, Blanque chose to remain in New Orleans.[3]

Delphine's mother, Marie Jeanne Lerable de Macarty, had died on February 26, 1807, five weeks before Delphine wed Jean Blanque.[4] Madame de Macarty divided her considerable estate between a daughter by her first marriage, Adelaide Lecomte Piernas, and the children of her marriage to the Chevalier de Macarty, Louis Barthélémy and Delphine. Did Blanque perhaps see a financial opportunity? There was no formal marriage contract between Delphine and Jean Blanque, but Delphine agreed that the sum of $33,070 "accruing to her from the estate of her mother, as well as every other property which she should happen afterwards to acquire," would constitute her dowry. This inheritance would have the purchasing power of about $613,000 today.[5]

There is no evidence that Delphine's mother, the fun-loving hostess described in the 1796 letters of Joseph Xavier de Pontalba, died of anything but natural causes. A persistent element of the Lalaurie legend, however, says that both of Delphine's parents were killed in the Saint-Domingue slave rebellion or that Madame de Macarty was killed by family slaves brought from Saint-Domingue. Delphine allegedly retaliated by punishing the perpetrators. In reality, the Macartys never lived in Saint-Domingue, and the Chevalier de Macarty owned only one female slave from that island, Bonne, acquired in 1816, long after his wife's death. Bonne later came into the possession of Madame Lalaurie and plays a part in her story.

The idea that one or both of the elder Macartys were murdered by slaves first turns up in the research notes of George Washington Cable's assistant, Dora Richards Miller. Miller had interviewed a number of local residents, and in a report to Cable she offered two theories about Madame Lalaurie's motivation for excessive punishment of her bondspeople. One was that her "parents were from St. Domingo and were massacred or injured in the insurrection there, and that she had vowed vengeance on all negroes for this." The other was that her mother was a "cruel woman," who was "set upon and murdered" by her slaves while returning to her plantation by carriage one night. "Madame Lalaurie suspected a certain nine and had them brought to her house and tortured them in revenge." Miller did not identify her informants; she noted that she had been unable to verify either story, but that the notion that Delphine's parents died at the hands of rebellious slaves in Saint-Domingue was "from the most reliable source."[6]

Another version, given by John P. Coleman in his 1924 article from the *New Orleans States*, relates that "after the death of Mr. McCarthy [sic], his house and his vast estate, including many slaves, remained under the control of his widow, a woman gifted in many things, and withal an excellent business manager." (The Chevalier de Macarty, who died in 1824, actually outlived his wife by seventeen years.) Coleman went on to postulate that during a "negro uprising . . . fourteen of the white population were murdered, including Mrs. McCarthy . . . presumably by some of the slaves . . . brought over from San Domingo." Coleman extolled the virtues of "this benevolent old lady" and the "ingratitude" of her slaves for her "efforts to ameliorate the wretchedness of their condition. . . . At her own expense she brought teachers here . . . to educate and train these negroes in some specialized handcraft."[7]

In *Louisiana: A Guide to the State*, produced by the WPA Louisiana Writers' Project in 1941, Delphine's father was portrayed as a "cruel slave-master." According to this guidebook, the Chevalier de Macarty sent to his neighbor, Monsieur Chalmette, a severed black ear with a note reading "My friend, this is the way to treat a renegade slave." The guidebook goes on to say that "Macarty's wife was later murdered by her slaves."[8]

Bob Brown's article in the *New Orleans States*, also from 1941, reported that Delphine's parents came to New Orleans from Saint-Domingue, bringing their slaves with them, and that the slaves later revolted and killed Madame de Macarty. This account was supplied to Brown by Miriam DeBuys.[9]

Several factual incidents have been conflated here, none of them having anything to do with the death of Marie Jeanne Lerable de Macarty in 1807. One of Delphine's uncles, Baptiste Césaire le Breton, actually *was* murdered by his slaves in 1771. And in 1811 there was, in fact, an uprising in St. John the Baptist Parish that was thought at the time to have been instigated by slaves from Saint-Domingue; this incident is described below in more detail. Less well known is the abortive insurrection plot of October 1812 that involved slaves on several upriver plantations, including the one formerly owned by le Breton and later by Delphine's uncle Jean Baptiste de Macarty and his son-in-law Paul Lanusse. Only one slave belonging to Macarty and Lanusse was named in the criminal proceedings against those who had "knowingly, wickedly, maliciously, and feloniously persuaded and encouraged" others to participate in "an insurrection against the white inhabitants of this Parish." Nobody was killed.[10]

·

Delphine and her new husband, Jean Blanque, had already inherited from her mother's succession a downtown plantation on the bank of the Mississippi valued at $50,000, fifty-two slaves valued at $31,953, plus livestock and farm equipment.[11] In June 1808, Delphine's father made the couple a gift of household furnishings, another plantation below the city, a lot on Chartres Street, and twenty-six slaves. The value of Delphine's inheritance plus her father's donation was approximately $130,850, more than

$2 million today.[12] In July, Delphine's father also sold two plantations and fifty-three slaves to his son Louis Barthélémy and his son-in-law Jean Blanque, as joint owners.[13]

In 1808 Blanque purchased a two-story brick townhouse on Royal Street near the corner of Conti, next to the Bank of Louisiana of which he was a director. The house, designed and built by the architect Godefroy

During her marriage to Jean Blanque, Delphine Macarty lived in this townhouse, now 409 Royal Street near the corner of Conti. The building to the left was the Bank of Louisiana, of which Blanque was a director. The ground floor of the Blanque house is now a fine antiques shop, and the adjacent bank building is now a restaurant. (Photograph by the author, April 2009.)

du Jarreau, had been seized in a lawsuit against du Jarreau, and Blanque acquired the property at the ensuing sheriff's auction for $8,100.[14] Later, this dwelling was described as "a two-story brick house, slate roofed, with two iron balconies, the second story containing eight rooms; the ground floor being divided into two stores, with a large passage in common, and having over them an entresol." Behind the residence was "a three story brick building used for a kitchen and servants' lodging," with a "yard well paved, large cistern, water works put up, &c."[15]

The Blanques divided their time between the Royal Street townhouse and a plantation near the property of Delphine's father and brother. The 1815 Tanesse Map shows a strip of land with buildings, labeled "Mr Jn Blanque," fronting the river and extending back into the cypress swamp (see p. 14).[16] Stanley Clisby Arthur noted in *Old New Orleans* that both "the stylish Royal Street home" and "the Villa Blanque, a charming country place," were "resorts for the socially elect."[17]

"Villa on Levee Road below New Orleans." Illustration by Ellsworth Woodward, in Grace King's *Creole Families of New Orleans* (1921), p. 77. The "Villa Blanque" may have resembled this unidentified house, now demolished. (Collection of the author.)

Delphine had three daughters and a son with her second husband. Louise Marie Pauline was born in 1809. The next child, Louise Marie Laure, did not arrive until 1813, indicating that Delphine might have lost at least one infant during that four-year interval. After that, the babies came every twelve to fifteen months. Louise Marie Jeanne was born in 1814, and Jean Pierre Paulin in 1815. All were baptized at St. Louis Cathedral. In each case Delphine's father stood as godfather to the children, with one of their young sisters as godmother. Borja and Pauline were under the age of six years when they served as godmothers, and Laure was only eighteen months old.[18]

Since arriving in New Orleans, Jean Blanque had been involved in local politics and was perceived by the Americans as an adversary of the United States government. In 1810 Territorial Governor William C. C. Claiborne wrote to President Thomas Jefferson regarding Blanque's nomination to the new Legislative Council for the Territory of Orleans: "Mr Jean Blanque . . . resides near New Orleans, and is a merchant in high credit. About three years ago he married a very beautiful Creole lady, possessing a large estate and connected with one of the most numerous and respectable families in the County [sic] of Orleans. Mr Blanque is a man of genius and education, and possesses considerable influence in the city. . . . He is a member of the City Council, a Director of the Louisiana Bank, and has been for the last three years a member of the House of Representatives for the Territory." Claiborne nevertheless doubted Blanque's loyalty to the United States: "Mr Blanque is much disliked by most of the native Americans residing in and near New Orleans; his attachments are supposed to be wholly foreign, and they consider him a dangerous man."[19]

Another description of Jean Blanque appears in a report written in 1814 by Louis de Clouet to a representative of King Ferdinand of Spain. Clouet, a Louisiana native, was one of those involved in the plot to oust the Americans and restore Spanish rule. Even after the Territory of Orleans had become the State of Louisiana in 1812, Clouet continued to act as an agent for Spain while also keeping alert to French ambitions in Louisiana. Through his spying, Clouet learned that the French faction hoped to manipulate the electoral process to ensure that men sympathetic to their cause occupied major governmental positions; Jean Blanque was named as a potential state senator. Clouet characterized all of those favored by the French as "men of a corruption and immorality unparalleled, all of them enemies of Spain and agents of Bonaparte." Regarding Jean Blanque, Clouet wrote that "This clever and daring man is persuasive of tongue, whereby he sways the crowd. Blanque is regarded as one of the persons [financially] interested in the piracies of Barataria, which he openly protects." Clouet submitted his own roster of "citizens [who are] attached to the Spanish monarchy." Among them were "Louis the Chevalier Macarty, a respected resident, as is his son, Bartolomé." Clouet also named Fray Antonio de Sedella, pastor of St. Louis Cathedral, as a Spanish partisan.[20]

Governor Claiborne definitely suspected Antonio de Sedella of collaborating with the Spanish. Archbishop Patrick Walsh referred to the "unfortunate schism that has recently taken place in this city . . . proceeding from the ambition of a refractory monk [Sedella], supported in his apostasy by the fanaticism of a misguided populace." Walsh reported that "two individuals . . . instigated by a certain foreign agent" had gone to Havana to "procure a reinforcement of monks to support Father Antonio de Sedella in his schismatic and rebellious conduct." Claiborne later wrote to Henry Dearborn, Secretary of War, that "We have a Spanish priest here who is a very dangerous man; he rebelled against the superiors of his own church, and [would] even . . . rebel against the government whenever a fit occasion may serve. . . . This seditious priest is Father Antoine. He is a great favorite of the Louisiana ladies, has married many of them and christened all their children. He is by some citizens esteemed an accomplished hypocrite, has great influence with the people of color, and report says, embraces every opportunity to render them discontented under the American government. . . . If his conduct should continue exceptionable, I shall send him off."[21]

Delphine was caught between her husband, who was a French sympathizer, and her father, her brother, and her pastor, who were allied with Spain. None of them favored the American cause.

·

During the early years of the nineteenth century, as business and agriculture began to flourish under the American administration, Louisianians were desperate for enslaved workers. López y Ángulo had reopened the African slave trade in 1800, but in 1804 the inhabitants learned, to their dismay, that the American government had banned the importation of slaves from "any port or place without the limits of the United States" into the Territory of Orleans after October 1 of that year.[22] This exclusion of slaves from Africa and the Caribbean elicited howls of protest from the citizens. Cotton and sugar plantations, they argued, would become value-less without a plentiful supply of black, non-free labor because free white men would not work in the unhealthy semi-tropical climate.[23]

Governor Claiborne faced a vexing dilemma. He personally disap-proved of the "inhuman traffic" in slaves, and he believed that slavery was "a galling yoke" from which the enslaved would ultimately rebel. He was well aware of the revolution in Saint-Domingue, and he was therefore apprehensive about the introduction of insurrectionary slaves from that island and elsewhere in the Caribbean into the Territory of Orleans.[24] On the other hand, he had no wish to deal a "serious blow to the commercial and agricultural interest" of the Territory, and so he reluctantly took the side of the Louisianians against the American government.[25]

Meanwhile, the people of the Territory were buying any slaves they could get. Jean Blanque's associates, the brothers Jean and Pierre Laffite, were a major supplier of enslaved workers of questionable provenance. The Laffites, described by one historian as "smugglers, merchants of con-traband, revolutionaries, spies, privateers, and pirates as well," were na-tives of the Bordeaux region of France between the River Garonne and the Pyrénées Mountains. The brothers had arrived in Louisiana sometime shortly after the Louisiana Purchase; like so many others, they had come from Saint-Domingue. By around 1809 the Laffites had created a complex of buildings and wharfs on the barrier island of Grand Terre, where the Gulf of Mexico flows into Barataria Bay, creating an ideal harbor. The Laf-fites' headquarters became known as "Barataria."[26]

There is ample evidence that the buying and selling of human mer-chandise, both legal and illegal, was also one of Jean Blanque's primary occupations. In 1806 and 1807, even before the Laffites had established their center of operations at Barataria, Jean Blanque began acquiring small lots of slaves designated as *brut*, meaning a "raw" or "uncivilized" worker imported from Africa. His suppliers were two ship captains oper-ating between New Orleans and Charleston, Antoine Laporte, master of the *Aura* and the *Lanna*, and Edouard Lauve, master of the *Franklin*. In response to the ban on slave imports into the Territory of Orleans, South Carolina had reopened its African trade in late 1803.[27] Blanque circum-vented the 1804 law by procuring captives by way of Charleston instead of engaging in the more dangerous activity of smuggling them directly from Africa. Blanque sold these men, women, and children, most of whom had not even been assigned a "Christian" name, to local planters for approximately $550 each.[28]

A search of Gwendolyn Midlo Hall's *Louisiana Slave Database* shows that ships from Charleston were supplying Africans not only to Jean Blanque but also to many of the leading merchants and planters of Orleans Parish. Some of these recently arrived captives were designated as Mandinga, Congo, Senegalese, Mina, or simply as *brut*. Sellers include the aforementioned captains Antoine Laporte and Edouard Lauve, as well as captains Jean Dupuy of the *Favorito*, William Flagg and A. H. Villechaise of the *Caroline*, Laford of the *Bellone*, P. Walsh of the *Cliopiene*, Campbell of the *Agent*, and Lorenzo Olivier of the *Dos Hermanos*, as well as unidentified captains of the ships *Adventure*, *Glory*, *Neutrality*, and *Mary Masson*. A French historian used newspaper advertisements to discover even more ships, importing a total of 1,661 enslaved Africans by way of Charleston between 1804 and 1808.[29]

In 1807, President Jefferson signed into law a bill to abolish the African slave trade altogether. The bill went into effect on January 1, 1808, after which it became illegal "to import or bring into the United States or territories thereof from any foreign kingdom, place, or country, any negro, mulatto, or person of colour, with intent to hold, sell, or dispose of such . . . as a slave, or to be held to service or labor."[30] Slave smuggling was therefore rife, and the illegal trade in enslaved persons from Africa and the Caribbean flourished during the early antebellum period and continued sporadically until the eve of the Civil War.

If Jean Blanque was still engaged in this illicit commerce after 1808, it was "off the books" and does not appear in the notarial records. He nevertheless continued to buy and sell slaves in large numbers; by the time of his death in 1815, a total of 367 enslaved persons had passed through his hands.[31]

·

In 1804, one year after the Louisiana Purchase, the thirteen-year-long slave revolt in Saint-Domingue culminated in the founding of the Republic of Haiti. During the 1790s and into the first decade of the nineteenth century, thousands of refugees fled the fighting and political upheaval. Among them were the free women of color CéCé Carpentier, Totote Destrés, and Helöise Croy, who became the concubines of Delphine's kinsmen Jean Baptiste Barthélémy and Eugène Macarty, as well as those enterprising businessmen the brothers Jean and Pierre Laffite. In 1803, following the final defeat of Napoleon's troops, thirty thousand people sought shelter in nearby Cuba, hoping eventually to resume their lives in Saint-Domingue. After war broke out between Spain and France, the Saint-Dominguen refugees who refused to swear allegiance to the Spanish government were forced out of Cuba, and many of them came to New Orleans.[32]

During the spring and summer of 1809, thirty-four vessels arrived from Santiago de Cuba and Havana carrying nearly ten thousand passengers. Some were natives of France and some were white and free colored Creoles of Saint-Domingue. Those whose slaves had not joined the revolution brought this valuable property, mostly women and children, with them. The introduction of these bondspeople violated the 1808 prohibition against importation of "foreign" slaves, and for a time Governor Claiborne had them impounded and held on the ships that brought them. A special act of Congress was required to permit the entry of the Saint-Dominguen slaves.[33] By early 1810 the tide of immigrants had virtually ceased, and the newspaper Le Moniteur de la Louisiane announced on January 27 that the total number of men, women, and children arriving from Cuba in the past year numbered 2,731 whites, 3,102 free people of color, and 3,226 slaves.[34]

.

On January 8, 1811, just as the Carnival season was getting under way, an insurrection erupted in St. John the Baptist Parish, a rich sugar-producing area on the "German Coast" above New Orleans. The revolt was organized by an enslaved mulatto named Charles, property of the Widow Deslondes, who was employed as a driver on the adjacent plantation of Manuel Andry.[35] Over a long period of careful planning, Charles recruited slaves from neighboring sugar plantations. Some were Louisiana Creoles and some were "American Negroes" from the upper South. Among the insurgents there were also enslaved Africans; some would have been imported during the Spanish administration, some probably entered the Territory of Orleans by way of Charleston, and some might have been smuggled in by the Laffites. The slave army was joined by maroons who had been living in the swamps for years.[36] The insurgents wounded Andry and killed his son, and then, with a force of as many as five hundred men, set off for New Orleans armed with guns, cane knives, axes, and hoes. Along the way they also killed the planter François Trépagnier. The rebellion was put down by the militia, aided by local planters. They captured Charles, chopped off his hands, broke his thighs, shot him dead, and burned his corpse.[37] Twenty-one of the rebels were killed during the skirmish, and forty-five were executed by firing squad after a makeshift trial.[38] Replicating the gruesome spectacle of 1795, their severed heads were displayed on pikes along the river.[39]

In analyzing the causes of the uprising, white Louisianians chose to blame "outside agitators" rather than their own "faithful and contented" bondsmen.[40] It was believed until recently that Charles Deslondes was from Saint-Domingue and that among his band were dangerous, insurrectionary slaves smuggled in from that island by Jean and Pierre Laffite. The 1811 revolt may indeed have been inspired by the Haitian Revolution, but Charles was a Louisiana Creole, and there is no evidence that any of the other participants came from Saint-Domingue by way of Barataria.[41] This incident nevertheless intensified Governor Claiborne's determination to eradicate the Laffites and their operation.

·

Over the years, Jean and Pierre Laffite's privateering and outright piracy and their sales of smuggled goods and illegal African captives and slaves from the Caribbean had become increasingly bold and sophisticated, attracting the attention of state and federal authorities. In 1813, Governor Claiborne issued a proclamation commanding the "banditti" encamped at Barataria to "cease from their unlawful acts and forthwith to disperse." When this order was flagrantly ignored, Claiborne issued another proclamation cautioning the citizens against "giving any kind of succor to the said John Lafitte [sic] and his associates," and offering a $500 reward for their capture.[42] On July 8, 1814, the United States marshal finally arrested Pierre Laffite and had him locked in irons in the city jail behind the Cabildo. The grand jury indicted Pierre for "acts of piracy & robbery upon the high seas . . . and for having received & repeatedly introduced goods, wares, & merchandise arising from such piratical captures into this District." They refused to set bail.[43]

On September 3, while Jean Laffite was devising schemes to free his brother, a British warship approached the pirate headquarters. Captain Nicholas Lockyer of the British navy presented Jean with a packet of letters inviting "Monsieur Lafite . . . the Commandant at Barataria . . . with your brave followers, to enter into the service of Great Britain." The invitation

Jean Laffite. Wood engraving by John R. Telfer, published in Homer Thrall, *Pictorial History of Texas* (1879), p. 133. Thrall, writing of Laffite's arrival at Galveston in 1817 after leaving Barataria, described him as "a man in the prime of life, well-formed and handsome, about six feet and two inches in height, strongly built, with large hazel eyes, black hair, and generally wore a mustache, dressed in a green uniform and an otter-skin cap." Telfer, who had never seen Laffite in person, based his illustration on this description.

was accompanied by the promise of rewards and pardons if the Baratarians joined forces with the British, and threats of punishment if they did not.[44] Jean Laffite asked for fifteen days to consider. Seeing little advantage in the British offer, he decided to inform the American authorities of this development. He chose his associate Jean Blanque to act as go-between.

In a letter dated September 4, Jean Laffite wrote to Blanque: "Though proscribed by my adoptive country, I will never let slip any occasion of serving her, or of proving that she has never ceased to be dear to me." He went on to describe Captain Lockyer's offer, contending that as a "good citizen" of the United States he made a great sacrifice by not accepting it. Laffite offered Blanque "the secret on which perhaps depends the tranquillity of our country" and expressed his hope that "such proceedings may obtain amelioration of the situation of my unhappy brother," now imprisoned and ill. "I recommend him to you, in the name of humanity." Jean Laffite delivered his letter and transferred the British documents to Blanque's care, and that night someone unlocked Pierre Laffite's cell and enabled his escape.[45]

Jean and Pierre Laffite also wrote directly to Governor Claiborne. Their letters are masterpieces of contrition and flattery. Jean portrayed himself as a "stray sheep, wishing to return to the sheepfold." Later, romanticized versions of the story declare that the Laffites, motivated by patriotism, volunteered the services of their men to defend New Orleans against the British without any expectation of reward. The actual offer was for the Baratarians to defend their own strategic location on Grand Terre at the mouth of Barataria Bay in return for a cessation of the "current prosecutions and indictments" against them and a general pardon for all their past crimes.[46]

Jean Blanque delivered the Laffites' letters and the British documents to Governor Claiborne, protesting to Claiborne that he was only an intermediary and had "no acquaintance with either of the Laffites." After a good deal of dithering around by Claiborne and others, on December 18 General Andrew Jackson finally inducted about four hundred Baratarians into the volunteer militia and granted them immunity.[47] By then the British were on their way to the Gulf of Mexico. A few days later, on December 23, 1814, British troops launched an invasion. The famous Battle of New Orleans took place below the city at Chalmette on January 8, 1815, with Delphine's kinsman Augustin Macarty's plantation serving as General Jackson's headquarters. Unbeknownst to the combatants in Louisiana, Britain and the United States had reached a peace agreement at Ghent on December 24, 1814.[48]

·

Ten months after the Battle of New Orleans, Jean Blanque died at the age of fifty on October 7, 1815.[49] His death left twenty-eight-year-old Delphine a widow with five young children. Her first daughter, Borja López y Ángulo, was eleven; Pauline Blanque was six, Laure Blanque almost three, Jeanne Blanque a year and a half, and Paulin Blanque was only six months old.

It fell to Delphine to settle her deceased husband's estate, including his extensive holdings in land and slaves. In late 1815 her representatives took an inventory of Blanque's assets and obligations. She subsequently appeared before the Parish Court to declare that her late husband's succession was so "encumbered with debt" that she had "renounced the community of property" that existed between herself and Jean Blanque in order to prevent her personal assets from being seized by his creditors.[50] Delphine took this action in accordance with Louisiana civil law, which stated that a wife or widow has "the privilege of being able to exonerate herself from the debts contracted during the marriage by renouncing the partnership or community of gains," while allowing her to retain control of her dotal property.[51]

In early 1816 the syndics (representatives) of the creditors of Jean Blanque's estate testified before the Parish Court that Blanque owed a total of $160,000, almost $2.5 million today. The syndics concluded that since Blanque's monetary assets were "insufficient to pay the amount of their respective claims," and since "a large portion of the estate consists of negroes who are a perishable property," the slaves should be sold at public auction. As the legal tutrix of the Blanque children, who were her late husband's heirs, Delphine was required to authorize all sales of his property.[52]

During the spring, summer, and fall of 1816, Delphine, acting in cooperation with the syndics of the creditors of Jean Blanque, disposed of slaves and real estate through the auction house of Dutillet and Savory. Delphine and the syndics sold some of the laborers, field hands, and domestics to her father and some to other planters for a total of $50,945.[53] Her father and brother bought thirteen linear arpents of riverfront land below the city for $9,471, and her brother bought one of the houses on Bienville Street for $2,500.[54] She sold a plantation at Pointe de la Hache in Plaquemines Parish for $16,000.[55] Blanque had owned land in the Faubourg Pontchartrain on Bayou St. John, and Delphine sold the vacant lots for a total of $2,055.[56] The townhouse on Royal Street brought $17,800 at auction.[57] The sale of the slaves and real estate amounted to only $98,771, a little over half the amount required to cover Blanque's total indebtedness.[58]

In order to keep her country home, the "Villa Blanque," Delphine was compelled to buy the property from the syndics of her late husband's creditors. She paid $17,000 for the plantation fronting the river below the city, which consisted of a narrow but deep strip of land with a brick house and "various other edifices and dependencies."[59] She petitioned the court "to retain the diverse furniture, effects, and silverware" that she had brought to the marriage with Jean Blanque. She also asked to keep, "in payment of her matrimonial rights," fifteen enslaved adults and four children. The female domestics were Arnante, Genevieve, Hélène, Nancy, Rosette, Suzette, and Zoé, along with Hélène's daughter Elisa, Nancy's mulatto sons Ben and Nicolas, and Suzette's son Edouard. The skilled male slaves included Bastien the coachman; the shoemaker Jean Baptiste; George and Thom, gardeners; Lindor the cook; and Théodore, a cooper. Finally there was Françoise, referred to as "the old one" (*la vieille*) or "the hunchback" (*la bossue*). Five of these enslaved workers had been given to Delphine and her husband by Delphine's father in 1808, and the others were purchased by Blanque during their marriage.[60] In 1817 Delphine's father gave her a twenty-two-year-old mulatress named Pauline.[61]

On July 22, 1819, following the wishes expressed by her late husband, Delphine emancipated the slave Jean Louis. According to her petition to the Orleans Parish Court, Jean Louis was "a negro man of upwards of fifty years of age" who had "always led an honest conduct without running away nor committing any robbery or misdemeanor."[62]

Eight of Delphine's bondspeople died during her widowhood. Most were children or women of childbearing age; four of the deaths occurred in the "unhealthy" summer months and four in winter. The St. Louis Cathedral funeral entries gave the date of death (but never the cause), the name of the slave, with age and color, sometimes the place of birth or African nation, and the name of the owner or other family member who reported the death. If the deceased was a child, the mother's name was usually recorded.

Of the slaves retained by Delphine in 1816, those who died were Hélène's fifteen-year-old daughter, Elisa; Genevieve, age forty, described as a quadroon born in Illinois; Zoé, age twenty, specified as being of the Congo nation. Marie Françoise, for whom no age was given, might have been the "old hunchback," Françoise. In addition, several of the enslaved women listed in the inventory had children who died: Enriette, three-year-old daughter of Célestine; Jean, age five, mulatto son of Rosette; and Clemént, age twenty-two months, whose mother is not identified. A mulatto slave named Jean Pierre Paulin of unstated age also died.[63] There might have been more. The register of funerals for slaves and free persons

Table 2. Slaves retained by the Widow Blanque from the succession of Jean Blanque in payment of her matrimonial rights, Acts of Pierre Pedesclaux, July 9, 1816

Name, age, color, skills	Value	Acquired	Sold, freed, or died before 1828
Arnante, 40, black, cook, laundress, and domestic	Unlisted	Macarty donation 1808	
Bastien, 22, black, carpenter, coach driver, and domestic	$1,000	Purchased from Montegut 1815	
Genevieve, 35, quadroon, native of Illinois, domestic	$800	Macarty donation 1808	Died 1819
George, 60, black, gardener	$200	Unknown	
Françoise, "the old hunchback," black	$50	Unknown	Possibly died 1823
Hélène, 29, black, native of Senegal, domestic, with her daughter Elisa, 15, black	$1,000	Purchased from Piernas 1810	Elisa died 1816
Jean Baptiste, 25, black, shoemaker	$1,200	Purchased from Pavie 1814	
Lindor, 50, mulatto, cook	$400	Macarty donation 1808	
Marie Françoise, black, age unknown	Unlisted	Unknown	Died 1823
Nancy, 20, black, no occupation listed, with her mulatto sons Ben and Nicolas	$1,500	Purchased from Kenner 1812	Ben sold to Brugnière 1828
Rosette, black, no age or occupation listed; with her son Jean, mulatto, born about 1819	$800	Purchased from Laborde 1812	Jean died 1823
Suzette, 24, black, domestic and seamstress, with her son Edouard, 3, griffe	$1,000	Purchased from Laborde 1812	Both sold to Brugnière 1828
Theodore, 30, black, cooper and sawyer	$1,000	Unknown	
Thom, 50, black, gardener	$300	Unknown	
Zoé, 16, of the Congo nation, no occupation listed	Unlisted	Macarty donation 1808	Died 1820

of color for 1815–1819 is nearly illegible owing to the acidic iron-gall ink that has eaten and bled through the pages, and the register for late 1825 through 1828 has been lost.

.

Delphine's father, the Chevalier Louis Barthélémy de Macarty, died on October 21, 1824.[64] In 1819 Macarty had prepared a will in which he appointed his brother Eugène and his son Louis Barthélémy as his testamentary executors. Delphine and Louis Barthélémy were named as his legal heirs, who were to inherit his estate in equal portions. The Chevalier de Macarty also devoted several paragraphs to his natural daughter Delphine Emesie, "born of my cohabitation in lieu of marriage with the free woman of color Sophie Mousante." As a mark of his affection, Emesie, nine years old at the time of her father's death, was to receive $5,000 and two slaves. The bequest was to be administered by the child's mother.[65]

In 1825 Eugène and Louis Barthélémy Macarty petitioned the court to open the succession of the Chevalier de Macarty. If an inventory was taken at the time, it has been lost. Delphine and her brother divided the original Macarty plantation. A drawing attached to the notarial act shows the long, narrow strips of land extending back from the river. The central portion, which included the main house and the garden, was labeled "Louis B. Macarty," with the land on either side designated as belonging to "Mme Blanque." The Macarty holdings lay between the Montreuil and Olivier plantations.[66]

After 1824 Delphine was no longer a young girl under the influence of a husband or father. Even though the settlement of Jean Blanque's massive debts had brought her to the edge of financial ruin, this inheritance from her father, plus her own shrewd real estate dealings, put her back on a solid monetary footing. By the time she met Dr. Louis Lalaurie in 1825, she was a very wealthy lady indeed.

4

LALAURIE

Leonard Louis Nicolas Lalaurie, the man who was to become Delphine Macarty's third husband, was born December 6, 1802, in Villeneuve-sur-Lot in southwestern France. His parents were solidly middle class. His mother, Françoise Depenne, was a housewife, and his father, Jean-Marie Lalaurie, was a medical doctor who was also the president of the local agricultural society.[1] The medieval town of Villeneuve, on the River Lot, is near the port city of Bordeaux, along the Atlantic Ocean and the Pyrénées mountain range on the border with Spain.

Much of what we know about Louis Lalaurie comes from letters to Louis from his father and siblings in Villeneuve, Louis's account of his voyage to Louisiana, and one letter written by Louis to Delphine's son-in-law, Auguste DeLassus, in New Orleans. This correspondence came into the possession of the Missouri History Museum through the DeLassus family, who had ties to Missouri. The letters have been preserved in the DeLassus–St. Vrain Collection.

In 1823 Louis Lalaurie studied medicine at the Sorbonne in Paris, and in 1824 he was a medical student at the University of Toulouse. During these years he was in close touch with his family, who wrote to him at least once a month. By October 1824, he was preparing to leave France to seek his fortune in Louisiana.[2]

On December 8, 1824, one day after his twenty-second birthday, Louis and five other travelers boarded the merchant ship *Fanny* at the Port of Bordeaux. The passenger list submitted by Captain John Mathias includes the name of L. Lalaurie, occupation doctor, and a gentleman named Charles Lanusse who would later marry into the Macarty clan.[3] Lalaurie wrote a detailed description of the ship's progress along the coasts of Guadeloupe, Montserrat, Antigua, Nevis, and Saint-Christophe at Christmas time. By the first of February they had sighted the island of Haiti.[4] On February 17, 1825, the shipping news column of the *Louisiana Courier* announced that the *Fanny* had docked at the Port of New Orleans. The cargo included bales of paper, hogsheads of wine, cases of liquor and brandy, iron ware, cheese, oil, corks, "cotton looms" and other weaving implements, and a load of paving stones, each lot destined for some local merchant.[5]

In 1825, when Louis Lalaurie arrived in New Orleans, two newspapers, the *Courier* and the *Louisiana Gazette*, were published daily. These periodicals consisted of two pages in French and two in English. While there were always several columns of national and international news, local events were generally not reported. Most of the space was devoted to announcements from the courts and the mayor's office, notices of runaway servants and strayed livestock, the arrival and departure of sailing vessels, and advertisements for the sale of land, slaves, and merchandise. Occasionally a doctor or lawyer would proclaim the opening of his practice.

On March 19, 1825, Louis Lalaurie addressed such a letter to the editor of the *Courier*: "Sir—I pray you to announce . . . that a French Physician has just arrived in this city, who is acquainted with the means, lately discovered in France, of destroying hunches." In the French edition the word *hunches* was rendered as *gibbosités* or *bosses*, meaning a crooked, humped, or hunched back. "The individual submitting to the operations required sees his deformity gradually diminish, and after a treatment longer or shorter according to the extent of the deformity, the body resumes its natural form. The discovery has met with the greatest success in France, and everything induces the belief that it will have the same result in this country." Dr. Lalaurie went on to say that he had "complied with the laws" of the United States and been "duly licenced to practice physic," meaning that his credentials had been examined by the Comité Médical of New Orleans. It was not his intention to "devote himself exclusively" to the treatment of physical abnormalities, and he hoped that "those who honor him with their confidence will be satisfied with the punctuality with which he will discharge the duties of his profession. He will attend *gratis* on the indigent." Finally, Dr. Lalaurie announced that he could "be found every day between the hours of eleven and three o'clock at Mr. Dalché's apothecary store, corner of Dumaine and Bourbon streets."[6]

New Orleans had few professional medical practitioners at the time, although many free women of color served as nurses and midwives. The city directory listed twenty druggists and twelve physicians. There were no specialists in orthopedics; an "Orthopaedic Institution" for the "surgical treatment of all deformities of the body, both congenital and acquired, such as club-foot, wry-neck, distortions of the spine, anchylosis, [and] dislocations" did not open until 1859.[7]

When Louis Lalaurie came to New Orleans in 1825, the French and Creole population was still uncompromisingly alienated from the newly arrived Americans. Dr. Lalaurie would have found his place in the French-speaking, Roman Catholic society of the Vieux Carré and surrounding residential neighborhoods and outlying plantations along the river. During his first months in the city, he lodged in the home of a family friend from Villeneuve, Pierre Dulcide Barran, formerly the solicitor general for the Spanish government. Letters to Louis from his father were addressed to Chez Maitre Barran.[8]

New Orleans must have seemed like a provincial backwater to the young French doctor fresh from his studies in Paris and Toulouse. Entertainment consisted of visiting among friends, attendance at theatrical performances and balls, and gambling. The Théâtre d'Orléans on Orleans Street between Royal and Bourbon presented French operettas, comedies, one-act vaudevilles, and tragedies. The Camp Street Theater offered similar fare in English. The Salle St. Philippe, at the corner of St. Philip and Royal Streets, advertised public dances, to which admittance cost one dollar, and potential patrons were assured that "managers will be appointed in order to keep good harmony." The Vieux Carré sported many gambling establishments, and most social gatherings featured card games and dancing. That winter Lalaurie would have experienced his first Carnival season, which at that time consisted of private parties leading up to the climax of Mardi Gras day.[9] The new doctor was probably invited to some of these events.

Louis Lalaurie had been a member of the Masonic lodge Les Amis des Bourbons during his student days, and as a newcomer to New Orleans he might have joined a local organization. The Grand Lodge of Louisiana

Etoile Polaire (Polar Star) was a Masonic lodge chartered in 1798 by the Grand Orient of France. Louis Lalaurie may have joined Etoile Polaire or one of the other French lodges when he arrived in New Orleans. The building still stands on North Rampart Street corner of Kerlerec, just outside the Vieux Carré. (Photograph by the author, May 1997.)

was comprised of the five original French lodges: Parfaite Union, Etoile Polaire, Charité, Concorde, and Persévérance. Shortly after Lalaurie arrived in town, the Grand Lodge posted notices in the newspapers inviting "Masons residing in New Orleans who are desirous of participating in the banquet" in honor of the visiting Marquis de Lafayette to submit their names. Three hundred Freemasons, possibly including Dr. Lalaurie, attended this event on April 14, 1825.[10] In 1827 one of Lalaurie's former lodge brothers from Les Amis des Bourbons asked if Freemasonry was popular in the United States, and if it had "provided some appeal" for him.[11] Lalaurie's answer has not been preserved.

·

We can only guess at how Louis Lalaurie met Delphine Macarty Blanque and how their relationship developed. His shipmate Charles Lanusse, who in 1826 married Elénore Mirtile de Macarty, or his landlord, the former Spanish official Pierre Dulcide Barran, might have introduced him into the Macartys' social circle. As we will see below, it is also possible that Delphine and Louis met and became romantically involved when she consulted the new doctor, a specialist in "straightening crooked backs," about the orthopedic condition of one of her children.

Delphine was living at the "Villa Blanque" on the river below the city, near the Macarty plantation.[12] She was thirty-eight years old at the time, but even as she approached middle age she was still described as a great beauty. She was from one of the wealthiest and most powerful families in Orleans Parish—a useful connection for an ambitious young doctor. Her father had died the year before, leaving her a sizable inheritance, and she had used this bequest to enrich herself even more. Popular legend has characterized Louis Lalaurie as an "inconspicuous" and "colorless" nonentity, a "meek, mousy little man" who "cowered at [his wife's] every word."[13] The archival evidence, however, reveals that Delphine found Lalaurie quite engaging. By late 1826 their relationship had become intimate, and Delphine was pregnant.

Louis Lalaurie's letters to his parents and siblings have not been discovered, so we must reconstruct the details of his life in New Orleans from their letters to him. The name of "Madame Blanque" appeared frequently in communications from his father in 1825 and 1826, indicating that Louis had at least mentioned his new friend to the family back in Villeneuve. Papa Lalaurie apparently viewed Delphine as an influential older lady who was taking a kindly interest in his young son and could help establish his career.

In October 1825, Lalaurie *père* mentioned a box of table linens that he had sent to Madame Blanque: "If the work and delicacy suit her, next spring I will send six more sets of twelve place settings. There is nothing I would not do, my dear friend, for the people who wish to show interest in you." There was some talk of sending Delphine's ten-year-old son, Paulin Blanque, to Dr. Lalaurie's parents in France. The elder Lalaurie wrote: "I would welcome the son of Madame Blanque as my own child, and she can be certain that I will watch over his health and his education with the same care that she would take herself. I would be happy for the opportunity to reward her for all the attention she has shown you." This, according to Papa Lalaurie, would be like "exchanging families for a time, giving ourselves the consolation of thinking that we are close to our children."[14] This statement clearly indicates that Lalaurie *père* thought of Delphine as a substitute parent to his "child" Louis, not as a potential daughter-in-law.

Louis appears to have confided to his brother, Laurent Eugène Lalaurie, that he was facing some sort of ethical dilemma. Did he reveal the fact that he had impregnated Madame Blanque, the woman viewed as his patron by the family back in Villeneuve? On Christmas Eve of 1826,

Laurent wrote that "moral troubles are the hardest, and your separation [from your kin] in a country completely new to you could only bring you many regrets." Regarding Louis's career, Laurent, who was also a doctor, advised that the medical profession could be "a path to fortune," through which he could ally himself with "a rich and honest family" and "make a marriage . . . that would shelter you from the uncertainties of fate." After that, Louis's brother hoped that "the remembrance of your country, your family, and your friends will speak to your heart, and you will return so we can all share your happiness."[15]

A popular element of the Lalaurie legend says that one of Delphine's children suffered from some crippling disability, probably curvature of the spine (kyphosis or scoliosis), and that Dr. Lalaurie had undertaken to cure this young person in exchange for the lady's hand. Madame Lalaurie's defenders, particularly her DeBuys descendants, argued that it was this primitive orthopedic treatment, and not the torture of family slaves, that accounted for the screams emanating from the Lalaurie mansion. Corinne DeBuys was quoted in a 1936 *New Orleans Morning Tribune* article, where she claimed that Dr. Lalaurie attempted to straighten the "twisted body" of Delphine's "deformed son" with chains. The boy's anguish supposedly plunged Madame Lalaurie into "fits of screaming, hence the rumors of chained and beaten slaves." In a 1941 article from the *New Orleans States*, Miriam DeBuys told a reporter that "one of Madame Lalaurie's daughters was a cripple," that Dr. Lalaurie "had promised to effect a remedy during his courtship of the widow, and that after the marriage, with the crude implements at hand in those days, the daughter was probably given treatment that proved painful, causing her to voice her agony."[16]

Delphine's son Paulin Blanque was perfectly healthy, but she indeed had a disabled daughter—probably Pauline Blanque—whose "crooked back" Dr. Lalaurie undertook to straighten. In the early nineteenth century, practitioners of the branch of medicine called "orthopraxy" would have prescribed braces or subjected their patients to rack-like mechanisms that stretched and rotated the body to bring it into alignment.[17]

In a letter of July 25, 1825, Papa Lalaurie spoke of the therapy that Madame Blanque's daughter, "the hunchbacked young lady" (*la Mademoiselle bossue*) was receiving from Dr. Lalaurie. The December 24, 1826, letter from Louis's brother Laurent also mentions his care of a "young deformed person" (*une jeune personne contrefaite*). Laurent cautioned Louis "not to promise too much [because] the difficulties are immense,

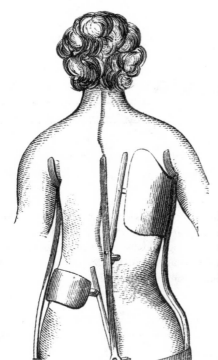

Device for the correction of "double lateral curvature of the spine." Henry Heather Bigg, *Orthopraxy* (1865), "Deformities," pp. 264–66, detail plate 87. (National Museum of American History, Smithsonian Institution.)

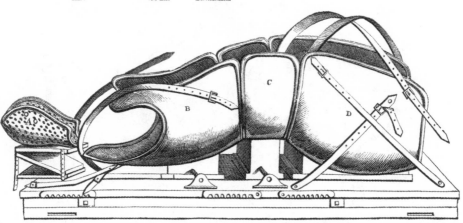

Device for "inclination, compression, and extension." This "form of apparatus . . . used in Paris . . . is called a 'corsetlet' and, as its name implies, forms a bed or couch, in which the patient is placed recumbent, and is fixed there by a series of corsets. The apparatus is divided into three sections, moving by screws, in opposite horizontal directions; whilst elongation is also obtainable at the will of the operator. The head rests in a padded receptacle (a), the position of which can be varied to suit the condition of the case. . . . The thorax is received by a padded shield (b); the lumbar region rests in a movable sheath (c), whilst the pelvis is firmly embraced by the lower part of the apparatus." Henry Heather Bigg, *Orthopraxy*, "Deformities," 280–82, plate 92. (National Museum of American History, Smithsonian Institution.)

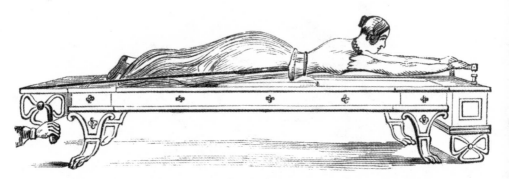

Coles' Orthopaedic Sofa "consists of a padded sofa on which the patient is placed in a prone posture. A soft belt surrounds the hips, and terminates by lateral straps in a winch turned by the hand of an attendant. The hands of the patient grasp firmly a rod placed at arms's length, and extension of the spine is made by means of the winch. This is a very ingenious piece of mechanism for the purpose it is intended to effect." Henry Heather Bigg, *Orthopraxy* (1865), "Deformities," 281–82, plate 93. (National Museum of American History, Smithsonian Institution.)

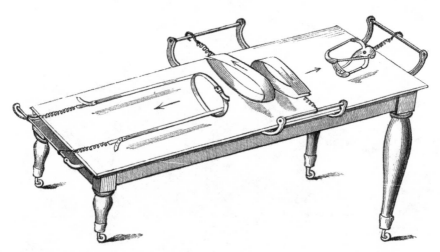

The spinal couch "consists of a well-padded surface, having a rest for the head, which can be moved obliquely upwards by means of an elastic cord fixed to the upper rail of the plane. At the lower edge of the plane, another rail is arranged for the attachment of two elastic bands belonging to a padded belt, which is fastened round the hips. Another rail is arranged at the side corresponding with the dorsal curve, and a fourth rail is fixed at the lateral edge of the plane answering to the lumber curve. To both these rails soft webbing bands are fastened by elastic cords, and these webbing bands pass in antagonistic directions over the arcs of dorsal and lumbar deflections." Henry Heather Bigg, *Orthopraxy* (1865), "Deformities," 285–86, plate 95. (National Museum of American History, Smithsonian Institution.)

Spinal gymnastics. "The following drawing represents one of the most useful exercises in cases of double lateral curvature. . . . The patient's pelvis is fixed by a strap to the seat; whilst over the arc of the dorsal curve, and acting in a direction calculated to diminish it, a band passes which is attached to the side of the apparatus. Another band is also placed on the apposite side of the body over the lumbar curve, and similarly fastened to the side. Both hands are acted upon by weights carefully proportioned to the degree of curvature." Henry Heather Bigg, *Orthopraxy*, "Deformities," 350–52, plate 130. (National Museum of American History, Smithsonian Institution.)

especially if the patient is over the age of seventeen years." The treatment of such abnormalities was "still a very new branch of our art," and a cure required "at least two years." But, wrote Laurent, if Louis succeeded in straightening the spine of this young woman, his reputation would be assured.[18]

The year 1827 began with tragic news from France. In a letter from Papa Lalaurie dated January 5, Louis learned of the death of his mother on Christmas day from an "attack of apoplexy." Papa Lalaurie was nearly hysterical with grief for his "excellent spouse, this friend so dear to my heart, this woman so good, so virtuous, so well-regarded by all, my tender helpmate, my other self."[19]

Three months later, the elder Lalaurie was still overwhelmed by sadness. On March 7, 1827, he wrote to Louis that "you cannot ignore the immensity of the loss that we have experienced. . . . This letter . . . will serve to remind you of the one who gave you life, who believed so much in you, and for whom I will cry until the day that I go to join her. The same stone will cover your father and mother, and if you ever see your country again, visit the gravesite and let a tear fall on it."[20]

After the death of the mother, Louis Lalaurie's family became even more insistent that he wind up his affairs in New Orleans and return to Villeneuve. His brother Laurent wrote in February 1827 that he "desired before anything to have a wife one day, and to have created a small fortune for myself. I work with ardor; I have the happiness of having obtained some success. If my wishes are fulfilled, I will especially enjoy dreaming that, if you fail in your hopes, I can offer you a shelter from need."[21] Laurie *père* also wanted his son established in a "good" marriage and back in the protective circle of the family. In a letter of March 1827, he referred to a communication in which Louis had expressed his intention to "acquire an honest existence" before returning to France. But why, asked his father, do you "remain in a country where you will only be rejected," instead of coming home where "you will be able to make a suitable establishment?" Papa Lalaurie warned Louis that in New Orleans, he would be unable to bring about an advantageous match because no rich young woman would marry a man with no fortune.[22] Nothing in these letters gives any indication that Louis's family was aware of a romantic relationship between Louis and the Widow Blanque.

In the March 1827 letter, Papa Lalaurie also made a pronouncement regarding his late wife's estate. By law, Louis and his siblings would have inherited her half of their parents' community property, amounting to two thousand francs each, but the father wanted to retain control of the funds: "Nothing has changed . . . and I will administer [the money] as I did when [your mother] was alive. . . . I intend for each of you to give me . . . a renunciation in my favor of your portion of the inheritance." He went on to say that if any of his children should "fall into need, it is in my house that you will find a retreat."[23] On August 9, 1827, just before Delphine was delivered of her child, Louis signed his portion of his mother's estate over to his father. He declared this arrangement valid "until the day when I will ask that a rendering be done of the account," and authorized his father to use the funds as he saw fit.[24]

On August 13, 1827, Delphine gave birth to a son named Jean Louis Leonard Lalaurie. Within a short time Dr. Lalaurie was making plans to leave New Orleans, and in mid-October he authorized a friend to oversee his financial affairs during his "absence from the state."[25] Where was he going, and why? Was he leaving town on pressing business—perhaps some money-making scheme to support his new family, or was he skipping out on the mother of his child?

Whatever the nature of Lalaurie's mysterious journey, he was back in New Orleans on January 12, 1828. Five months after the birth of Jean Louis, Louis Lalaurie and Delphine Macarty Blanque appeared before a notary to negotiate their marriage contract. Louis declared that he had $2,000; this would have been the inheritance from his mother, which his father still controlled. The inventory of Delphine's property included $5,000 worth of jewelry and clothing; $2,800 worth of household furniture and silverware; promissory notes in the amount of $4,900; a carriage, carts, horses, and mules worth $1,000 and $43,200 worth of real estate. Delphine also declared ownership of twelve adult slaves and three children valued at $10,500: Bonne, a laundress, cook, and pastry-maker, with her children Juliette, Florence, and Jules; the sisters Célestine and Louise, domestics; the coachmen Bastien and Célestin; the shoemaker Devince; the laborers Louis and Lubin; Nicolas, a cook; Théodore, a cooper; and William, a gardener. Some of these probably had come from her father's estate. Also listed was John, a fifteen-year-old "American Negro" purchased by Delphine on the day before her marriage to Lalaurie and perhaps intended as a manservant for her new husband. John was specified to be "of a feeble constitution."[26]

After subtracting $1,000 in personal debts, the bride was worth $66,389.58, an amount having the purchasing power of approximately $1.5 million in today's currency. In a marginal note, Delphine stipulated that she would retain title to her "paraphernal goods," meaning all of the property that she brought into the marriage. The contract ended with the statement that "the future husband and wife recognize their natural son Jean Louis Lalaurie, born in this city the thirteenth of August, 1827 . . . and [convey to him] all the rights of a child born during their marriage."[27]

Having settled their business affairs, the couple proceeded to St. Louis Cathedral, where they recited their nuptial vows. In recording the marriage, the priest appended to the usual particulars the statement that "the parties by the said marriage expressed their wish to legitimize their child Jean." Jean Louis Lalaurie was baptized the next day. None of Delphine's relatives signed the sacramental register as witnesses to the marriage or stood as godparents for Jean Louis.[28] In an attempt to conceal the fact that Jean Louis was born out of wedlock, later defenders of Madame Lalaurie have given the date of the marriage as June 12, 1825, instead of the actual date of January 12, 1828.[29]

We can only speculate about the relationship between this unlikely couple. Did the lady, who had been widowed for ten years, develop a passion for Louis Lalaurie and maneuver the naive young man into her bed? Was her pregnancy an accident, or was it calculated to entrap him? Or was it Lalaurie, infatuated by her charm, and especially by her money and status, who pursued Delphine in response to his father's injunction to marry a lady with wealth and social connections? Maybe, to take a less cynical view, the two were simply in love.

The response from Louis Lalaurie's father and siblings to news of his marriage is unknown. The last letter from Lalaurie *père*, quoted above, is dated March 7, 1827. There are a few inconsequential letters from Louis's sisters, the last written on December 1, 1827, and then silence. If more correspondence exists to indicate whether the family sent happy congratulations or reacted with disapproval, it has not come to light.

Delphine was forty years old at the time of her marriage to Louis Lalaurie, who had just celebrated his twenty-fifth birthday. Delphine's first daughter, Borja López y Angulo, was only two years younger than her mother's new husband. Borja had married the planter and businessman Placide Forstall in 1821 and was already the mother of three youngsters.[30] Delphine's other children, Pauline, Laure, Jeanne, and Paulin Blanque, ranged in age from eighteen to twelve. In antebellum New Orleans, men routinely married or entered into domestic partnerships with much younger women, but the marriage of a man in his mid-twenties to a forty-year-old grandmother is virtually unheard of.

Some very revealing observations about Delphine and her new husband are found in the Ste-Gême Family Papers at the Historic New Orleans Collection. The Baron Henri de Ste-Gême was a French nobleman who settled in Saint-Domingue after the French Revolution, became involved in privateering in the Caribbean, and immigrated to Louisiana in 1809. He had business dealings with Delphine's father and her second husband, Jean Blanque.[31] In 1816 Ste-Gême married a New Orleans widow who owned a sugar plantation in the Gentilly area.[32] In 1818 Ste-Gême and his wife returned to France, leaving Jean Boze as his New Orleans business manager. Over a period of many years Boze sent his employer periodic newsletters filled with reports of current events and gossip about Ste-Gême's neighbors and associates in New Orleans.[33]

On December 1, 1828, Jean Boze wrote that the Widow Blanque had "married a young French doctor, newly arrived [in the city]. They do not have a happy household; they fight, often separate, and then return to each other, which would make one believe that someday they will abandon each other completely." Boze again referred to the remarriage of the Widow Blanque on July 20, 1829, adding that before the wedding she had given birth to a child.[34] As we will see in the next chapter, Boze's December 1828 and July 1829 letters also contain the earliest mention of Delphine's cruelty to her slaves.

During the early years of their marriage, Delphine and Louis lived at Delphine's plantation below the city with the Blanque children and their young son Jean Louis Lalaurie. The 1830 census shows the family and their twenty-four slaves among the "inhabitants of the bank of the Mississippi River between the Faubourg Danois [D'Aunoy] and the Fisherman's Canal."[35]

Apparently, country living did not suit the Lalauries. Delphine had set her sights on a fine new townhouse under construction at the corner of Royal and Hospital (now Governor Nicholls) in the Vieux Carré, and during the spring and summer of 1831 she undertook to raise the purchase price by selling or mortgaging some of her properties.[36] In May 1831 she transformed the former "Villa Blanque" into a new subdivision called the Faubourg Delphine and sold residential building lots at public auction.[37] The scheme was short-lived, and a few months later Delphine and the buyers of the lots sold the land to the Levee Steam Cotton Press Company for $30,100. The site of the Faubourg Delphine, between today's St. Ferdinand and Montegut Streets, became Press Street.[38] Delphine was now prepared to buy the home she considered suitable for her station in life.

John P. Coleman incorrectly stated in his 1924 *New Orleans States* article "The Famous Haunted House in Royal Street" that the Lalaurie house was built in 1773 by two French "adventurers," Jean and Henri Ramaie, and was later purchased by Delphine's father and passed on to Delphine.[39] In reality, she acquired the property from Edmond Soniat Dufossat on August 30, 1831. The land was part of a large tract granted in 1726 to the Ursuline nuns by King Louis XV of France; their right of ownership was renewed by a patent from the United States government in 1824. In 1825 the Ursulines sold six lots to Germain Ducatel, who in 1828 sold the two corner lots to Edmond Soniat Dufossat.[40]

It was these lots that Delphine purchased in August 1831. Lot number one, facing Royal Street, was bounded on the uptown side by the property of the attorney John Randolph Grymes. The back lot, number two, faced Hospital Street, and was bounded on the river side by the property of Julie Duralde, widow of John Bruce Clay. Along with the two lots, Delphine also acquired the house and outbuildings, which were still under construction. Soniat Dufossat declared in the act of sale that "the whole will be finished and ready to be delivered at the latest within thirty days . . . at his own cost and expense. . . . The work that remains . . . will be done under the direction and according to the taste of Sieur Soniat . . . [relying] on the judgement of experts . . . accepted by the said Dame Lalaurie." The total price was $33,750, of which Delphine paid $6,000 cash and owed a balance of $27,750 payable in two years at 8 percent interest.[41]

In 1830, when Jean Boze was seventy-seven years old, he moved from Gentilly into the Vieux Carré and rented a room near the corner of Royal and Barracks, less than a block from what would become the site of the Lalaurie mansion. Boze commented to Ste-Gême in his August–November 1831 newsletter that Madame Lalaurie had just bought "a beautiful brand new home with an iron balcony and many amenities." He also mentioned in this letter that she had made an offer on one Ste-Gême's houses at the corner of Levee and Quartier (now Decatur and Barracks). Boze, who obviously disliked Madame Lalaurie, later expressed "pleasure, contentment, and satisfaction" when Ste-Gême's property was sold to another buyer.[42]

The Lalaurie mansion, when built in 1831, was a two-story townhouse

LALAURIE HOUSE
ERECTED 1831

Pencil sketch by preservation architect Samuel Wilson Jr., 1962, showing how the Lalaurie mansion would have looked at the time of construction. Architectural historians have determined that the dwelling, finished in 1831, had only two stories and an attic, topped by a hipped roof and dormers. The third story was added when the house was rebuilt after the fire. (Vieux Carré Survey, Square 50, courtesy of The Historic New Orleans Collection.)

fronting directly on the street. The interior layout, with its center hall and staircase, shows more American than French influence. The building now familiar as the "Haunted House" is quite different from the original. The present flat-roofed third story replaced a hipped roof with dormers. The balcony would have had delicate, wrought-iron railings; the wider gallery with heavy cast-iron railings supported by iron colonnettes is a later addition. The ground floor of most townhouses of the time was used as a storage and work space or was occupied by retail shops, although this might not have been true of the Lalaurie residence. The living quarters, consisting of parlor, dining room, and bedchambers, were on the second floor, and the finest materials and ornamentation were used for this level of the house. The attic under the hipped roof might have had quarters for the most favored domestic servants.

Within the enclosed courtyard behind the main residence was a well, cistern, and privy, and it is here that the enslaved workers would have performed household chores. A multi-story service wing extended at a

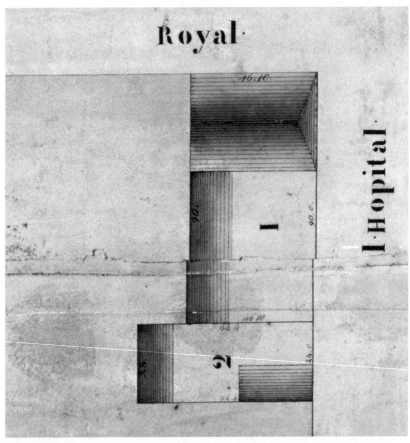

"Plan de 2 lots de terre dans le Carré de la Ville." This plan was created on February 24, 1837, when the Lalaurie property was sold after the fire. Presumably the configuration of the buildings had not changed since Madame Lalaurie bought the two lots and the nearly completed house and dependencies in 1831. The plan shows the main residence on lot 1 measuring forty-six feet, ten inches, fronting on Royal Street; the slope of the hipped roof is indicated by a gradation of the lines from heavier at the peak to finer at the edges. The attached service wing is ninety feet long, with the shed roof also indicated by a gradation of the lines. Lot 2 shows a shed-roofed outbuilding across the back of the property and another perpendicular to Hospital Street. (Plan Book 73, folio 49, courtesy of the Notarial Archives Research Center.)

right angle from the back of the main residence. This building had a slop-
ing shed roof, narrow balconies, and an outside stairway, and would have
contained the kitchen and slave quarters. The other outbuildings on the
back lot might have been a stable, carriage house, laundry, or additional
slave quarters. A wide gate in the outside wall of the courtyard opened
onto Hospital Street.[43]

The family moved into their new townhouse in late 1831, and "L. Lalaurie, M.D." was listed in the 1832 city directory at the corner of Royal and
Hospital.[44] The household included the four Blanque siblings—twenty-
three-year-old Pauline, nineteen-year-old Laure, eighteen-year-old Jeanne,
and seventeen-year-old Paulin—and Jean Louis Lalaurie, age five. Jeanne
Blanque moved out in 1833 when she married Pierre Auguste DeHault
DeLassus, son of Charles DeHault DeLassus, former governor of Spanish
West Florida and governor of the Missouri Territory under the American administration.[45] Paulin Blanque also left home in 1833 to enroll as a
freshman at Yale University.[46]

Dwelling within a few blocks of the Lalaurie mansion were not only
Delphine's married daughters Borja and Jeanne but also the free colored
concubines and the nearly white natural sons and daughters of Delphine's
male relatives.[47]

In 1816, shortly after the death of Jean Blanque, Delphine and her
brother Louis Barthélémy had stood as godparents to their colored half-
sister Emesie Macarty. In early 1834 Delphine and Louis Barthélémy donated to eighteen-year-old Emesie a young slave from their father's succession as a "demonstration of their affection." The girl's mother, Sophie
Mousante, was present and signed the notarial act.[48] Most elite white
women did not socialize with or even acknowledge their relations of
mixed race.[49] While Delphine's dealings with Emesie and Sophie do not
prove that she treated them as equals, she apparently felt no animosity toward her father's concubine and his natural child. This liberal attitude may
not have extended to her other non-white kin, but there is no evidence
that she harbored such a grudge against them that she tortured her slaves
in retaliation, as some writers have claimed.

The Lalauries are said to have lived lavishly in their new home. Dr.
Lalaurie had not yet established a lucrative medical practice, indicating
that their lifestyle was financed by Delphine's wealth and resources. Delphine filled the house with the finest furnishings and works of art, and
the Lalauries held extravagant parties to which the best society of New
Orleans were invited.

The move to the Royal Street mansion and their more luxurious mode of living did not improve the relationship between Delphine and Louis. Jean Boze's observation of discord within their household was accurate. On November 16, 1832, Delphine petitioned the First Judicial District Court for a separation from the bed and board of her husband; in French this was termed a *séparation de corps et de biens*, literally a "separation of body and goods." The Louisiana Civil Code of 1825 allowed several grounds for such an uncoupling. The husband could "claim a separation in case of adultery on the part of the wife," but the wife could only claim a separation when her husband "has kept his concubine in their common dwelling." Married persons could also separate "on account of excesses, cruel treatment, or outrages . . . if the ill treatment is of such a nature as to render their living together insupportable," for "public defamation," for "abandonment," or for "an attempt of one of the married persons against the life of the other."[50]

Delphine quoted the law almost verbatim when she claimed that Lalaurie had "treated her in such a manner as to render their living together insupportable." She further stated that "on the 26th of October last [1832] in the presence of many witnesses, the said Louis Lalaurie went so far as to not only ill treat her, but even to beat and wound her in the most outrageous and cruel manner." She testified that Lalaurie was staying in rural Plaquemines Parish, and asked the judge to "authorize her to live separately from her husband in the home she now occupies with her family at the corner of Royal and Hospital streets." She was, according to this court record, "already . . . separated of goods from her husband by her marriage contract."[51] The Civil Code of 1825 stipulated that "The wife, even when she is separate in estate from her husband, cannot alienate, grant, mortgage, or acquire [property] . . . unless her husband concurs in the act or yields his consent by writing." But "The woman separated from bed and board has no need in any case for the authorization of her husband, as this separation carries with it not only a separation of property, but a dissolution of the community of acquests and gains."[52]

On April 11, 1833, five months after Delphine had petitioned for a separation from bed and board, Louis Lalaurie declared before a notary that his medical practice required his residence in Plaquemines Parish, and that he therefore gave permission to his wife to "administer their goods and affairs without his consent and authorization."[53]

What was the true story behind this estrangement? Was Lalaurie indeed an overbearing and abusive husband, or was he reacting to his wife's erratic behavior? It is easy to imagine that Delphine became increasingly possessive and demanding, and that her mental unbalance prompted Dr. Lalaurie to spend more and more time away from home. His activities in Plaquemines Parish are unknown. It is difficult to imagine that he was pursuing a career in orthopedics in this remote outpost instead of establishing his medical practice in the city of New Orleans. Maybe he served as a general practitioner for the planters and their slaves. Had he also, perhaps, found a more agreeable female companion?

Delphine's separation from the bed and board of her husband does not seem to have been permanent. As Jean Boze had observed in 1828, the couple's fights, separations, and temporary reconciliations were notorious. In subsequent business transactions, Delphine was referred to as the "wife separated in property of Louis Lalaurie," not the "wife separated from bed and board." When she appeared before a notary to buy and sell real estate or slaves, Dr. Lalaurie was stated to be "present and accepting for his wife" and his signature appears next to hers on the notarial acts. He would have been in and out of the Royal Street house. As we will see, he was there on April 10, 1834, the day of the fire.

5

"PASSIVE BEINGS"

The institution of slavery was not only tolerated but considered a necessity in colonial Louisiana, and this attitude continued under the American administration. In this slave-owning society it was understood that, in order to control one's bondspeople, a degree of chastisement was indispensable. Excessive cruelty, however, was prohibited by law and abhorrent to public sentiment.

The 1724 French *Code Noir* forbade "killing . . . [or] mutilating slaves in . . . any part of their bodies, under the penalty of the confiscation of said slaves; and masters, so offending, shall be liable to a criminal prosecution." It was nevertheless permissible to "put slaves in irons, and to have them whipped with rods or ropes."[1] The somewhat more liberal Spanish *Codigo Negro*, although it still permitted physical punishment, allowed slaves to petition to be sold away from a vicious master.[2]

After Louisiana was purchased by the United States, lawmakers formulated an American Black Code at the 1806 session of the first legislature of the Territory of Orleans. It afforded little protection for the enslaved. Section 16 states that "In case any person . . . should inflict any cruel punishment, except flogging, or striking with a whip, leather thong, switch, or small stick, or putting in irons, or confining such slave, the said person shall forfeit and pay for every offence a fine not exceeding five hundred and not less than two hundred dollars." According to Section 17, "if any slave be mutilated, beaten, or ill-treated . . . the owner or other person having charge of the slave . . . shall be deemed responsible and guilty of said offense, and shall be prosecuted without further evidence, unless said owner . . . can prove the contrary by good and sufficient evidence, or can clear himself by his own oath." The slave owner's oath was seldom contested because, in most cases, the only witnesses to the cruel treatment were other slaves, who were not permitted to testify against white people.[3]

In 1808 the distinguished jurists Louis Casimir Moreau Lislet, a Saint-Domingue immigrant, and James Brown, an American, compiled the *Digest of the Civil Laws Now in Force in the Territory of Orleans with Alterations and Amendments Adapted to Its Present System of Government.* There was some confusion about whether slaves were to be regarded as "persons" or "things," and the lawmakers finally decided on the ambiguous term *passive beings.* In the chapter titled "Of Slaves," article 16 declares that "The slave is entirely subject to the will of his master, who may correct and chastise him, though not with unusual rigor, nor so as to maim or mutilate him, or to expose him to the danger of loss of life, or to cause his death." Article 27 provides that "When the master shall be convicted of cruel treatment of his slave, the judge [may] deem proper to pronounce, besides the penalty established for such cases, that the slave shall be sold at public auction, in order to place him out of the reach of the power which his master has abused."[4]

It was not until 1822 that Moreau Lislet, Edward Livingston, and Pierre Derbigny were commissioned by the Louisiana Legislature to produce a complete text of the civil law, published in 1825 as the *Civil Code of the State of Louisiana.*[5] Article 173, regarding cruel treatment of slaves, is identical to article 16 of the 1808 *Digest,* and article 192, which provides that slaves may be sold at auction to remove them from an abusive owner, is identical to article 27 of the *Digest.* Article 177 reiterates that a slave "cannot be a witness [against a white person] in either civil or criminal matters."[6] The 1825 law was in effect when Madame Lalaurie was first denounced for cruelty in 1828, and it was still in effect in 1834 when the fire at the Lalaurie mansion revealed her starved and tortured slaves to a horrified public.

·

Delphine Macarty Lalaurie had lived her entire life in a society in which slavery was omnipresent. Her parents and all of her relatives owned numerous slaves, as did her second husband, Jean Blanque. Legend says that both her father and mother treated their bondspeople with cruelty, and Blanque, a major slave dealer who was engaged in the marginally legal importation of African captives into Louisiana, probably had little regard for his chattel as human beings.

In New Orleans, domestics who served within the household and the skilled male and female workers who hired themselves out usually experienced a relatively mild form of bondage. Plantation laborers had a much harder lot. Evidence of cruelty in the city and in the rural parishes crops up in family letters, travelers' accounts, newspaper stories, and court cases from the colonial period until just before the Civil War. Some of these sources indicate that Creole women were the most likely to mistreat their bondspeople, and that female slaves were frequently the target of their abuse. The mistress of the household had more direct interactions with female domestics, who would have been more vulnerable to corporal punishment than larger, stronger male servants or laborers. In addition, there might have been real or imagined sexual relationships between enslaved women and the master, resulting in jealousy on the part of his wife and punishment of the slaves.

This is not to say that men were not also guilty of abusing their bondspeople. In 1796 Joseph Xavier Delfau de Pontalba, in letters to his wife, offhandedly mentioned that he had his manservant whipped because he failed to bring Pontalba his breakfast on time, and that another slave, sent into the city as a milk vendor, was put in the stocks because she failed to sell the expected quantity. Pontalba's friend Guy Dreux killed a house servant discovered "ransacking his armoir in order to rob him." The authorities investigated the incident, and Dreux faced a sentence of "several years in the penal colonies." Pontalba advised him to "arrange matters with money if possible," which was evidently the case, since Dreux was never convicted.[7]

The Frenchman Claude-Cézar Robin wrote in his *Voyages dans l'Interieur de la Louisiane, 1802–1806* that plantation slaves "who are guilty of serious offenses" were "stretched naked between [four] stakes, face down" and given up to a hundred strokes of the whip. "Women escape nothing of this rigorous punishment," and for those who are pregnant, "before attaching them to the stakes, a hole is made in the ground where . . . the belly will lie." Robin particularly noted the cruelty of the white Creole women. If a slave did not obey orders promptly, the mistress would "watch with a dry eye as she sees the victim attached to the four stakes. She counts the blows and if the arm of him who strikes begins to falter or if the blood does not run fast enough, she raises her voice in menacing tones." Robin believed that the women had come to crave this "horrible spectacle" as a stimulant: "In order to revive themselves, they require to hear the sharp cries and to see again the flow of blood."[8]

Major Amos Stoddard, an American military officer and anti-slavery advocate from New York who was stationed in Louisiana during the territorial period, wrote that the white Creole women "are remarkably loquacious, and their manners are more polished than those of the men; they are hospitable, and manifest much pleasure in offering to their guests and visitors the best things they are able to furnish. They have but one fault not easily extenuated; they are habitually cruel to their slaves."[9]

The famous architect and engineer Benjamin Henry Boneval Latrobe, in New Orleans in 1819 to oversee the building of the municipal waterworks, also noted the savage treatment of slaves by white Creole women: "It is impossible to imagine that [their] fair, mild, & somewhat languid faces could express any feeling but kindness and humanity. And yet . . . those soft eyes can look on the tortures of their slaves, inflicted by their orders, with satisfaction, & cooly prescribe the dose of infliction." Latrobe's landlady, Madame Tremoulet, punished a domestic for not making a bed at the hour prescribed. The enslaved woman was "stripped quite naked, tied to a bed post, & [Madame Tremoulet] herself, in the presence of her daughter, whipped [the servant] with a cowskin until she bled." Latrobe also described the first wife of Bernard de Marigny as "a beast of the same kind. A gentleman whom I will not name saw her stand by, some years ago, when a naked woman was tied to a ladder by her order to undergo the punishment of the whip."[10]

In addition, Latrobe reported that "another of these hellcats," Madame Lanusse, wife of the president of the Bank of Louisiana, had "whipped a negress to death, and treated another so cruelly that she died a short time after. Mr. _____, a principal merchant of this place, stated the facts to the Grand Jury, but it was hushed up from respect to the lady's husband." The viciousness of Madame Lanusse is born out in a letter written by Jean Boze to Henri de Ste-Gême at the time of the 1834 fire, in which Boze reported that she was "accused of the same crime" as Madame Lalaurie.[11]

Madame Lanusse was Delphine's cousin Céleste de Macarty. Céleste's brother Jean Baptiste Barthélémy had successive relationships with the free women of color Henriette Prieto and CéCé Carpentier and fathered a total of seven biracial children, including a daughter named Céleste Macarty. The white Céleste might have found it insulting that a person of color had the same name as herself. The Swedish writer Fredrika Bremer declared in her 1851 travel memoir, *Homes of the New World*, that "Madame Lallorue's [*sic*]" abuse of her slaves was motivated by "the behavior of her brother toward his mistress of the colored race. . . . [She] mistreated [them] because she enjoyed and relished their sufferings." Bremer's informants might have confused Delphine Macarty Lalaurie with the equally reprehensible Céleste Macarty Lanusse. In Bremer's opinion, the horrifying tale served to reinforce the impression formed during her sojourn in the South that "women not infrequently were found to be the cruelest slave owners."[12]

Occasionally the abused slaves fought back. On June 20, 1829, a brief notice in the *Bee* announced that "the negro-wench named Phoebe, who murdered her mistress Madame Leonard, was condemned to be hung." Jean Boze later provided more details when he wrote that a "young American negress," having suffered mistreatment by her elderly white owner, had killed the woman with an axe and was executed on June 26.[13]

In the 1850s, when newspapers regularly featured a column of "local intelligence," one finds articles denouncing owners, many of them women, who were accused of slave abuse. A free woman of color named Marguerite Peyroux was arrested for "putting her slaves to torture."[14] A Mrs. Padron was arrested for "inflicting cruel and unlawful punishment on a slave girl, her own property."[15] A police officer discovered "a slave boy belonging to Mrs. Woods . . . bearing marks of extreme cruel treatment, unable to walk from the severity of his injuries, and appearing as if he were starved."[16] The "inhuman woman" Fanny Smith, alleged to be the "keeper of a house of prostitution," had tortured two young enslaved boys by "burning them with red-hot rods," and had "thrown her slave woman Eliza into the street naked" with her back "beaten and mangled . . . in a horrible manner, the blood flowing from her wounds." Another of Smith's bondswomen, Aglave, had "surrendered herself up" at the police station, asking to be given a refuge from her mistress.[17] The newspapers also reported on other abused slaves who had come to the police for "protection from ill-usage on the part of their owners," as in the case of Rose, the property of Madame Leguise, and Queen Victoria, belonging to the free woman of color Madame Aimer.[18]

Evidence of slave abuse also appears in court records. Most of these atrocities occurred on the plantations, not in the city of New Orleans. Both civil and criminal cases involving cruelty to enslaved persons were tried in the lower courts, and some made their way to the state supreme court on appeal. Few of the lower court records have survived, but Judith Kelleher Schafer has analyzed the supreme court cases in *Slavery, the Civil Law, and the Supreme Court of Louisiana* (1994).

Civil cases involved the death or injury of slaves as property, and owners brought suit against overseers and others for the price of the dead worker or the amount by which the injury had diminished his or her value. In an 1842 civil case, an overseer beat a pregnant slave so severely that she delivered her baby prematurely and both mother and child subsequently died. In 1855 an owner sued his overseer, who had stripped an enslaved man naked, tied him down on the cold ground, whipped him, and poured castor oil down his throat; the slave died within a few hours. In 1856 an overseer nailed a man's penis to a porch post, and "inflicted blows upon him until said negro pulled loose from the post." This slave also died.[19]

Criminal cases of masters charged with excessive cruelty to their own slaves were infrequent, but they did exist. The worst was an 1849 instance of a defendant who "gouged out a hole" in his slave's abdomen and beat him to death. The slave owner was convicted of manslaughter, and the supreme court upheld the conviction. The sentence was not specified.[20]

The examples given by Pontalba, Robin, Stoddard, Latrobe, and Boze, the 1850s newspaper articles, and the supreme court cases cited by Judith Schafer illustrate that the reports of Madame Lalaurie's barbarous deeds are not necessarily exaggerated, and that such atrocities, although rare, did take place in colonial and antebellum Louisiana.

·

Delphine owned at least fifty-four men, women, and children between 1816, when she settled the estate of her second husband, Jean Blanque, and 1834, when she fled New Orleans after the fire. Notarial and court records and the funeral registers of St. Louis Cathedral provide evidence of their names, ages, color, and skills.

Following the 1816 resolution of Jean Blanque's succession, Delphine kept fifteen enslaved adults and four children as her "matrimonial right." In January 1828, the names of twelve additional slaves were included in the inventory of Delphine's property attached to her marriage contract with Louis Lalaurie.

After marrying Lalaurie, Delphine purchased eighteen more slaves, substantially increasing her workforce. In early November 1828, while still living on her downriver plantation, she acquired Cyrus, Matilda, Maria, Nelson, Rochin, and Samson.[21] She purchased a slave named Lucinda in April 1830.[22] In 1831, prior to moving into the Royal Street mansion, she paid for Abram, Amos, Frederick, James, Mary, Sally, and Patsy. Patsy was described as being "five feet ten inches tall" with a "good moral character, not in the habit of running away."[23] Delphine acquired Diana and Mary Anne in 1832.[24] In 1833 she bought Lively and Priscilla.[25] These individuals ranged in age from twelve to thirty-one years; most were in their teens or early twenties. All were black and all except Rochin had English names, indicating that they were "American Negroes." Delphine had in fact acquired some of them from slave traders from Virginia, Kentucky, and Mississippi. Only a few were described as having any particular skills. Abram and Nelson were carters. James was a blacksmith and carpenter. Diana was a laundress, ironer, and domestic. Sally was a seamstress "capable of making dresses, shirts, trousers, and waistcoats."

On November 22, 1828, a few weeks after acquiring the first of her new American slaves, Delphine sold six of her original bondspeople: the sisters Célestine and Louise; Suzette and her sixteen-year-old son, Edouard; Nancy's sixteen-year-old mulatto son, Ben; and Bonne's ten-year-old daughter, Juliette. The buyer was a family friend, Louis Brugnière of St. Bernard Parish. Within three months Brugnière sold Célestine, Edouard, Juliette, and Ben to another family friend, Andre Dussumier. Louise and Suzette might have died; the funeral register for 1828 is missing. In May 1830, Dussumier sold Célestine, Edouard, Juliette, and Ben back to Delphine.[26]

Despite her reputation as a cruel mistress, Delphine did grant freedom to some of her slaves. She had already emancipated Jean Louis in 1819. In 1828 she liberated her children's nurse, the Senegalese woman Hélène, for "faithful service." Hélène had been with the Macarty family for years; Delphine's half-sister Adelaide Lecomte Piernas had acquired Hélène from the succession of their mother, and Jean Blanque had purchased her from Madame Piernas in 1810.[27] In 1832 both Lalauries petitioned the Parish Court for permission to free the shoemaker Devince and asked that he be allowed to remain in the state, declaring that "the motives which now influence them . . . are to reward his fidelity and to stimulate other slaves to observe the like good condition."[28]

.

Delphine may have been an abusive slave owner for all of her adult life, but she was never accused of mistreating her bondspeople until after her 1828 marriage to Louis Lalaurie. Later that year the rumors began to fly. In Jean Boze's December 1, 1828, newsletter to Henri de Ste-Gême, Boze mentioned that Madame Lalaurie's abuses had come to light: "Finally justice descended on her home and, after being assured of the truth of the denunciations for barbarous treatment of her slaves contrary to the law, [the authorities] found them still all bloody. She had them incarcerated, letting them be given only the bare necessities." On July 20, 1829, Boze wrote to Ste-Gême that Madame Lalaurie's case had come before the criminal court, but she had been "absolved [from blame] by an indulgent jury, who contended that no witness had come forward to declare that she was seen beating the slaves . . . with her own hands." Boze went on to say that this case, "which caused such a public outcry, should serve as a lesson for her to avoid the cruelty that characterizes this family."[29]

Fredrika Bremer's New Orleans informants were probably referring to the 1828 and 1829 incidents when they reported that Madame "Lallorue" had "ruled with arbitrary sway" over the slaves on her plantation below the city. Her viciousness "roused her neighbors in arms against her. They announced that they would no longer hear of such actions, and in case they did, she should become amenable to law." According to Bremer, she "derived an income by hiring out her slaves, who every week were compelled to bring home their pay to her. . . . Woe to them [who] did not return on time or [whose] earnings were less than thought proper. Her house-slaves had no better fate; on the slightest occasion . . . she confined them to the cellar, fettered with iron chains, where she visited only to practice her cruelty on them."[30]

By the time of Boze's May 1832 newsletter, the Lalauries had moved to their new townhouse on Royal Street and were quarreling so violently that Delphine would petition the court for a separation from bed and board. Boze himself was living only a block away, at the corner of Royal and Barracks. He wrote to Ste-Gême that Madame Lalaurie had been indicted by the criminal court. Again he described the cause as the "barbarous treatment of her slaves," but went on to say that by paying a sum of money she was able to clear herself of the charge. While the case was being settled, one man, referred to as the "martyred negro," was held in protective custody at the guardhouse at the Cabildo, where he "received the treatment that humanity demanded."[31]

Armand Saillard, the French Consul to New Orleans, later sent a similar report to the French Minister of Foreign Affairs. Saillard stated that "one of the relatives of Madame Lalaurie denounced her to the authorities a few years ago." When she appeared before the criminal court, she followed the advice of her lawyer to "swear under oath that she had not maltreated her slaves. She thus raised her hand and was discharged."[32] In other words, she and her attorney used the loophole in the Civil Code that allowed an accused slave owner to "clear himself by his own oath" without having to provide further proof of innocence.

Another contemporary witness, Amédée Ducatel, had served during the early 1830s as a clerk in the office of the Lalauries' notary, Felix de Armas, and was undoubtedly well informed about Delphine's affairs. Ducatel subsequently became a notary himself and handled many transactions for Delphine's family members.[33] Years later, Amédée Ducatel told George Washington Cable's research assistant J. W. Guthrie that he was "quite positive" that Madame Lalaurie was never convicted by the Criminal Court, but that she "was condemned to pay a fine for her ill-treatment of the slaves."[34]

The English author Harriet Martineau visited New Orleans in 1836. When her curiosity was aroused by the sight of the ruined Lalaurie mansion, local friends were eager to recount the story and provide additional details not published in the 1834 newspaper articles. Martineau later wrote in her memoir, *Retrospect of Western Travel*, that "it had long been observed that Madame Lalaurie's slaves looked singularly haggard and wretched," and that she would "beat her two daughters by a former marriage [Pauline and Laure Blanque] . . . as often as they attempted in her absence to convey food to her miserable victims. She always knew of such attempts by means of the sleek coachman, who was her spy." But, said Martineau's informants, "the lady was so graceful and accomplished, so charming in her manners and so hospitable, that no one ventured openly to question her perfect goodness." Martineau heard from an American friend, "an eminent lawyer," that he had been induced by the rumors about Madame Lalaurie to send a Creole associate to acquaint her with the law, which "ordains that slaves who can be proved to have been cruelly treated shall be taken from their owner, and sold in the market for the benefit of the State." The young man sent to deliver this warning "returned full of indignation against all who could suspect this amiable woman of doing anything wrong."

Shortly after this, wrote Martineau, a lady, "living in a house which joined the premises of Madame Lalaurie," heard "a piercing shriek from the next courtyard" and saw "a little negro girl, apparently about eight years old, flying across the yard towards the house, with Madame Lalaurie pursuing her, cowhide [whip] in hand." The neighbor saw the child "run from story to story, with her mistress following, until both come out upon the top of the house." Putting her hands over her eyes in horror, the lady did not witness the girl's fall, but she heard the body hit the courtyard, and later saw her lifeless form taken up, the "limbs hanging as if every bone was broken." That night the neighbor "saw the body brought out, a shallow hole dug by torchlight in the corner of the yard, and the corpse covered over."[35] Martineau maintained that she heard this story from reliable witnesses, but the incident was not mentioned by Jean Boze, Armand Saillard, or Amédée Ducatel, nor was it included in the newspaper reports of 1834.

If the death of the enslaved child happened as Martineau's informants said it did, the woman who reported seeing her fall must have resided in the home of Julia Duralde Clay, who owned the house next door at 57 Hospital Street. The outbuilding at the back of the Lalaurie property, possibly a one-story stable or carriage house, would have been lower than the upper floor of the Widow Clay's residence, allowing a person in an upstairs window to see into the Lalaurie courtyard. (The Clay house is now 618–22 Governor Nicholls. Note that 628 Governor Nicholls, the house adjacent to the Lalaurie courtyard, was built in the 1840s on the back lot of the Lalaurie property and was not there in the 1830s.)[36] On the Royal Street side, the neighboring house and service wing at 1134 Royal belonged to the attorney John Randolph Grymes. This building shares a wall with the Lalaurie house and its service wing, and it would have been impossible for anyone at that address to see what was happening next door.

In her sensationalized 1946 telling of "The Haunted House of the Rue Royale" from Ghost Stories of Old New Orleans, Jeanne Delavigne invented the name "Lia" for the girl who reportedly fell from the roof. Delavigne portrayed her as "Madame's own personal maid," who had been "schooled in the arts of dressing hair and laying out skirts and selecting handkerchiefs. Lia was slim and chocolate-colored, swift and keen and quiet. . . . But one morning Lia's body came hurtling down from the roof, smashing onto the banquette with a sickening thud."[37] The creators of later Web sites, taking their cue from Delavigne, have elaborated on the story of "Lia" or "Leah," asserting that as the servant was dressing Madame Lalaurie's long hair, she accidentally pulled a strand with her comb. In a fury, her mistress snatched up a whip and chased the girl to the roof-top, from whence she fell.[38]

·

Jean Boze would write to Henri de Ste-Gême after the fire that Madame Lalaurie had "killed her slaves without pity."[39] The funeral records of St. Louis Cathedral reveal the deaths of twenty of her bondspeople, almost all women and children. In addition to the eight who died before Delphine's marriage to Louis Lalaurie, at least twelve died between 1831 and 1833. Among them were the Saint-Dominguen woman Bonne and all of her children. Bonne's ten-year-old daughter Florence died on February 16, 1831, while the Lalauries were still living on Delphine's country planta-tion. On August 26, 1831, a few days before Delphine finalized the pur-chase of the Royal Street mansion, Bonne's youngest daughter Leontine (born since Bonne came into the possession of Madame Lalaurie) died at the age of twenty-two months. On February 7, 1833, while Delphine resided with her family on Royal Street and Dr. Lalaurie was pursuing his own interests in Plaquemines Parish, Bonne herself died at age thirty. Bonne's daughter Juliette died less than two weeks later. At thirteen, Ju-liette is a bit too mature to have been the "little girl" who fell from the roof, but she is a possibility; she was among the slaves sold to Brugnière and later returned by Dussumier. Bonne's son Jules, age six, died on May 29, 1833.[40]

Bonne had arrived in New Orleans from Saint-Domingue along with her mistress, a free woman of color. When purchased by Delphine's father in 1816, she was described in the act of sale as a chronic runaway.[41] Was Bonne one of those potentially dangerous Saint-Dominguen slaves who were so greatly feared by New Orleanians of the time, and did some act of rebellion incite Delphine to do away with this woman and her children?

In addition to Bonne's family, seven other Lalaurie slaves turn up in the funeral registers of St. Louis Cathedral. Célestine, about thirty-three years old, died on June 20, 1831, and Edouard, age eighteen, died ten days later. These two, like Juliette, had been returned to Delphine by Dussumier the year before. Nancy's twenty-six-year-old mulatto son Nicolas, brother of Ben, died on September 30, 1832. A nineteen-year-old woman named Rose, for whom there is no other record, died on September 24, 1832. In addition, three of the recently purchased "American Negroes" died: a funeral was held for twenty-two-year old Mary Ann on February 17, 1833; for Maria, age twenty, on November 22, 1833; and for Sally, about twenty-four, on November 26, 1833.[42]

What are we to make of the demise of these twelve (or more) young and presumably healthy enslaved persons during the very years when Delphine was alleged to be committing acts of cruelty against them? We know that children were particularly at risk, and even young adults regularly died from the tropical fevers that plagued New Orleans in the early nineteenth century. Did the Lalaurie slaves succumb to the usual ailments and accidents, or were they the victims of starvation and torture, their bodies presented to the priest in closed coffins to hide their condition? How many others, particularly among the Protestant American slaves, were buried without benefit of a Roman Catholic funeral service?[43]

．

Martineau wrote that following an inquiry into the death of the little girl, "illegal cruelty was proved in the case of nine slaves" who were confiscated by the court and sold at a sheriff's auction. "It afterward came out that [Madame Lalaurie] induced some family connexions [sic] of her own to purchase these slaves, and sell them again to her, conveying them back to her premises in the night."[44] The Conveyance Office Index to Vendors does not show that any of the Lalaurie bondspeople were sold at auction by the sheriff of Orleans Parish. It is, however, significant that Delphine sold Célestine, Louise, Suzette, Edouard, Ben, and Juliette to her friend Brugnière on November 22, 1828, and that on December 1, 1828, Jean Boze wrote that justice had finally descended on her home when an investigation proved the truth of the denunciations against her. Might these six slaves have been victims of Delphine's chastisement, whom she temporarily removed to Brugnière's rural plantation? As we have seen, Louise and Suzette disappear from the record, and Célestine and the teenagers Edouard, Juliette, and Ben were returned to Delphine by another family friend. Célestine, Edouard, and Juliette later died in the Lalaurie household, and Ben might have been the "mulatto boy" cited in the 1834 newspaper articles as one of the slaves rescued from the fire.

·

Jean Boze and Armand Saillard, and later on Henriette Martineau and Fredrika Bremer, reported that as a result of complaints from her relatives and neighbors, Madame Lalaurie had been investigated or called before the criminal court for cruel treatment of her slaves. Boze specified that this had occurred in late 1828, in the early summer of 1829, and again in the spring of 1832. Excessive cruelty was a criminal offense that could only be prosecuted by the State of Louisiana. Masters who were accused by another person of abusing their own slaves were seldom brought to trial. In one such case, a judge ruled that a private citizen did not have the right to institute such a suit and that to allow it opened the door for charges motivated by envy or malice.[45]

At the time of the accusations against Madame Lalaurie, a case involving cruel treatment of slaves would have been heard before Judge Felix Grima of the Criminal Court of the First District for Orleans Parish. The Criminal Court, along with the Parish Court, the Court of Probates, and the Supreme Court, were all crowded into the Presbytere, the building adjacent to St. Louis Cathedral at the corner of Chartres and St. Ann Streets. The Criminal Court handled crimes against persons: murder, assault and battery, and cruelty to slaves; and crimes against property: burglary, larceny, receiving stolen goods, harboring runaway slaves, swindling, forgery, counterfeiting, and fraud. There were also a number of instances in which free people of color were charged with "insulting a white person."[46]

All surviving court records for Orleans Parish have been deposited in the City Archives, Louisiana Division, New Orleans Public Library. The pre-1846 records of the Criminal Court of the First District no longer exist, so there is no direct documentation of the 1828, 1829, or 1832 criminal cases against Delphine Macarty Lalaurie. There are, however, two "minute books" from the Criminal Court, one for February 1, 1830, to January 25, 1832, and one for February 6, 1832, to October 30, 1834. The minute books contain summaries of around four hundred cases, giving the name of the defendant, the charge, and the outcome of the case. These books also contain the "true bills of indictment" returned by the grand jury if the evidence was sufficient, as well as the occasional "no true bill," indicating that there was not deemed to be enough evidence to prosecute the case.

Because the existing minute books only begin in 1830 and the pɪ court records have been lost, there is absolutely no documentatioɪ 1828 and 1829 cases against Madame Lalaurie. If the 1832 accusatio.. ᴐᴗ. to trial before a judge and jury, or was even considered by the grand jury, it should have turned up in the 1832–34 minute book. Disappointingly, it did not. The defendants in these criminal cases were overwhelmingly male. The few female defendants were free women of color or lower-class Irish women, and there are no records for white women of Delphine's elite status.

The minute books do contain three other cases of cruel treatment of slaves, and one case of the murder of a slave. In 1831 Bernard Chapiau denied the charge of "cruelly beating a slave." When the jury returned a guilty verdict, his attorney, John Randolph Grymes, was "given leave by the court to file grounds for a new trial." The final outcome of this case is unknown. Charges of "inflicting cruel punishment on a slave" against the free man of color Pierre Soulé were dismissed in 1832, when "the Deputy Attorney General . . . entered a *nolle prosequi.*" This Latin term, which literally means "do not prosecute," is an entry in the court record indicating that the state will proceed no further in a particular action. The case against Patrick Sheeran for "assaulting and cruelly beating a slave" also resulted in a *nolle prosequi* in 1834. In addition, there was an 1832 case in which Louis Donnet was charged with killing a slave; the jury found him not guilty.[47]

The testimony of contemporary observers, the 1834 newspaper articles, and the further elaborations of Harriet Martineau and Fredrika Bremer offer convincing evidence that monstrous happenings in the Lalaurie household had attracted public scrutiny and disapproval, leading to a criminal prosecution. The absence of documentation in the records of the Criminal Court of the First District is frustrating, but not really surprising.

There is, however, one very significant piece of evidence that Madame Lalaurie faced criminal charges in 1829. Tucked away in an unrelated civil suit before the Parish Court is a document signed by Delphine's Royal Street neighbor, the prominent American attorney John Randolph Grymes. Here Grymes stated that on June 22, 1829, he "Received of Madame Lalaurie three hundred dollars for my fee for defending the prosecution of the State against her in the Criminal Court." The seemingly piddling sum of three hundred dollars is equivalent to around $7,000 today.[48]

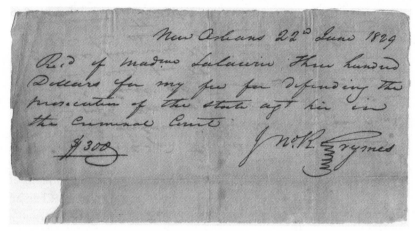

Receipt from John Randolph Grymes dated June 22, 1829, for "three hundred dollars of Madame Lalaurie for defending the prosecution of the State against her in the Criminal Court." This important piece of evidence was attached to an unrelated case involving a small debt owed by Grymes to Madame Lalaurie. The receipt confirms the July 20, 1829, statement by Jean Boze that justice had finally descended on Madame Lalaurie's house and that city authorities had investigated the "barbarous treatment of her slaves." (*Delphine Macarty, wife of L. Lalaurie, v John R. Grymes, Parish Court*, June 28, 1830, docket no. 5673, City Archives, courtesy of the Louisiana Division, New Orleans Public Library.)

This supports the statement by Jean Boze, written on July 20, 1829, that Delphine had been brought before the criminal court for "the barbarous treatment of her slaves," but was absolved for a lack of accusers willing to testify that they had actually seen her in the act of beating the slaves. Although Grymes' receipt does not specify the charge, it is unlikely that a woman of Delphine's stature was charged with any of the other crimes handled by the criminal court.

As all of the contemporary witnesses intimated, Madame Lalaurie's wealth and social position allowed her to evade the accusations of cruelty brought by her fellow New Orleanians. This process would have been facilitated by her attorney, the flamboyant Virginia native John Randolph Grymes, characterized as "one of the ablest lawyers of Louisiana."[49] One wonders if Grymes was the "eminent" American attorney interviewed by Harriet Martineau in 1836.

John Grymes handled some of the most famous cases of his day. He served as a prosecutor for the State against the pirates Jean and Pierre Laffite. He also served as defense attorney for those on the wrong side of law or morality. As noted above, the Minute Books of the Criminal Court

Portrait of John Randolph Grymes by Theodore Sidney Moise, ca. 1842. Grymes was said to be possessed of an acute analytical mind, a keen wit, and an acerbic tongue; he was also known as a stylish dresser, a favorite of the ladies, a gambler, and a man who on a point of honor would immediately appeal to the arbitration of the duello. (Accession no. 1959.83, courtesy of The Historic New Orleans Collection.)

of the First District reveal that he was involved in at least one other slave cruelty case, when he defended Bernard Chapiau against these charges in 1831. He represented Myra Clark Gaines in her suit against the estate of her alleged father, the millionaire Daniel Clark. He argued for the slave owner in the case of the "German slave girl," a woman portrayed by her supporters as a German immigrant illegally held in bondage. He defended a riverboat pilot accused of murdering a prostitute.[50]

For John Randolph Grymes, it must have been a simple task to resolve the Lalaurie matter privately before Judge Felix Grima of the Criminal Court. Grymes would have advised Delphine to swear under oath that she had not maltreated her slaves, dissuaded the witnesses from testifying, and arranged for his client to evade the charges by paying a fine. Because the court records no longer exist and no collection of Grymes' personal papers has come to light, we cannot know exactly what transpired between Delphine, John Grymes, and Judge Felix Grima. Although there is no proof that the accusations of cruelty to her slaves resulted in an actual criminal trial and the seizure of her bondspeople, the rumors that had been swirling around Delphine Macarty Lalaurie since at least 1828 were finally verified by the events of April 10, 1834.

6

THE FIRE

Fire broke out at the Lalaurie home on the morning of Thursday, April 10, 1834. New Orleans newspapers of that time rarely devoted much space to local news, but in this instance *Le Courier de la Louisiane/Louisiana Courier* and *L'Abeille de la Nouvelle-Orléans/New Orleans Bee* carried detailed eyewitness accounts of the shocking discoveries revealed by the blaze. J. C. de St. Rome, editor of the *Courier*, and Jérôme Bayon, editor of the *Bee*, were men of French ancestry. Both newspapers were intended primarily for the Creole community, although they were published in French and English. The *Louisiana Advertiser*, edited by the American John Gibson and published only in English, also reported on the story but made only brief comments. Owing to the antagonism between Creoles and Americans, one would suppose that the editors of the Creole newspapers would try to absolve Madame Lalaurie from guilt, while the American newspaper editor would heap denunciations upon her. The opposite is true. The *Courier* and the *Bee*, especially in the French editions, were much more extreme in their criticism than the *Advertiser*. The newspaper articles of April 10–15 provide an important narrative of what transpired during those calamitous days.[1]

The story first appeared in the afternoon edition of the *Courier* on April 10. The *Courier* stated that the fire had started "in the kitchen of Madame

Lalaurie," which was "soon wrapped in flames." The Lalaurie kitchen, as in other nineteenth-century New Orleans houses, was located in the attached multi-story service wing with slave quarters above. The *Courier* went on to say that it was "known to some of the neighbors that the upper part of this building was used as a prison and that it was then tenanted by several unfortunate slaves, loaded with chains." This statement, indicating that rumors of Madame Lalaurie's vicious treatment of her bondspeople were already in circulation, supports Jean Boze's letters of 1828, 1829, and 1832.

Among the anxious crowd that began to gather in response to the fire was Judge Jacques François Canonge, who had replaced Felix Grima as judge of the Criminal Court on January 1, 1834. Canonge lived just across Royal Street from the Lalaurie mansion.[2] While some bystanders helped the Lalauries transfer their valuables to a safe place in case the fire spread to the house, concerns regarding the captive bondspeople were communicated to Judge Canonge. The *Courier* reported that Judge Canonge, "in a polite manner," asked permission of Dr. Lalaurie to "have the slaves removed to a place of safety." Lalaurie, however, replied to the judge "with much rudeness" that "there are those who would be better employed if they would attend to their own affairs instead of officiously intermeddling with the concerns of other people."

The flames were "gaining rapidly on the building," and Judge Canonge gave orders to break down the doors. According to the *Courier*, the group of citizens who entered the service wing were greeted by an "appalling sight," as "several wretched negroes" emerged from the smoky interior, "their bodies covered with scars and loaded with chains." Among them was "a female slave upwards of sixty years of age."[3]

The *Bee*'s French edition of Friday, April 11, reported that the rescuers found "seven slaves, more or less horribly mutilated . . . suspended by the neck with their limbs stretched and torn from one extremity to the other. . . . They had been confined . . . for several months in the situation from which they had thus been providentially rescued, and had merely been kept in existence to prolong their sufferings and to make them taste all that the most refined cruelty could inflict." The "elderly negress . . . whose great age should have created pity," had "declared to the mayor that it was she who set the house afire with the intention of terminating the sufferings of herself and her companions, or perishing in the flames."[4]

The editors of the *Courier* and the *Bee* went in person to Mayor Denis Prieur's office, adjacent to the guard house at the Cabildo, where the seven rescued slaves had been taken "to protect them from the cruelty of their owner." J. C. de St. Rome of the *Courier* wrote that the sight of these mutilated men and women "inspired us with so much horror that even at the moment of writing this article we shudder from its effects . . . the most savage heart could not have witnessed the spectacle unmoved." St. Rome had observed "one of these miserable beings" and found the sight "so horrible that we could scarce look upon it. . . . He had a large hole in his head, his body from head to foot was covered with scars and filled with worms!! Those who have seen the others represent them to be in a similar condition." Jérôme Bayon of the *Bee* called the "painful circumstances" of the victims "one of those atrocities, the details of which seem to be too incredible for human belief." He only spoke of such matters out of "a sense of duty, and the necessity of exposing and holding up to the public indignation such a wretch as the perpetrator renders it indispensable for us to do." Bayon declared that he had seen the slaves and the chains with which they were confined "with my own eyes," and had been told that "for several months they have been in that situation, having only some meal porridge and water in insufficient quantity for nutriment."[5]

After the injured slaves were taken to the Cabildo, reported the French edition of the *Bee*, "at least two thousand persons visited the jail to be convinced . . . of the sufferings experienced by these unhappy ones. Several have also seen the instruments which were used by these villains: pincers that were applied to their victims to make them suffer all manner of tortures, iron collars with sharpened points, and a number of other instruments for punishment impossible to describe."[6]

The *Courier* ended with the hope that "the Grand Jury will take cognisance of this unparalleled outrage and bring the perpetrator of it to the punishment she so richly deserves."[7] The French edition of the *Bee* expressed confidence that "the community shares with us our indignation, and that vengeance will fall, heavily fall, upon the guilty culprit. . . . Monsieur [Etienne] Mazureau, attorney-general, will prosecute this new Lucrezia Borgia, this fury escaped from hell, where she must have learned the lessons by which she has profited too well, and we are certain that public indignation will call upon the head of this atrocious mistress the full rigor of the law."[8] The *Advertiser* also hoped that "Justice will be done and the guilty be brought to punishment."[9]

The Cabildo, located at the corner of Chartres and St. Peter Streets adjacent to St. Louis
Cathedral, served as New Orleans' city hall and is now part of the Louisiana State Museum.
The identical building on the other side of the cathedral, the Presbytere, housed the city
courts. After the slaves were rescued from the fire at the Lalaurie mansion, they were
carried to the mayor's office at the Cabildo and laid under the arches. Charles Gayarré, J. C.
de St. Rome of the *Courier,* and Jérôme Bayon of the *Bee* wrote of having seen them there.
The newspapers reported that "at least two thousand persons" had gathered to witness
for themselves "the sufferings experienced by these unhappy ones." (Historic American
Buildings Survey, reproduction number LA-36-NewOr, 4-4, 1937, Division of Prints and
Photographs, Library of Congress.)

On April 12, the *Bee* published in its entirety a deposition made on the day of the fire by Judge Canonge before Gallien Préval, judge of the Parish Court for the City of New Orleans. The editor stated that "Coming from the source it does, it is entitled to full credence. We shall make no comments, but let the document speak for itself." Canonge's account agrees with those published earlier in the *Courier* and the *Bee*. It also provides additional details about the discovery and condition of the slaves.

Judge Canonge stated to Judge Préval that "on arriving he was apprized of there being in one of the apartments some slaves who were chained and were . . . exposed to perish in the conflagration." When other friends of the family seemed "indifferent" to his concerns, he "determined upon addressing both Monsieur and Madame Lalaurie, who replied to his inquiries . . . that [the allegation] was a slander." When he again "demanded of M. Lalaurie if he had any slaves in his garret," Lalaurie "replied in an insulting tone" that Canonge would "do much better by remaining at home," rather than "dictating to them the laws."

Judge Canonge then asked Messrs. Montreuil and Fernandez to "go into the garret [of the service wing] to make the necessary search, observing that he had himself once attempted to do so, but was almost suffocated by the smoke." Canonge further stated that Felix Lefebvre "said that he had broken the bars of one of the apartments and that he had discovered some slaves." Judge Canonge, accompanied by Ducatel, Fernandez, Fouché, Gottschalk, Guillotte, Lefebvre, Montreuil, and other citizens, found "two negresses incarcerated, whom they liberated from this den." One of them "was wearing an iron collar, very large and heavy, and was chained with heavy irons by the feet [and] walked with the greatest difficulty; he had no opportunity of examining the other who was behind." It was Monsieur Guillotte who located the "old negress," lying on a bed under a mosquito bar. She "had a deep wound on her head [and] appeared to be quite feeble." She was taken "to the mayor's office, where the first two had been removed."[10]

After helping to deliver the injured slaves to the Cabildo, Judge Canonge would have walked the short distance past St. Louis Cathedral to Judge Préval's chambers at the Presbytere, where he gave his sworn statement. The document was signed by Judge Canonge, with Fouché and Gottschalk as witnesses who "appeared and attested to the truth of this deposition." This second witness was Edward Gottschalk, whose son Louis Moreau

Gottschalk, age five at the time of the fire, became the internationally famous concert pianist and composer.[11]

Madame Lalaurie, presumably accompanied by her family, fled the Royal Street mansion on the afternoon of the fire. The next day, in an article titled "Application of the Lynch Law," the *Courier* commented that her "successful escape from the hands of Justice so exasperated the populace that they assembled last evening in the vicinity of her dwelling, and about the hour of eight began a regular and fatal attack upon it. In a few minutes the doors and windows were broken open; the crowd, composed of persons of all classes and colors, rushed in and the work of destruction commenced."

> In one short hour, every article of furniture was thrown into the street and smashed into a thousand pieces; the very panels and floors were doomed to destruction, indeed nothing that they could lay hands on escaped the fury of the people—it was cut and smash until the interior of the building was stripped of its elegant contents and completely laid waste. The valuable furniture, jewelry, and plate, which had been removed at the time of the fire, were returned to the house in the course of the afternoon and became a prey to popular vengeance. The mob continued their operations on the roof and walls of the building until a late hour this morning. . . . The house . . . is a complete wreck.[12]

On the same day, the *Advertiser* related that "last night the infuriated populace . . . in their just indignation sought the wretch [Madame Lalaurie], but not finding her, demolished her dwelling and destroyed her property."[13]

The *Bee* of Saturday, April 12, reported that the rioting, "consequent upon the barbarous and fiendish atrocities committed by the woman Lalaurie upon the persons of her slaves, continued unabated for the whole of the evening before last and part of yesterday morning."[14]

According to both the *Courier* and the *Bee*, the melee was quelled only by the intervention of Sheriff John Holland and his officers. By then, "nearly the whole of the edifice" had been pulled down, and "nothing remains but the walls," which the angry crowd had "ornamented with various writings expressive of their indignation and the justness of their punishment." The loss of property was estimated at $10,000:

The furniture alone was of the most costly kind, consisting of pianos, armoires, buffets, &c., &c., which were removed to the garret and from thence thrown into the street, for the purpose of rendering them of no possible value whatever. . . . All the wainscots, floors, stairs, balusters . . . and even some of the iron balconies were torn down. . . . The street was encumbered with the debris and the scattered objects were rapidly heaped up, and all this under the light of torches made a sad and hideous spectacle.

Both newspapers, although the editors obviously felt that Madame Lalaurie got what she deserved, expressed concern about the dangerous precedent set by this demonstration of mob justice.[15]

Jean Boze lost no time in conveying the latest scandal to Henri de Ste-Gême. On April 13 he described the fire at the "beautiful mansion at the corner of Royal and Hospital streets," noting that he had "experienced only the inconvenience of being disturbed in my sleep" on the morning of the fire. Judge Canonge, he wrote, "was the first to arrive . . . to call for help in this time of urgent need." Boze, by then eighty-one years old, did not join the other citizens in their attempts to rescue the slaves. Concerned that the fire might spread to the building where he was a tenant, he watched events unfold from his "upper room above a courtyard," which he described as being "about 23 steps away" from the Lalaurie mansion. That evening he heard "the cries of riot and the fracas" as those bent on destroying the house "did not fear to send overboard, in their fury, the peacekeepers [who tried to stop them], from the balconies to the street. Fortunately the heads of the onlookers softened their falls and they were put back on their feet without danger." In this letter Boze again expressed revulsion at the "cruel and barbarous character" of Madame Lalaurie, who "killed her slaves without pity. This involved her in a criminal procedure, but with her fortune, she was always able to succeed in extricating herself."

Boze referred to Delphine's escape, with her husband and children, from "the pursuit of justice and the rage of a people who gathered by the thousands." All were "animated with the desire to punish her in the fire because of her cruelty toward her slaves." He later wrote that the damage to the house was such that *la Famille Lalaurie* could no longer live there.[16]

Boze also commented on Delphine's cousin, Céleste Macarty Lanusse, described by Benjamin Latrobe in 1819 as a "hellcat" who had flogged at least two of her slaves to death. Boze wrote that "Madame Widow Lanus

[Lanusse] is accused of the same crime [as Madame Lalaurie]. Because she had killed [all of her slaves], not even one remained to serve her." She was living in a rented house, but "If [the mob] had been able to discover any property belonging to her, she would have undergone the same fate as Madame Lalaurie."[17]

On Monday, April 14, the *Louisiana Advertiser* reported that "one of the negroes saved from the fire has since died, and in digging up the yard, bodies have been disinterred, and a condemned well being uncovered, others, particularly that of a child, were found in it." This brings to mind Harriet Martineau's story, heard from a local informant, of the girl chased to her death by Madame Lalaurie and buried in "a shallow hole dug by torchlight in the corner of the courtyard."[18]

The *Louisiana Advertiser* article was reprinted in the English edition of the *Bee* on April 15, with a disclaimer by J. C. de St. Rome that "Our contemporary [editor John Gibson] is misinformed. . . . None of the slaves are dead, nor have human bodies, from the best information we can claim, been found. As we avail ourselves of this article, it is necessary to correct him in these particulars." It is difficult to decide which report to believe. George Washington Cable's research assistant Dora Richards Miller commented that "it seems to me this denial must be taken with much doubt. Throughout the issues of the *Bee* that I looked at, the editor evinced a most bitter feeling against the *Advertiser* and its editor and seems to miss no occasion to contradict and put him in the wrong."[19]

Within a few weeks the story of the fire had been picked up by two newspapers with a national circulation, the *Daily National Intelligencer* of Washington, D.C., and *Niles Weekly Register* of Baltimore. The *National Intelligencer* of April 29 repeated the reports from the New Orleans newspapers and added several interesting details. According to the *Intelligencer*, one of the victims was "a mulatto boy, [who] declares to have been chained for five months, being fed daily with only a handful of meal, and receiving every morning the most cruel treatment." The *Intelligencer* also reported that the citizens had rescued from the burning kitchen "a negro woman, found there chained." Later versions of the story assert that the cook was chained to the kitchen stove, and that it was she who started the fire. On May 3, even though the Lalauries were long gone from New Orleans, *Niles' Weekly Register* expressed the hope that the facts would be presented to the grand jury, and that the perpetrators of this crime would be punished.[20] The Lalaurie catastrophe was also seized upon by the abolitionist press. In an article titled "Horrid Fruits of Slavery," the *Emancipator* asserted that it "could have originated only in the spirit, and been perpetuated in the opportunity, produced by American slavery."[21]

Armand Saillard, the French Consul to New Orleans, sent a report to his employer, the Minister of Foreign Affairs, on August 20, 1834. We have seen that within a few weeks the story of the slaves and the fire had been circulated by American newspapers. Although the Paris journals *Le Temps* and *Le National* made no mention of the scandal, it was apparently known overseas as well.[22] Saillard commented that the "noise" of the Lalaurie affair "must have already resounded in Europe. Allow me to quote the facts to you, because you could not believe them if they were not confirmed to you by sufficient authority." Madame Lalaurie, "related to the most distinguished families of New Orleans . . . condemned her servants to dreadful torments: blows, wounds, tortures, deprivations of food." On the day of the fire, Saillard had walked to the Cabildo from his office on Royal Street to observe the victims: "I never saw a more horrible spectacle! The dislocated heads, the legs torn by the chains, the bodies streaked [with blood] from head to foot from whiplashes and sharp instruments." Because she "bound their hands and did not bandage their wounds," flies had settled on their raw flesh, and "when [the slaves] were discovered, they were already devoured by maggots."

Saillard joined in the general outrage when no charges were brought against "this sanguinary woman." The people, "made indignant by the [lack of] control of the authorities, went to the house where so many infamies had been committed with impunity." Saillard described the destruction of the Lalaurie mansion, and commented sarcastically that "Madame Lalaurie will complain that city officials failed to take the necessary measures for the conservation of her property! None of them thought of bringing this woman to judgment and besides, if she reappeared before the criminal court, a new perjury would still be enough to exonerate her."[23]

In addition to the attestations of Canonge, Boze, and Saillard, some eyewitnesses gave their accounts of the fire and its aftermath many years later. Amédée Ducatel had been a young clerk in the office of the Macarty family notary, Felix de Armas, in 1834. When interviewed by George Washington Cable's research assistant J. W. Guthrie in 1889, Ducatel related that he "remembered the riot very well." Upon hearing of "the trouble going on at the corner of Royal and Hospital streets," he hastened to the site and joined the crowd, and "was among those who went into the building by force to liberate the slaves imprisoned in the garret." Ducatel told Guthrie that on the evening of the fire "the mob exceeded one hundred . . . in the house, and a great concourse of people outside. They destroyed the furniture, breaking and smashing everything." In "The Haunted House in Royal Street," Cable identified Ducatel as "Young D____, a notary's clerk, who was "one of those who had found and helped carry out Madame Lalaurie's victims."[24]

Another contemporary observer was the jurist and historian Charles Gayarré, who in 1834 was the presiding judge of the New Orleans Court of Appeals and made his residence on Hospital Street near the Lalaurie mansion. In his youth, Gayarré had been a classmate of Amédée Ducatel at the College d'Orléans. In the 1890s, Gayarré described to the younger writer Grace King how he "saw [the slaves] carried out on stretchers and laid under the arches of the portico [of the Cabildo]. They had changed from black to ashen gray, and were barely breathing." The sight of these "unfortunate wretches so excited whoever looked at them that a mob collected." Madame Lalaurie was barricaded inside her house, "agonized with terror. She feared that [the angry populace] would lynch her . . . which they would have done." He also attested to the "total destruction" of the house. Gayarré never mentioned Madame Lalaurie, the slaves, and the fire in his published works. Grace King, who allied herself with the defenders of Madame Lalaurie, concealed Gayarré's account in her private journal and ignored the Lalaurie scandal in her popular histories.[25]

Later, second-hand versions of the story, although they are based on interviews with eyewitnesses, should not be given quite the same weight as the testimony of the newspaper editors, Judge Canonge, Jean Boze, Armand Saillard, Amédée Ducatel, and Charles Gayarré, who were present at the time of the fire and actually saw the victims.

In *Retrospect of Western Travel*, Harriet Martineau presented additional information about the Lalaurie incident. Martineau heard the story from New Orleanians in 1836, only two years after the fire. Her account generally supports those given by observers at the time. According to Martineau's informants, the citizens broke into an "outbuilding," meaning the kitchen with slave quarters above, and found "seven slaves that could scarcely be recognized as human. Their faces had the wildness of famine, and their bones were coming through the skin. They were chained and tied in constrained postures, some on their knees, some with their hands above their heads. They had iron collars with spikes which kept their heads in one position." Here Martineau adds other gory details: "The cowhide, stiff with blood, hung against the wall, and there was a stepladder on which this fiend stood while flogging her victims, in order to lay on the lashes with more effect. Every morning, it was her first employment after breakfast to lock herself in with her captives and flog them till her strength failed." On the day of the fire, the unfortunate slaves "were brought out into the air and light. Food was given them with too much haste, for [as the *Advertiser* had reported] two of them died in the course of the day. The rest, maimed and helpless, are pensioners of the city."[26]

The 1834 newspaper accounts noted Madame Lalaurie's getaway on the afternoon of the fire without elaborating on how she accomplished this brazen act. It was Harriet Martineau who provided the detailed description of the lady's escape from the infuriated mob, and it is here that we first learn of her "sleek" and "obsequious" enslaved coachman, who reportedly received preferential treatment in return for informing on the other domestic workers. As the streets outside the mansion "filled from end to end with a yelling crowd," this favored servant "advised that Madame Lalaurie should have her carriage brought to the door after dinner, and appear to go forth for her afternoon drive as usual." When the coachman brought the carriage at the appointed hour, Madame Lalaurie "was ready, and stepped into it. Her assurance seems to have paralyzed the crowd. The moment the door was shut they appeared to repent having allowed her to enter, and they tried to upset the carriage, to hold the horses, to make a snatch at the lady. But the coachman laid about him with the whip, made the horses plunge, and drove off."[27]

The probable escape route can be traced on Zimpel's 1834 "Topographical Map of New Orleans and its Vicinity." The coachman would have galloped the horses out Hospital Street to the Bayou Road, turned left at the canal that intersects the small fishing settlements of Faubourg St. John and Faubourg Pontchartrain, and taken the road that follows Bayou St. John through the swamp to the New Orleans Navigation Company's docks on Lake Pontchartrain.[28] There, according to Martineau, Madame Lalaurie "boarded a schooner that was lying ready. The crowd met the carriage returning from the lake. What became of the coachman I do not know. The carriage was broken to pieces and thrown into the swamp, and the horses stabbed and left dead upon the road."[29]

In 1838 a fictionalized adaptation of Harriet Martineau's memoir by "L. Souvestre" (possibly Madame Lesbazeilles-Souvestre) appeared in *Le*

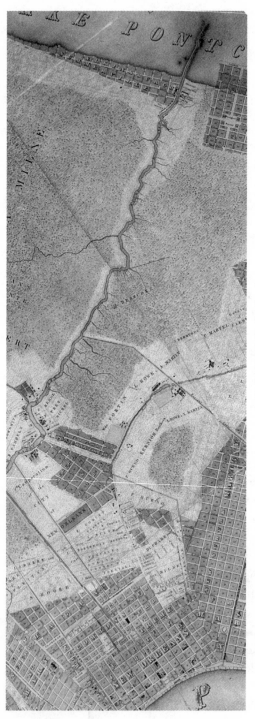

"Topographical Map of New Orleans and its Vicinity, Embracing a Distance of twelve miles . . . " (Charles F. Zimpel, 1834), showing Madame Lalaurie's escape route. (Accession no. 1955.19, detail sections b, c, and f, courtesy of The Historic New Orleans Collection.)

Courrier des États-Unis, a French-language newspaper published in New York. This version incorporates all of the major themes from Martineau's account: the gaunt and dejected household slaves, the coachman "glowing with good health," the child chased from the roof, the inquiry in which illegal cruelty was proven, the nine slaves confiscated and sold at public auction, the horrible discoveries made on the day of the fire, the attack on the house by the angry mob, and Madame "Lalorie's" escape in the carriage driven by her favored coachman. This piece from *Le Courrier des États-Unis* served to further disseminate the story of Madame Lalaurie to American and European readers.[30]

Fredrika Bremer's 1851 account is even further removed from the date of the fire. Without mentioning the dramatic event that led to the revelation of the tortured slaves, Bremer said only that their "doleful cries" attracted an indignant crowd that attempted to rescue them and pull down the house. The arrival of the mayor with an armed force afforded an opportunity for Madame Lalaurie to escape. Bremer was told by her New Orleans acquaintances that the lady's husband, a Frenchman, "still resides in New Orleans and is said to be a man of good character."[31]

George Washington Cable's "The Haunted House in Royal Street," from his 1889 collection *Strange True Stories of Louisiana*, was an imaginative retelling of the newspaper reports and Martineau's account of the fire, with some additional information provided by his two research assistants. Although Cable's "Haunted House" did not shed much new light on the Lalaurie incident, the popularity of *Strange True Stories* ensured that the tale reached a much wider audience than any of the earlier publications.[32]

·

The 1834 newspaper articles and most of the other published accounts agree that seven people were carried out of the locked rooms above the kitchen on April 10. By piecing together the various reports, we can conclude that there were four women and two men, plus another who is unidentified by gender. None of these sources refer to the victims by name. The elderly negress might have been Françoise, called "the old one" and "the hunchback" in the 1816 inventory of slaves retained by Delphine from the succession of Jean Blanque. The woman found in the kitchen might have been Arnante, a cook, laundress, and domestic also listed in the 1816 inventory. Nancy's son Ben was the only "mulatto boy" that Delphine owned in 1834; he, like the others, came from the 1816 Blanque succession.

Beyond that, it is impossible even to speculate. Françoise and Arnante disappear from the archival record after 1816 and might have died earlier of natural causes, but, as we will learn, Ben was sold in 1836.

With the exception of the *Advertiser's* April 14, 1834, report that one of the seven victims had died, and Martineau's later statement that two had succumbed to their injuries, the newspaper stories and eyewitness accounts are silent about what happened to the seven slaves after being rescued from the fire. Logic indicates that following their conveyance to the mayor's office at the Cabildo, the "maimed and helpless" bondspeople would have been treated at Charity Hospital, the city's medical establishment for the indigent. They may have been transported to some smaller, private care facility, but a search of the Charity Hospital admission books shows no slaves registered there. Nor are there any funeral records for the Lalaurie bondspeople in the spring of 1834. If any of them died, they were buried privately without benefit of a Catholic Church funeral.[33]

Twentieth-century popular historians and local-color writers have attached the name "Bastien" to the enslaved coachman who, according to Martineau, saved Delphine from the angry populace. Stanley Arthur wrote in *Old New Orleans* that "During the excitement, Madame Lalaurie . . . took to her carriage, and with her faithful . . . coachman Bastien on the box, swept through the howling, cursing rabble." In an article for the *Southern Architectural Review*, Lyle Saxon mentioned "Bastien," who "made a fine figure in his plum-colored livery and his beaver hat, as he sat high on the box of Madame Lalaurie's carriage." Herbert Asbury, in his popular history of New Orleans, *The French Quarter*, commented on Delphine's "plump and well-fed" butler and coachman without giving him a name: "He was clearly Madame's favorite. Later it was hinted that his position in the household was even higher than that of trusted servant," implying that Delphine had made the slave her accomplice or even taken him as a lover. It was the coachman, according to Asbury, who accompanied Madame Lalaurie to the attic, and "wielded the whip . . . while she watched in ecstasy."[34]

Later writers made the story of the enslaved coachman even more fantastic. A 1958 biography of Louis Moreau Gottschalk, whose father had helped rescue the slaves and signed Judge Canonge's deposition, asserts that "Madame Lalaurie and her handsome mulatto coachman got away to no one knew where, but hangdog Monsieur Lalaurie was still in New Orleans, living in a cheap boarding house." In 1981, Jay Robert Nash elaborated on the scenario created earlier by Herbert Asbury, describing how, when Madame became fatigued, "her mulatto butler continued the torture . . . as she stood by in an ecstatic swoon, her eyes glazed, spittle dripping from her gaping mouth." Christopher Benfey, who included a discussion of Delphine Macarty Lalaurie in his 1997 study *Degas in New Orleans*, went even further. Instead of Dr. Lalaurie having a "quadroon mistress," wrote Benfey, Delphine may have had a sexual relationship with "the mulatto coachman who seemed to be her true partner."[35]

As we have seen, Delphine did, in fact, own a coachman named Bastien, retained "in payment of her matrimonial rights" from the succession of Jean Blanque. This man was always described as a negro, not a mulatto. Blanque had purchased Bastien from the creditors of Joseph Montegut *père* in 1815.[36] The coachman would have been around forty years old at the time of the fire.

Stanley Arthur and Lyle Saxon, both writing in 1936, might have learned the name "Bastien" from Delphine's DeBuys descendants, who were busily disseminating her story at the time. While there is no proof that Bastien was the man who drove the coach through the mob and saved Delphine's life, the coincidence that there actually *was* a Bastien listed in her slave inventories as a coachman makes it unlikely that Arthur or Saxon simply pulled that particular name out of thin air.

·

In his 1934 *Times-Picayune* article, Meigs Frost placed blame for the destruction of Madame Lalaurie's reputation on the jealous spite of a man named Montreuil: "Through the smoky accusations in those century-old stories one figure looms clear. He knew everything, he saw everything that would hurt Delphine Lalaurie. He survives in those records only as Monsieur Montreuil." Frost identified Montreuil as Delphine's next-door neighbor and kinsman, providing a convoluted and inaccurate explanation of how Montreuil had been deprived of the rightful portion of his father's property by his widowed mother, a Macarty. In defiance of logic, Frost concluded that since Madame Lalaurie "was known to all New Orleans as the real brains, the competent business administrator, of the great Macarty estate," she must have appropriated most of the assets for herself, thereby inciting the enmity of Monsieur Montreuil: "Does anybody who ever knew a family squabble over a rich inheritance need a blueprint to know how M. Montreuil must have felt" toward Delphine Macarty Lalaurie?[37]

According to the 1834 coverage of the *Courier* and the *Bee*, Montreuil had been one of the men who entered the burning building to rescue the slaves. The French edition of the *Bee* added the comment that Madame Lalaurie had "long been celebrated in New Orleans for such atrocities, which drew upon her . . . the reprimand of the authorities. M. Montreuil made several times useless attempts to deliver these unhappy ones that the criminal Lalaurie without doubt hoped to see burn to satisfy her ferocious soul." The French Consul Armand Saillard might have been alluding to Montreuil when he reported that Madame Lalaurie had been "denounced to the authorities by one of her relations."[38]

Who was this mysterious "M. Montreuil"? The reports in the *Courier* and the *Bee* and the Canonge deposition never identified Montreuil by his given name, but a little research reveals his identity. The Montreuils were, like the Macartys, a wealthy Orleans Parish family whose landholdings were adjacent to the Macarty plantation. Barthélémy Robert Montreuil and his brother Théodule Joseph Montreuil were the sons of François Robert Gauthier Montreuil and Marie Marthé "Manette" de Macarty. Manette was the younger sister of Delphine's father, making the Montreuil brothers Delphine's cousins. Théodule died in 1832. Therefore Barthélémy, a city tax collector, must have been the person referred to by the newspaper reports at the time of the fire.[39]

When François Montreuil made his will on October 1, 1797, he designated his wife Manette as tutrix to their minor children, who were his sole heirs. He died soon afterward.[40] In compliance with Louisiana Civil Law, Manette retained half of the couple's community property, and the other half was divided equally between Barthélémy, his brother, and their two sisters when they came of age. The many documents related to François Montreuil's complicated succession show that Manette Macarty Montreuil, acting in her own name and as "attorney in fact" for her children, was selling land and slaves from the early 1800s until her death in 1837. There is no evidence that any part of the family estate was taken away from Barthélémy Montreuil, or that Delphine was ever involved in any business dealings with the Montreuil family.[41] There may have been some enmity between the Macartys and the Montreuils, and Barthélémy may have held a grudge against Delphine, but he was not a disgruntled heir to the Macarty fortune.

1134 Royal Street, adjacent to the Lalaurie Mansion. In 1828, Delphine's attorney, John Randolph Grymes, contracted with the builders Ogier and Williams to construct a residence for him on the lot closest to the Lalaurie home. Grymes owned the property until 1835. (Photograph by the author, April 2009.)

Meigs Frost was also mistaken in his identification of Montreuil as Delphine's next-door neighbor. A search of city directories and the Vieux Carré Survey shows that no member of the Montreuil family ever lived or owned property anywhere near the Lalaurie mansion. Barthélémy Montreuil and his wife and children resided at the corner of what is now Decatur and Mandeville in the Faubourg Marigny. He died at his home on June 12, 1834, two months after the fire.[42]

All of the nineteenth-century accounts examined in this chapter assumed that Madame Lalaurie was guilty. Does blame for the cruel treatment of the Lalaurie slaves rest entirely on Delphine, or might Dr. Lalaurie have been an accessory to the crime or even the chief perpetrator of these atrocities? Louis Lalaurie seems to have been a fairly innocuous young man who had emigrated to Louisiana to establish his medical career and find a rich wife; he almost certainly regretted having become involved with the mentally unbalanced Delphine. The rumors of Delphine's crimes were in circulation by 1828, shortly after the couple married, and by at least 1832 Dr. Lalaurie was spending much of his time in Plaquemines Parish. Did he absent himself from the Royal Street mansion because of his wife's abuses and the fear that he would be drawn into the criminal charges against her? Or did she torture the slaves out of frustration because he had abandoned her?

Dr. Lalaurie's insolence to Judge Canonge and refusal to cooperate with efforts to locate and save the slaves indicate that he was fully cognizant of the situation and realized the consequences should the victims be discovered. None of the 1834 newspaper articles accused Louis Lalaurie of torturing the slaves. Jean Boze never suggested that he was guilty, but Armand Saillard reported in 1834 that in executing her "dreadful torments" Madame Lalaurie had acted "with the agreement of her husband." Later writers also expressed opinions on Dr. Lalaurie's involvement. In 1836 Harriet Martineau stated flatly that Delphine's spouse "had nothing to do with the management of her property," and that he was "in no degree mixed up with her affairs and disgraces." But George Washington Cable wrote in 1889 that Martineau was "misinformed," and that Dr. Lalaurie was "as deep in the same mire as passive complicity could carry him." In 1997 Christopher Benfey, in *Degas in New Orleans*, suggested that the doctor practiced "unorthodox treatments" on the slaves.[43]

The creators of Web sites and other popular media have eagerly embraced the notion that both Lalauries, with the doctor playing the role of mad scientist, were conducting "unspeakable medical experiments" on their bondspeople. These fantasies exceed even the nauseating inventions of Jeanne Delavigne's "The Haunted House of the Rue Royale." According to the Web sites "Famous Haunted Crime Scenes" and "The Haunted Mansion," one man had been "surgically transformed into a woman." Another victim "had her arms amputated and her skin peeled off in a circular pattern, making her look like a human caterpillar." A slave, confined to a tiny cage, "had all of her bones broken and reset at odd angles so she resembled a human crab."[44] An illustration from

Crab Scrambly's interpretation of the Lalaurie chamber-of-horrors "medical experiments" in Serena Valentino's 2007 *Nightmares and Fairytales*. (Collection of the author.)

Serena Valentino's 2007 graphic novel *Nightmares and Fairytales: 1140 Rue Royale*, shows Dr. Lalaurie and his wife in a subterranean operating room where the doctor performs sadistic procedures.[45]

Is it possible that the young doctor, rather than joining his wife in rituals of torture, had been trying out some new apparatus or cure on these captives, particularly the "old hunchback" Françoise? Some southern doctors did, in fact, use their slaves as experimental subjects, and historians have gleaned some particularly egregious examples from medical journals, plantation records, and newspapers of the 1830s–1850s.[46] Dr. Lalaurie's specialty was "straightening crooked backs." Might the men and women "suspended by the neck with their limbs stretched" have been undergoing treatments to realign their bodies? Might the "pincers" and other "instruments for punishment" actually have been the tools of Dr. Lalaurie's profession? Lalaurie did attempt to cure Delphine's "hunchbacked" daughter and discussed the treatment with his father and brother, both of whom were physicians. Because no letters later than 1827 have survived in the DeLassus-St. Vrain Collection, there is no evidence to support the idea that he also performed orthopedic procedures on her slaves.

The fact that the enslaved men and women were starved, beaten with a cowhide whip, had infected wounds full of maggots, wore heavy iron collars with sharpened points, and had their feet chained together precludes the possibility of curative therapy, however misguided. This was torture.

Whether the responsibility for the crimes revealed by the fire fell only on Delphine or whether Dr. Lalaurie was involved as well, it was obvious that in that one fateful day they had lost everything. Delphine's reputation and her elite social status were destroyed; Louis's ambitions for a successful career and a comfortable life with a respectable family were in ruin. Subsequent events would prove that they could never again show their faces in New Orleans.

7

EXILE

Jean Boze wrote to Henri de Ste-Gême that Madame Lalaurie had "fled from her beautiful mansion with her husband and children" on the afternoon of the fire. Harriet Martineau later described the lady's frantic carriage ride out the Bayou Road to Lake Pontchartrain, where she boarded a schooner.[1] Either alone or with her family, she crossed the water to the town of Mandeville in St. Tammany Parish. The Lalauries spent several weeks in the area as the guests of Delphine's niece and her husband, the English lumberman John Nelder.[2] Seven-year-old Jean Louis Lalaurie probably would have been with his parents. The whereabouts of Pauline and Laure Blanque, both in their early twenties, is unclear. Paulin Blanque, age nineteen, was away at Yale University.

On April 21, while still in Mandeville, Delphine signed a power of attorney placing Placide Forstall, the husband of her daughter Borja López y Ángulo, in charge of her affairs. Dr. Lalaurie assigned power of attorney to Auguste DeLassus, the husband of Delphine's daughter Jeanne Blanque. A few days later, on April 30, Forstall and DeLassus appeared in the New Orleans office of Notary Louis Feraud to register the documents. Perhaps embarrassed by the circumstances, the men chose Feraud instead of the family's usual notaries, Felix and Octave de Armas. A transcription of these long and complex legal instruments was entered into the notarial record. Delphine and her husband authorized Forstall and DeLassus to manage all of their affairs and business transactions in the state of Louisiana: to open and answer all letters addressed to them, to make promissory notes in their names, to write checks and withdraw money from their bank accounts, to collect dividends, to sell or rent real estate, to sell slaves or hire them out, to deal with their creditors, and to pay their taxes. Delphine made no provision for the emancipation of any of her slaves, not even the coachman who had allegedly saved her life.[3]

Journalists and writers of popular histories have put forward various theories about Madame Lalaurie's movements after the fire of April 10, 1834. One version of the story says that she never left Louisiana. Some asserted that, calling herself the Widow Blanque, she lived quietly in New Orleans on the Bayou Road near her daughters Pauline and Laure; others maintained that she and her husband lived in seclusion somewhere across Lake Pontchartrain. Some reported that the Lalauries journeyed from Mandeville to Mobile and there boarded a ship for France. Others said that they went from Mobile to New York City, but that Delphine was recognized and their stay was "made unbearable by social insults," forcing the family to depart for Europe.[4] A persistent rumor alleges that their voyage was financed by Delphine's longtime admirer, Tulane University founder Paul Tulane. One tourist booklet makes the absurd claim that she had become Tulane's lover after being taken prisoner during the 1791–1804 Haitian Revolution, was held on shipboard by "drunken Negroes," and was subsequently rescued and brought to New Orleans by the pirate Dominique You, a confederate of Jean Laffite.[5]

The account of the Lalauries traveling along the Gulf coast to Mobile and from there to New York City turns out to be true. The facts come from a particularly unexpected source, the published journal of the American poet William Cullen Bryant. Bryant wrote that on June 24, 1834, he set sail from New York for the French port of Le Havre on the ship *Poland*. He noted that he "was seasick until my arrival at Le Havre and consequently had little disposition to study the characters of my fellow passengers," although he did observe "a pretty-looking French woman . . . a Madame Lalaurie." Bryant was familiar with her story, either from reports in the national press or from the gossip of the other travelers. The lady, he wrote, was the same one who had "committed such horrible cruelties upon her slaves last winter in New Orleans. Her house took fire and she was unwilling that the firemen should use any means to extinguish it. This led to suspicions that all was not right, and the fire being put out, the house was searched, and an apartment was discovered in which several negroes were confined, some chained in painful postures and others horribly wounded and scarce alive. The populace were so enraged that they would have torn her in pieces had she not made her escape disguised in men's clothes."

Bryant's journal entry confirmed that Madame Lalaurie "took refuge for a time in Mobile," traveled to New York, and "was now returning with her husband to his . . . native country." He noted that she "seemed much affected by the reserve with which the other ladies on board treated her and was frequently seen in tears." The Lalauries, at least in public, maintained the appearance of marital solidarity. Bryant observed that Delphine's "husband, Dr. Lalaurie, was as kind and assiduous as if his wife had been a miracle of female excellence."[6] Bryant failed to mention whether the couple traveled with other family members, and the passenger list for the *Poland* has not survived, but we can assume that they were accompanied by their young son, Jean Louis.

The Lalauries disembarked in Le Havre on July 14, 1834, and made their way to Louis Lalaurie's ancestral home in Villeneuve-sur-Lot. Louis appears to have heeded the invitation extended by his father in 1827, before his marriage to Delphine: "If you [or any of your siblings] should fall into need, it is in my house that you will find a retreat."[7] Papa Lalaurie had urged Louis to make an advantageous match with a woman of property, undoubtedly hoping for a rich, young, and compliant daughter-in-law. The middle-aged, strong-minded Delphine was not what he had in mind.

News of the spectacular crime of which Delphine was accused had spread like wildfire in the United States, and (according to a later letter from her son-in-law Auguste DeLassus) by the summer of 1834 the story had even reached the French village of Villeneuve.[8] How would Louis Lalaurie have presented this to his family? Would he have justified the incident as a simple misunderstanding and explained that they needed to leave New Orleans for a time until the excitement blew over?

Existing documents and letters indicate that, although Delphine was treated politely, she was not embraced by Louis's father and siblings. On November 17, 1834, Louis and his sisters Rosalie, Victoire, Hélène, and Hortense assembled before a notary in Villeneuve to open their late mother's succession. They were also settling the estate of their brother Laurent Eugène Lalaurie, who had left the country and was presumed to be dead. It was Laurent who had been Louis's confidant in 1826–27, when Louis was trying to establish himself in New Orleans. Louis now inherited a small house that had belonged to Laurent. Since the value of this property exceeded the portion of the estate allotted to each of the four sisters, Louis was required to pay them a balance of 16,000 francs over three years with 5 percent interest. In addition, the sisters claimed the entire contents of Laurent's house.[9] Delphine, Louis, and young Jean Louis moved into Laurent's modest dwelling, without servants and bare of furniture, linens, and other amenities—a considerable step down from their dozens of slaves and beautifully appointed mansion in New Orleans.

Delphine was dissatisfied with these arrangements, and Louis, no longer playing the devoted husband, was becoming exasperated by her complaints. Later, when Auguste DeLassus and his wife, Jeanne Blanque, visited with them, DeLassus wrote to his father that "My poor mother-in-law is disgusted with France. . . . Owing to the falsehoods and slander that followed them . . . the poor thing . . . was confined [to Laurent's unfurnished house] by that riffraff (*canaille*) Lalaurie family, without a bed to lie on. . . . She tells me of her sorrows and can't stop herself from breaking down in tears, and each time, her husband is more Jean Fr—— than ever." Note that DeLassus did not spell out the slang appellation "Jean-Foutre." A French dictionary defines the term as "a useless and unreliable fellow," although native French speakers give it a more coarse and insulting meaning.[10]

·

Back in New Orleans, Delphine's sons-in-law, Auguste DeLassus and Placide Forstall, were disposing of the couple's slaves and the partially demolished house. DeLassus, acting as agent for Louis Lalaurie, sold an enslaved family that Lalaurie had acquired in Plaquemines Parish.[11] Forstall, acting as agent for Delphine, disposed of eleven of her bondspeople. On September 19, 1834, he sold Priscilla and Eulalia, both domestics. A few days later he sold Abraham, a carter. On October 30, 1834, Forstall sold four more men: Nelson, a carter; James, a blacksmith and carpenter; Célestin, a coachman and domestic; and Théodore, a gardener. Almost two years passed before Forstall sold Frederick and Ben to his brother Felix Forstall on June 11, 1836. No occupation was given for Frederick or Ben.[12] Ben might have been the "mulatto boy" mentioned by the *National Intelligencer* as one of the slaves rescued from the fire.

Bastien, said to be the coachman who rescued Madame Lalaurie from the angry horde, was sold by Placide Forstall on September 19, 1834, along

Placide Forstall. Carte de visite from the Villere family photograph album. The photograph appears to have been taken in the 1860s, long after Forstall served as Madame Lalaurie's agent and attorney in fact. (Accession no. 1976.130.14, courtesy of The Historic New Orleans Collection.)

Auguste DeLassus, from Goodspeed's *History of Southeast Missouri* (1888). (Courtesy of the Missouri Historical Museum, St. Louis.)

with the domestic servant Diana. The buyer, claiming to be unable to make the agreed-upon payments, later canceled the sale. On June 11, 1836, Bastien and Diana were resold to the business firm of Robert and Buxton Layton and Nathaniel Hyde.[13] Bastien was finally manumitted, at age fifty-seven, by the testamentary executors of Robert Layton in 1849. According to the petition to the Council of the First Municipality, Bastien had always "conducted himself honestly and properly, without ever having run away, [and] without having . . . been guilty of any criminal misbehavior." Therefore Layton wished to "emancipate him as a reward for his industry and good conduct." The council gave permission for Bastien to remain in Louisiana.[14]

Delphine owned thirty enslaved men and women on the day of the fire.[15] The sale of these eleven individuals still leaves nineteen people unaccounted for in the archival record. Some of them might have died earlier of old age or illness, some could have been informally distributed among friends and family, and some perhaps seized the opportunity to run away after the fire. Still, given the strict ecclesiastical and civil record-keeping characteristic of New Orleans, the disappearance of so many people without a trace is unusual and has sinister implications.

On March 24, 1837, Placide Forstall sold the house at the corner of Royal and Hospital to Pierre Edouard Trastour for $14,000. This sale did not include the back lot on Hospital Street, on which there were only two small outbuildings. In 1831 Delphine had paid $33,750 for the double lot with the unfinished house and dependencies. The extreme drop in value is indicative of the damaged condition of the main residence and service wing caused by the fire and the ensuing riot. Three months later, on July 3, 1837, Trastour sold the house to Charles Caffin, still for $14,000, demonstrating that Trastour had made no improvements.[16]

·

Snippets of gossip about Madame Lalaurie's activities in France turn up in nineteenth-century published sources. According to Harriet Martineau's *Retrospect of Western Travel*, rumors of Delphine's crimes had followed her everywhere, and at the time of Martineau's visit to New Orleans in 1836 she heard that "Madame Lalaurie was skulking about in some French province under a false name." Writing in 1851, Fredrika Bremer declared in *Homes of the New World* that Madame "Lallorue" lived the rest of her life in Paris, and "received there the income of an immense property acquired in Louisiana, by what means we [already] know. She died, it is

Table 3. All slaves owned by Delphine Macarty Lalaurie between 1816 and 1834

Name, date of birth, color, skills	Age 1834	Acquired	Sold, freed, died, or unaccounted for
Arnante, born about 1776, cook/laundress/domestic	58	Macarty donation 1808, Blanque estate 1816	**UNACCOUNTED FOR**
Bastien, born about 1794, black, carpenter/coach, driver/domestic	40	Blanque estate 1816, inventory 1828	Sold to Louis Moreau 1834; sold to Layton & Co. 1836; freed 1849
Céléstine, born about 1798, black, washer/domestic		Macarty donation 1808, inventory 1828	Céléstine sold to Louis Brugnière 1828; returned by Andre Dussumier 1830; died 1831
Daughter Enriette, born about 1819			Enriette died 1821
Clemént, born about 1820			Died 1822
Françoise, "the old hunchback," black		Blanque estate 1816	**UNACCOUNTED FOR** Possibly died 1823
Genevieve, born about 1792 in Illinois, mulatto, domestic		Macarty donation 1808, Blanque estate 1816	Died 1819
George, born ca. 1756, black, gardener	78	Blanque estate 1816	**UNACCOUNTED FOR**
Hélène, born about 1787 in Senegal, black, domestic		Purchased from Piernas 1810	Hélène freed 1828
Daughter Elisa, born about 1801, black		Blanque estate 1816	Elisa died 1816
Jean Pierre Paulin, birth date unknown, mulatto			Died 1819
Lindor, born about 1771, mulatto, cook		Macarty donation 1808, Blanque estate 1816	Sold to Emile Johns 1829
Louise, born about 1808, black		Inventory 1828	Sold to Brugnière 1828
Marie Françoise, birth date unknown, black			Died 1823
Nancy, born about 1796, black	38	Blanque estate 1816, inventory 1828	**NANCY UNACCOUNTED FOR**
Mulatto son Nicolas, born about 1806, cook/coachman	19		Nicolas died 1832
Mulatto son Ben, born about 1815			Ben sold to Brugnière 1828; returned by Dussumier 1830; sold to Felix Forstall 1836

continued

Table 3—*continued*

Name, date of birth, color, skills	Age 1834	Acquired	Sold, freed, died, or unaccounted for
Rosette, born about 1791, laundress/seamstress	43	Blanque estate 1816	**UNACCOUNTED FOR**
Mulatto son Jean, born about 1819			Jean died 1823
Suzette, born about 1792, black, domestic/seamstress		Blanque estate 1816	Suzette and son sold to Brugnière 1828
Son Edouard, born about 1813			Edouard returned by Dussumier 1830; died 1831
Théodore, born about 1786, black, cooper/sawyer/coachman		Blanque estate 1816, inventory 1828	Sold to Marie Labostrie 1834
Thom, born about 1766, black, gardener	68	Blanque estate 1816	**UNACCOUNTED FOR**
Zoé, of the Congo nation, born about 1800, black		Macarty donation 1808, Blanque estate 1816	Died 1820
Bonne, born about 1791 in Saint-Domingue, black, cook/laundress		Purchased by Macarty from Lacroix 1816; inventory 1828	Bonne died 1833
Daughter Florence, born about 1808			Florence died 1831
Daughter Juliette, born about 1810			Juliette sold to Brugnière 1828, returned by Dussumier 1830; died 1833
Son Jules, born about 1813			Jules died 1833
Daughter Leontine, born about 1831			Leontine died 1831
Pauline, mulatto, born about 1794	40	Macarty donation 1816	**UNACCOUNTED FOR**
Celestin, born about 1807, domestic/coachman	27	Inventory 1828	Sold to Françoise Daubert 1834
Devince, born about 1792, shoemaker		Inventory 1828	Freed 1832
John, born about 1812, black, domestic	22	Purchased from Louis Miller of Natchez 1828, inventory 1828	**UNACCOUNTED FOR**
Louis, born about 1796, black, carter/ laborer	38	Inventory 1828	**UNACCOUNTED FOR**
Lubin, born about 1768, black, carter/ laborer	66	Inventory 1828	**UNACCOUNTED FOR**

Name, date of birth, color, skills	Age 1834	Acquired	Sold, freed, died, or unaccounted for
William, born about 1790, black, gardener	44	Inventory 1828	**UNACCOUNTED FOR**
Abram, born about 1810, black, carter	24	Purchased from J. B. Diggs of Norfolk 1831	Sold to David Adams 1834
Amos, born about 1810, black	24	Purchased from Diggs 1831	**UNACCOUNTED FOR**
Cyrus, born about 1816, black	18	Purchased from Stephen Peillon 1828	**UNACCOUNTED FOR**
Diana, born about 1811, griffe, laundress/ironer/domestic	23	Purchased from Jos. Hardy 1832	Sold to Louis Moreau 1834 and to Layton & Co. 1836
Eulalia alias Lively, born about 1811, black	23	Purchased from Sarah Lee 1833	Sold to Antonio Miranda 1834
Frederick, born about 1809, black	25	Purchased from Diggs 1831	Sold to Felix Forstall 1836
Jack, born about 1806, black	28	Purchased from Peillon 1828	**UNACCOUNTED FOR**
James, born about 1809, black, blacksmith/carpenter	25	Purchased from Diggs 1831	Sold to Louis Dansac 1834
Lucinda, born about 1811, black	23	Purchased Thornton Alexander of Virginia 1830	Sold to Louis Tabary 1833
Matilda, born about 1808, black	26	Purchased from Peillon 1828	**UNACCOUNTED FOR**
Maria, born about 1800, black		Purchased from Peillon 1828	Died 1833
Mary, born about 1800, black	34	Purchased from Francis Herriet 1831	**UNACCOUNTED FOR**
Mary Anne, born about 1815		Purchased from L. F. Feisturies 1833	Died 1833
Nelson, born about 1807, black, carter/domestic	27	Purchased from Peillon 1828	Sold to J. J. Jandot 1834
Patsy, born about 1812	22	Purchased from Wm. Eldridge of Kentucky	Possibly freed 1850 from Delphine's succession
Priscilla, born about 1816, black	18	Purchased from W. C. German of Jefferson Parish 1833	Sold to Eugène Dilatte 1834
Rochin, born about 1809, black	25	Purchased from Peillon 1828	**UNACCOUNTED FOR**

continued

Table 3—*continued*

Name, date of birth, color, skills	Age 1834	Acquired	Sold, freed, died, or unaccounted for
Rose, born about 1813, black			Died 1832
Sally, born about 1809, black, seamstress		Purchased from J. B. Philippi 1831	Died 1833
Samson, born about 1814, black	20	Purchased from Peillon 1828	**UNACCOUNTED FOR**
Oreste			Freed in 1849
Elodie			Possibly freed 1850 from Delphine's succession

Note: Birth dates were derived from age at time of purchase or listing in inventory. Age in 1834 is given for slaves who were still owned by Delphine at the time of the fire. Color and place of birth were derived from inventories and funeral records. Skills were derived from inventories and acts of sale. Macarty donation indicates slaves donated by Delphine's father in 1808; Blanque estate indicates slaves inherited by Delphine from the estate of Jean Blanque; 1828 inventory indicates slaves listed in the inventory taken at the time of Delphine's 1828 marriage to Lalaurie. Slaves sold in 1834 and later were sold by Delphine's agent after the fire.

said, a short time since. Who can doubt a hell after death when they see the life and pleasure of such persons on earth?" In 1892 the New Orleans journalist Marie Points insisted that Madame Lalaurie "kept a handsome establishment [in Paris], where her home was the resort of the cultured and intelligent, and her gracious manners, great wealth, and high connections made her a welcome guest in the most exclusive circles. When the story [of the tortured slaves] did reach Paris it was looked upon as the result of her well-known eccentricity and her high, ungovernable temper, which at times . . . almost bordered upon insanity."[17]

In 1895 Henry Castellanos related in *New Orleans as It Was* that "finding every door [in Paris] closed against her," Delphine had "adopted a strictly pious life and, spending her time in works of charity, was fast relieving her character from the odium that attached to it." Later in the 1890s the historian Charles Gayarré told Grace King that Madame Lalaurie was "once hissed at the Opera House in Paris on account of her treatment of her Louisiana slaves." But Gayarré also said that while traveling in France he "had conversed with her in Paris," and described her as a "beautiful, gentle woman, reputed to be very kind to her servants there." King added tartly that "it is said that she was crazy."[18]

Family letters and archival documents provide a more complete picture of Madame Lalaurie's life in exile. Delphine and her husband and their young son did not remain long with Louis Lalaurie's less-than-friendly family in Villeneuve-sur-Lot. By late October 1835, they were in Paris.

On October 29, Delphine wrote an affectionate letter to her grand-daughter Céleste Forstall, daughter of Borja López y Ángulo and Placide Forstall. Céleste, who was also Delphine's goddaughter, would have been about twelve years old at the time. Delphine apologized for not writing. Her "laziness," she explained, resulted from the "sorrows . . . [that] so overburden me, being separated from all of you, that I have not been able . . . to fix my attention . . . and arrange my thoughts in order." But Cé-leste's parents were also "lazy" about keeping in touch, and Delphine com-plained that they had been "neglecting" her. Eight-year-old Jean Louis, she wrote, had been in school for a week. She did not mention Pauline, Laure, and Paulin Blanque, indicating that they were not yet with the fam-ily. Dr. Lalaurie sent "an embrace" along with his greetings. On January 12, 1836, Delphine wrote again to Céleste, expressing the great pleasure that she received from the girl's letters. Having news of her "dear children" was her "great consolation" because she feared being permanently sepa-rated from them. She hoped for a visit from the Forstall family, saying that "Your uncle [Jean Louis] Lalaurie . . . makes grand projects to amuse you when you arrive." These loving messages certainly show Delphine's softer side, but even when writing to a favored child, she used the businesslike signature "Lalaurie née Macarty."[19]

By 1836 Delphine's daughters Pauline and Laure Blanque were in Paris. In July the family was joined by her other daughter, Jeanne Blanque, Jeanne's husband, Auguste DeLassus, and their children. It was a happy visit. According to a letter from DeLassus to his father, they behaved like typical tourists, visiting the Tuileries, the Palais Royal, and the Champs-Elysées, strolling on the boulevards, and spending an evening at the Cirque de Franconi. Jeanne wrote to her father-in-law: "I am so happy to be near Maman. You know with what tenderness I love her. She was, and is, always so good to me. Since I have been here, she has foreseen all that could trouble me and doesn't even want me to be busy with my chil-dren. . . . They have two nursery-maids." Delphine and Dr. Lalaurie, along with Jeanne, the DeLassus children, Pauline, Laure, and Jean Louis sent greetings to Papa DeLassus.[20]

Paulin Blanque had dropped out of Yale University after the disastrous events of 1834. By 1838 he too had arrived in Paris, and in June he wrote to Auguste DeLassus, who had returned to New Orleans, that he was living a slothful existence: "I get up so late that sometimes at 3 p.m. I am still in my dressing gown, smoking or chatting with Maman and Pauline." He was suffering from some unidentified illness and praised his mother's "kindness without equal. . . . It is she who prepares my medication and who sees to all the things that are necessary" for my care. Paulin was eager to return to New Orleans, but Delphine had persuaded him to stay, expressing the desire to have all of her children with her in Paris.[21]

For a few more years Louis Lalaurie remained with his wife in Paris, living on her money and catering to her emotional neediness, but he eventually grew weary of this life and departed for Cuba. His father had evidently lost confidence in him, and he left no bequest for Louis when he made his will in January 1840. Papa Lalaurie bequeathed the family home to his unmarried daughter, Rosalie, with the hope that it would "remain a place of meeting for his children," and made monetary donations to his other daughters. The elder Lalaurie died on October 26, 1842, and Louis was described in the succession record as being "in Havana at the present."[22]

A few weeks before his father's death, Louis Lalaurie wrote to Auguste DeLassus from Havana, asking DeLassus to send him some possessions that he had left in New Orleans. Lalaurie desired to have the medical books that had belonged to his father, as well as some other items "that I want very much to possess . . . a diploma of Master Mason and a diploma of the Lodge of Les Amis des Bourbons of Villeneuve-sur-Lot," along with two Masonic aprons, "one made of leather and one of silk, with its cord and a cross." Lalaurie asked DeLassus to send news of his family, especially "your oldest son, who is also mine . . . he will say that it is a very sad individual who rendered him into existence."[23] This boy, Charles Auguste DeLassus, was born in New Orleans September 18, 1833; Lalaurie evidently meant by this curious statement that he, who had assisted at Charles's birth, was now a ruined and melancholy man owing to the events of 1834. Louis Lalaurie's life in Cuba is a mystery. He died in 1863, and is buried in the Espada Cemetery in Havana.[24]

·

In September 1840 Placide Forstall permanently delegated responsibility for Delphine's finances to Auguste DeLassus. At the same time, Delphine's brother, Louis Barthélémy Macarty, left New Orleans for an extended trip to Europe, giving DeLassus power of attorney to "collect the rents accruing on his real estate . . . and to receive the amounts due to him by various persons." DeLassus was expected to send sizable payments to both

Delphine and Louis Barthélémy for living expenses.[25] His failure to do so resulted in a financial emergency for Delphine and a severe inconvenience for Louis Barthélémy.

For several years New Orleans had been in the grip of the worldwide financial crisis known as the "Panic of 1837." The problem began in Britain, where crop failures resulted in decreased demand for textiles and caused cotton prices in New Orleans to fall drastically. Fourteen New Orleans banks failed, and many local businessmen were bankrupted.[26] These conditions certainly would have affected the Macarty fortunes, but DeLassus also proved to be a bad steward of his in-laws' assets. Instead of sending the promised amounts to Delphine and Louis Barthélémy, he was using their funds for his own purposes. With Louis Barthélémy Macarty's money, DeLassus purchased two large tracts of land below the city on which to build a cotton press. But "being apprehensive" that Macarty might withdraw his power of attorney on learning that he was "embarked in a hazardous speculation . . . and thereby deprive DeLassus of the use of his funds," DeLassus had put the property in the name of a business partner. During this time he was living rent-free on Macarty's plantation, where he used Macarty's field hands to cut cypress logs for building the cotton press. When Louis Barthélémy returned to New Orleans in September 1842 to straighten out his finances, the Fourth District Court judged that DeLassus owed him $126,795.[27] Macarty had only four years to benefit from this settlement; he died in 1846.

Owing to DeLassus's mismanagement, Delphine had no source of income during the early 1840s. Despite these pecuniary difficulties, she continued to live in the style to which she was accustomed, renting comfortable lodgings and traveling to resorts with her children. In the summer of 1840, family friend Louis Brugnière of St. Bernard Parish was in Paris. In August, Brugnière wrote to Louis Barthélémy Macarty that "Your sister left here this past June along with Mademoiselle Pauline [Blanque] and my wife to go spend a good part of the Autumn under the beautiful sky of Gascony. At this moment, Madame Lalaurie, Paulin, and Mademoiselle Pauline are in the Pyrénées taking the waters of Saint Saveur. . . . The country air has done them good." Jean Louis Lalaurie, by then thirteen years old, was to join them later.[28]

This lifestyle was financed by heavy borrowing at exorbitant interest rates, and Delphine feared that her creditors would refuse to renew her promissory notes. A series of increasingly desperate letters to Auguste DeLassus ensued. In January 1842, Pauline Blanque wrote to her sister

Jeanne Blanque DeLassus in New Orleans asking her to ensure that Auguste would "hasten as quickly as he can" to send $2,500. Delphine herself wrote to DeLassus in May, asking the cause of the delay and saying that for nearly a year she had "waited in vain for the various steamships" hoping that she "would receive some news of my affairs." She complained that she had not had an accounting since Placide Forstall had put DeLassus in charge, and asked for $5,000 for that year's expenses.[29] When the money had still not arrived by August 15, Jean Louis Lalaurie wrote to DeLassus, saying that his mother was in bed sick and unable to write, but that she "charges me to make known to you that she will be in New Orleans [to settle her financial affairs] at the end of November or at the beginning of December" 1842.[30]

Paulin Blanque, by then twenty-seven years old, had become the "man of the house" and was taking charge of family matters. In an extremely significant letter to Auguste DeLassus, written on the same day as Jean Louis's, Paulin communicated that his mother was serious about returning to New Orleans. "She has been thinking about this for a long time. . . . We comfort ourselves with the hope that moments of bad humor alone could make her nourish such a thought." Referring to "the sad memories of the catastrophe of 1834," Paulin conveyed that he, who had "lived with her and studied her" for years had "seen that time hasn't changed anything in that indomitable nature, and that by her character she is again preparing many sufferings . . . for her children. I bemoan . . . the fate that awaits us if ever again my mother sets foot in that place, where her conduct elicited general disapproval. She has caused us to shed many tears, and where she goes we prepare ourselves for bad news owing to her presence. I truly believe that my mother never had any idea concerning the cause of her departure from New Orleans."

Paulin commented that his uncle Louis Barthélémy would certainly "make all possible objections" to this plan, which would prove "disastrous to all of us." He advised DeLassus to "see Placide [Forstall] when you receive my mother's letter announcing to you her arrival; deliberate together and don't let the fear of displeasing her cause you to recoil from what you will have to say on the impossibility of her return to New Orleans. . . . If I am unable to dissuade my mother from her insane project, I will tell her that Pauline and I won't go with her, and I will also make her see that living with one of her married daughters is impossible because they would never consent to it." Paulin ends by asking DeLassus to "greet my sisters and all the children for me as well as Placide and your father."[31]

The next letter to Auguste DeLassus came from Pauline Blanque, not Paulin, on December 1, 1842, again begging for money, not only for her mother but for herself. Pauline complained of "the little necessary expenses that cannot be avoided in spite of all my care to spend the least amount possible," and communicated that given their present circumstances, she could not ask her mother for funds. She stressed that DeLassus absolutely had to give Delphine an accounting of her financial affairs and send the money requested, in order to "avoid anything that might excite Maman's bad mood on the subject of your negligence." There was no more mention of a trip to New Orleans.[32] Pauline's letter is the last of the Lalaurie correspondence in the DeLassus–St. Vrain Collection.

The 1835–36 letters from the DeBuys Collection and the 1836–42 letters from the DeLassus–St. Vrain Collection have proven essential to the telling of this story. But excepting the affectionate notes written by Delphine to her granddaughter Céleste Forstall, the missives in her own hand are strictly concerned with business matters. Did she write more personal letters to her daughters Borja López Forstall and Jeanne Blanque DeLassus in New Orleans, in which she discussed the "catastrophe of 1834"? Did she admit wrongdoing and express defiance or remorse, or did she protest that the stories were fabricated and that there were no starved and mutilated slaves? If such letters exist, they are in private hands.

·

Madame Lalaurie was motivated by her need for money, and also perhaps by jealousy and resentment, to become involved in legal disputes over the successions of her uncle, Eugène Macarty, and her brother, Louis Barthélémy Macarty. Both of these men had long-term relationships and fathered children with women to whom they were not married. In each case those who considered themselves the legitimate heirs contested the amount of money diverted from the man's estate to his concubine and his natural children.[33]

The Louisiana Civil Code of 1825 made specific provisions regarding inheritance. The law followed the principle of "forced heirship." The surviving spouse of a married man or woman received half of the community property, and the deceased person's half was divided in equal portions between the legitimate children "without distinction of sex or primogeniture."[34] Only a portion of the estate could be willed to anyone other than the forced heirs, and the rules were particularly strict in the case of inheritance by concubines. The law never mentioned race, but it often served to obstruct the donation of property to the non-white partner of a white man.[35] The 1825 Civil Code also regulated inheritance by children who were "born outside of marriage." Such children "if acknowledged by their father [in the baptismal record or by notarial act], are called natural children; and those whose father is unknown are contra-distinguished by the appellation of bastards."[36] The Civil Code specified that in the absence of legitimate children, the natural children could receive one-quarter of their father's property if he had surviving parents, siblings, nieces, or nephews, and one third if he left only remote collateral relations.[37]

Although judicial opinion increasingly held that "the attempted transfer of property from a white man to his colored family . . . went against the very intent of Louisiana law," it was only in the revised Civil Code of 1870 that "those who have lived together in open concubinage" were barred from donating land to each other and were only allowed to donate movable property of one-tenth the value of the estate.[38]

Delphine's uncle Eugène Macarty died on October 25, 1845, at his residence on the corner of Dauphine and Barracks.[39] Eugène had lived for over fifty years with the free woman of color Eulalie Mandeville. A few days before his death, when Eugène was seventy-seven years old and Eulalie was seventy-one, the couple were married by a priest of St. Augustine's Roman Catholic Church.[40] The 1825 Civil Code stated that not only are "free persons and slaves . . . incapable of contracting marriage together," the "same incapacity . . . [exists] with respect to marriages contracted by free white persons with free persons of color."[41]

Even at St. Augustine's, where a large percentage of the congregation were free people of color, it is remarkable that at a time when interracial marriages were clearly illegal, and Eugène and Eulalie were undoubtedly known to the entire community, a priest would agree to perform this ceremony. This may have been a deathbed blessing of Eugène and Eulalie's long-standing union intended to confer a state of grace on a gravely ill parishioner.[42] Four years later the officiating priest, to avoid drawing attention to this act, quietly slipped the record of the marriage into the sacramental register for white persons.[43]

Eugène Macarty left an estate of only $12,000 to be divided among his kin. He made specific bequests totaling $4,500 to various relatives, and $300 to be divided between "the natural children that I have with Eulalie Mandeville." There was no mention of Eugène's other children with Totote Destrés and Helöise Croy.[44] The Macarty heirs challenged his succession in Second District Court. The suit was brought by Eugène's younger brother, Nicolas Théodore Macarty, joined by a long list of family members, including Delphine Macarty Lalaurie.

Eugène Macarty had not left a bequest of any sort to Eulalie Mandeville. The point of dissension was whether the $111,280 in cash (worth over $3 million today), plus real estate and slaves, possessed by Eulalie Mandeville at the time of Eugène's death actually belonged to his estate. The plaintiffs argued that Eugène had put all of his assets in Eulalie's name with the object of defrauding his legal heirs. The judge ruled against the family, commenting that fraud on the part of Eugène and Eulalie could not be proven, and that "No doubt parental love, the strongest tie on earth, suggested to both of them that their own children were better entitled to inherit the proceeds of their labor than collateral heirs for whom they felt little or no regard." In 1848, the year that Eulalie died, the claimants lost their appeal before the Supreme Court of Louisiana.[45]

In 1847 Delphine was the only plaintiff in the lawsuit over the succession of her brother. Louis Barthélémy Macarty, as described by Charles Gayarré in his 1890 *Harper's New Monthly Magazine* story, was in his youth "handsome, possessed of those clean-cut features which characterize the patrician of long descent, rich, and distinguished in every way." He was a bachelor on whom "mothers kept a steady eye . . . for there could not be a more eligible match for a beloved daughter." But suddenly, "he disappeared from the brilliant circles of which he was the ornament" and became a recluse on his plantation. He lived behind a "high wooden fence" within which he cultivated his "luxuriously perfumed garden" and enjoyed his library of the "most costly editions." All of his business was conducted through an agent, who invested his money in land and slaves to such an extent that Macarty amassed a fortune.[46]

Gayarré had actually known Louis Barthélémy Macarty and his father, but this description is only partially correct. Louis Barthélémy was indeed a wealthy and cultured recluse and he did rely heavily on his agent, but he was not lacking in female companionship. Sometime in the mid-1830s, when he was in his early fifties, he became romantically involved with eighteen-year-old Eugénie Adelaide "Pancine" Gormans, who for unexplained reasons used the surname Gomez. Her parents were not married, and her mother had died when she was ten years old.[47] Pancine was reportedly related to the wife of Macarty's agent, and it may have been through this connection that Louis Barthélémy Macarty became her "protector."[48] There was no legal impediment to a marriage between Louis Barthélémy and Pancine. She was not a person of color, nor was she

"Plan of a lot of ground with buildings thereon situated in the Suburb Washington, John Lehreiber, Engineer, May 27, 1836." This plantation house with garden and outbuildings was located on Levee Street between St. Ferdinand and Press near the Macarty Plantation. The Macarty house probably had a similar appearance during the time when Louis Barthélémy Macarty devoted himself to his gardens and orchards. (Plan Book 61, folio 55, courtesy of the Notarial Archives Research Center.)

another man's wife, but, possibly because her family was not of the same elite class as the Macartys, the couple never wed.[49] Instead, Louis Barthélémy treated Pancine as his concubine, donating to her some properties in the Faubourg Marigny and several slaves.[50]

On September 30, 1839, a daughter named Marie Jeanne Louise Philomène Macarty was born to the couple.[51] Six months later, Macarty donated houses, undeveloped lots, and five slaves to his baby daughter. The following year he gave "all the furniture, silver, and objects of his residence" to Pancine Gomez as a "testimony of his affection and recognition of the good and faithful services that she has rendered." He also gave $21,000 in cash to Pancine and their child. Auguste DeLassus was a witness to these notarial acts.[52]

Pancine and baby Louise accompanied Louis when he left for Paris in September 1840, and they shared a home at no. 28 rue Duphot.[53] One can only guess at Delphine's reaction to her brother's domestic partner, who was younger than her own daughters. Given the social conventions of the day, she probably chose to ignore the girl, and would most likely have resented the money and attention that Louis Barthélémy was lavishing upon Pancine and their child.

In his correspondence with Auguste DeLassus, Paulin Blanque never mentioned Pancine's presence, creating the impression that Louis Barthélémy was in Paris on his own. In December 1840, Paulin wrote to DeLassus in New Orleans that "my uncle occupies all my time. . . . He cannot be without me and at ten in the morning I go to his house and only leave him when he goes to bed. . . . I am not exempt from accompanying him on his errands, which is not always amusing for me." According to Paulin, Louis Barthélémy was having fun in Paris: "He goes very often to the theaters. . . . He especially admires the dancers at the Opéra, and it permits him to make little jokes when they lift their legs too high." Paulin prodded DeLassus to keep his uncle informed about his commercial projects in New Orleans. He noted that his mother was often sick, but that the family had "forced her to take care of herself" in order to prevent additional trouble and inconvenience.[54]

In March 1841, before leaving on an extended trip to Italy, Louis Barthélémy made another donation to his daughter Louise before a Paris notary, in which he gave the child a handsome two-story brick and granite building on Royal Street in New Orleans.[55]

Pancine, who was pregnant at the time, did not accompany Macarty on his excursion. Her child, to whom she gave the name Louis Barthélémy Paulin, was born on September 28, 1841. Macarty never acknowledged the boy, indicating that he doubted his paternity. Pancine later married Charles Casadavant, a native of Martinique, and with him had another son.[56]

Louis Barthélémy Macarty died at age sixty-two on his plantation below New Orleans on December 4, 1846.[57] In his will, enacted on September 19 of that year, he named Marie Jeanne Louise Philomène Macarty as his natural daughter and stated that he wished to leave her one-quarter of his estate, as permitted by law. Macarty also made a promise of freedom to his slaves for good and faithful service. He left the remainder of his estate to Delphine Macarty Lalaurie, and expressed the hope that "my sister and her heirs will respect my wishes relative to the freeing of my slaves."[58]

A few days after Macarty's death, a court-appointed assessor made an inventory of his possessions. The forty-eight-page document lists furniture, art objects, statuary, books, "casts, spheres, and globes," and Daguerreotype apparatus, indicating that, as Gayarré had described him,

509–11 Royal Street between Toulouse and St. Louis. Louis Barthélémy Macarty donated this building to his natural daughter, Louise, in 1841. Louise Macarty later became the wife of Henri Ferdinand Berthod. In 1874 she traveled from Paris to New Orleans to use the property as collateral for a loan. When she failed to make the required payment, the building was seized and sold at public auction by the sheriff of Orleans Parish. (Photograph by Frances Benjamin Johnston, Carnegie Survey of the Architecture of the South, lot 11836, Division of Prints and Photographs, Library of Congress.)

Louis Barthélémy was a man of learning and culture. Also listed were loans, promissory notes and contracts, land and buildings, horses, and eleven slaves, specified as *statu libers*, a legal term meaning that they had acquired the right to freedom in the future. The value of the entire estate was $261,224, equivalent to over $7 million in today's currency.[59] Paulin Blanque was back in New Orleans to represent his mother's interests, and was present and signed the inventory along with the family lawyer, Théodore Bailly Blanchard.[60] A notarial act lists the slaves and real estate to be received by Macarty's eight-year-old natural daughter Louise. The total value of the girl's inheritance was $65,306, or almost $2 million today.[61]

The auction of Louis Barthélémy Macarty's properties was announced in the *Bee* on May 14, 1847, by the sheriff of Orleans Parish. The list of over a hundred lots and houses took two full newspaper columns, and included properties in the Vieux Carré and Faubourgs Marigny, Tremé, and Washington (now the Bywater); store buildings in the central business district and warehouse district; and undeveloped lots in Jefferson Parish. The detailed description of the family plantation house, outbuildings, and grounds is of particular interest:

> A plantation or country residence . . . situated in Suburb Washington . . . on Levee between Independence and Barthélémy streets . . . facing the River Mississippi . . . rear on Good Children [now St. Claude] . . . with the batture, which is always rented, running between the plantation and the river. There is on said piece of land (1) a dwelling house bricked between posts, shingle roofed, the ground floor being divided into eight rooms, the second floor also into eight rooms, with a large gallery running around the building. (2) a frame house used as a kitchen, with two servants' rooms. (3) another frame building, shingle roofed, one room of which is used as a hospital, another as a washing room, and the three others with a gallery are given up to servants. (4) divers other outhouses, such as hen and pigeon roosts, two coach houses, a frame building with . . . a stable in the rear, negro huts, two cisterns, a greenhouse well glazed, flower gardens, ornamental trees &c. The property is half an hour's distance from the city, and the public road is well paved . . . offering a thousand conveniences to a rich man or considerable enticement to industry, as it may be made to yield a large income. The grounds are well stocked with . . . fruit trees of all kinds.[62]

Louis Barthélémy Macarty's long and complicated succession was opened in the Fifth District Court on November 18, 1847. Madame Lalaurie, represented by Paulin Blanque and Théodore Bailly Blanchard, contested the bequest to Louise Macarty on the grounds that the donations already made to Pancine Gomez and the child Louise constituted more than one-quarter of the estate. The appellants contended that young

Louise was entitled to only $49,418.68, and should be required to refund the balance of the money she had received. The attorneys for the defense argued that the disposition of the estate must be based upon the property owned by the deceased at the time of his death, and that donations made during Macarty's lifetime could not be counted against the one quarter share bequeathed to his natural daughter. They further stated that Macarty was only obliged by law to leave the remainder of his estate to his "legitimate relations," not necessarily to his sister Delphine, and that he had "already done more for her than he was bound to do." When the Fifth District Court upheld the terms of the will, Delphine's representatives took the case to the Louisiana Supreme Court, which also ruled in favor of Louise Macarty.[63]

These lawsuits do not substantiate the theory that Delphine tortured her slaves because she resented the colored concubines and natural children of her Macarty kinsmen, as some writers have claimed. She did not contest her father's relatively small bequest to his biracial natural daughter Emesie. She participated in a suit against the free woman of color Eulalie Mandeville over the estate of Eugène Macarty, but she also brought suit against her brother's natural daughter Louise by his white concubine Pancine Gomez, where much larger sums were involved. She may indeed have harbored some rancor against Mandeville and Gomez, but the two cases were about money rather than race.

·

Even while Delphine was still protesting the amount of the inheritance bestowed on her brother's natural daughter, her financial woes were ameliorated by the three-quarters of his estate—around $195,918, or over $5 million today—that she received under the terms of his will. By 1847 she and her adult children were domiciled at no. 72 rue de la Madeleine in the fashionable Quartier de la Madeleine in the 1st arrondissement (district) of Paris.[64] Delphine's cousin Céleste Macarty Lanusse, also accused of cruelty to her slaves in the early 1800s, lived nearby at no. 53 rue de la Madeleine. In 1848 Delphine and her family were at no. 6 rue Greffulhe, and in 1849 they lived at no. 8 rue d'Isly, also in the Quartier de la Madeleine.[65]

The streets once inhabited by Delphine and her family are located near the Champs-Elysées, the Place de la Concorde, the Tuileries Gardens, and the Church of la Madeleine. The nearby Boulevard Haussmann, the Gare

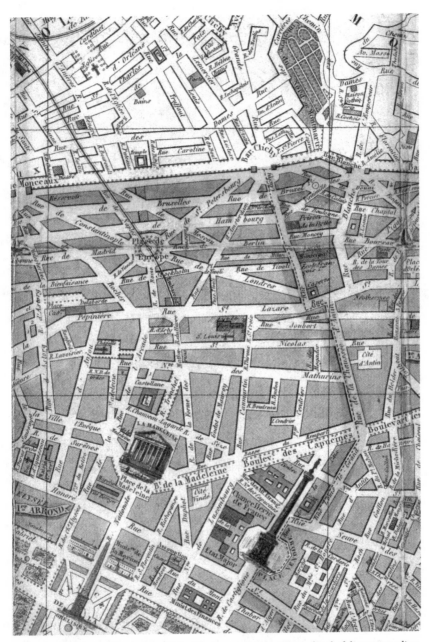

Paris Illustré et ses Fortifications, published by Auguste Logerot, 1849: detail of the 1st arrondissement. Madame Lalaurie lived on boulevard de la Madeleine, rue d' Isly, and rue Greffulhe
(not labeled), the short street between rue Nve. Des Mathurins and rue Castellane. Her funeral
was held at the Church of Saint Louis d'Antin on rue St. Croix between St. Nicolas and St.
Lazare. She was temporarily interred in the Cimetière de Montmartre, (upper right).
(Geography and Map Division, Library of Congress.)

"Boulevart de la Madeleine," from *Les Boulevarts de Paris 1820–1840*. This two-page hand-colored lithograph depicts Madame Lalaurie's neighborhood as it would have looked during her years of residence. The left side shows the Church of la Madeleine and rue de la Ferme des Mathurins. The right side shows rue Godot de Mauroy, rue Deséze, and rue Caumartin. (Lot 4363 (F), Division of Prints and Photographs, Library of Congress.)

Saint Lazare, and the Opera House in the Palais Garnier were constructed in the 1850s, a few years after Delphine's death. The Quartier de la Madeleine was, and still is, one of the finest neighborhoods in Paris, now filled with small hotels, luxury boutiques, chic department stores, theaters, and restaurants.

In 1849 Madame Lalaurie arranged for the manumission of a fifty-six-year-old enslaved man named Oreste. Oreste was never listed in Delphine's slave inventories, and there is no record of her having purchased him or of his being born in the Macarty household. Nevertheless, the Journal of Minutes and Proceedings of the Council of the First Municipality for April 16 shows that "Mrs. D^{ne} Macarty, wife of N. L. Lalaurie," sought permission to free Oreste and asked that he might remain in the state. Although the record does not indicate this, Delphine probably

Church of la Madeleine, lithograph plate 25 from *Paris Moderne et ses Environs* (Hautecolur Freres/ Imp. Lemercier de Seine, Paris, 1870). (Accession no. LC-USZ62–61294, Division of Prints and Photographs, Library of Congress.)

authorized the family attorney, Théodore Bailly Blanchard, to submit the petition. The manumission was finalized on April 20, 1849.[66]

Later defenders of Madame Lalaurie seized upon the liberation of Oreste to bolster claims for her benevolence. In 1934, *Times-Picayune* journalist Meigs Frost wrote that "Fifteen years after Delphine Lalaurie was a fugitive from justice in France," here in New Orleans she was setting free her slave Oreste. "This 'torturer and murderess of slaves' was emancipating one, with the full approval of city authorities . . . when Abraham Lincoln, the Great Emancipator, was an unknown Illinois country lawyer!"[67]

George Washington Cable, in his 1889 essay "The Haunted House in Royal Street," introduced the idea that Madame Lalaurie had been killed by a wild boar while on a hunting expedition. This is now a standard element of the Lalaurie legend. Cable's research assistant, Dora Richards Miller, provided the description of this incident, adding that "the information I have received relating to Mad. L.'s ultimate fate is said by my informant to come from an old colored servant of the Fernandez family." (A Monsieur Fernandez was one of the men who helped rescue the Lalaurie slaves from the fire.) According to Miller's source, "Madame Lalaurie was staying then at . . . Pau . . . in the Pyrénées Mountains. . . . [She] had gone out with a large, fine party of people . . . to hunt the wild boar. She got separated from the rest . . . and while alone encountered the infuriated beast, who sprang upon her and gored her to death before the others could get to her."[68] Cable's readers would have considered Delphine's death from mutilation by a wild animal to be a fitting retribution for her evil deeds.

In 1941, journalist Bob Brown's article "Proof that Madame Lalaurie . . . Rests Here" was published in the *New Orleans States*, and another piece, titled "Epitaph-Plate of 'Haunted' House Owner Found Here," appeared in the *Times-Picayune*. Both proclaimed that Delphine had died in Paris in 1842, and that her body was returned to New Orleans for interment in St. Louis Cemetery no. 1. According to the *States* and *Times-Picayune* articles, Eugene Backes, a marble cutter and former sexton at the St. Louis Cemeteries, had discovered "a mysterious epitaph plate: a rectangular piece of copper, turned green with age, nicked and cracked with corrosion, bearing the easily discernible words: *Madame Lalaurie, née Marie Delphine Maccarthy, decedée a Paris, le 7 decembre, 1842, a la age de 6—*" The rest of the inscription was missing because "a part of the plate had been eaten away by time." Miriam DeBuys confirmed the report and provided a photograph of the tomb in St. Louis Cemetery no. 1, say-ing that "the story was handed down [in the family] through the genera-tions that her body was buried here and they have attended to the tomb regularly."[69]

Delphine Macarty Lalaurie indeed died in Paris, but it was on Decem-ber 7, 1849. The 1842 death date given in the *States* and *Times-Picayune*

No. 8 rue d'Isly. Madame Lalaurie lived at this address with Jean Louis Lalaurie and her adult children Pauline, Laure, and Paulin Blanque during the last years of her life. She died there on December 7, 1849. (Photograph by Jérôme Malhache, September 2008.)

articles is incorrect because, as the journalists reported, the edge of the copper epitaph plate had "been eaten away by time," and 1849 was misread as 1842.

The death record issued by the Prefecture of the Department of the Seine identified Madame Lalaurie as "Marie Delphine Maccarthy [*sic*], *rentière*, aged sixty-four years, wife of Louis Lalaurie, aged forty-eight years," who expired "at her domicile no. 8 rue de l'Isly." Auguste DeLassus, also living at no. 8 rue de l'Isly, signed as a witness.[70] French death records never specify the cause of death, but the story of Delphine's being attacked by a wild boar while hunting at Pau is unlikely. As we have seen from the letters of her adult children, she had been ill for several years, and it was probably this illness that killed her.

Pauline, Laure, and Paulin Blanque and Jean Louis Lalaurie were painfully aware that their mother's spectacular crimes had forced them to leave New Orleans in 1834, and that the story of the starved and tortured slaves had followed them everywhere. What was it like for them to live in close proximity with her in their Paris apartment for thirteen years? It must have been especially difficult for Pauline and Laure. The Blanque sisters, then in their early twenties, had resided with their mother on her country plantation and in the Royal Street mansion during the time that the slave torture was taking place. Martineau learned from her informants that these young women were "thought to be spiritless and unhappy-looking," and that Madame Lalaurie punished them for trying to help the imprisoned slaves. Jean Louis was a little boy and may have been less aware of the abuse, but the three of them were present on the day of the fire and experienced the terrifying escape from the angry crowd. Paulin was away at college in 1834. Pauline and Laure remained unmarried and, as far as can be determined, Paulin and Jean Louis never worked at any occupation during their time in Paris. They all were financially dependent on their mother and subject to her idiosyncratic whims and fits of temper. Perhaps her death was a relief to them.

The funeral records of the Church of Saint Louis d'Antin in Paris show that on December 9, 1849, the body of Marie Delphine "Machaty" was presented for burial. A marginal note states that her third-class funeral was held at noon of that day—was her family unwilling to pay for a first-class ceremony?[71] The records of the Cimetière de Montmartre indicate that she was interred in the tomb of the Notta and Noël families on the day of her funeral, and that her body was exhumed on January 7, 1851, to be transported to New Orleans.[72]

Sepulture Notta et Noël, Cimetière de Montmartre. After her funeral at the Church of
Saint Louis d'Antin on December 9, 1849, the body of Madame Lalaurie was interred
in this tomb until it was exhumed in 1851 for reburial in New Orleans. (Photograph by
Jérôme Malhache, September 2008.)

This record verifies the story of Madame Lalaurie's remains being returned to her native city. The 1941 newspaper articles, based on information provided by Miriam DeBuys, state authoritatively that she was
reinterred in St. Louis Cemetery no. 1.[73] Because the Archdiocesan Archives burial books for this cemetery end in 1841 and resume in 1857,
there is no record of her 1851 interment. The Archdiocesan Cemeteries

Tomb in St. Louis Cemetery no. 1 alleged to be that of Madame Lalaurie. The inscription on the pediment reads simply "tombe de famille," and none of the individual tablets have inscriptions. One tablet is missing—might that have held the inscription for Madame Lalaurie, removed later by the family or by souvenir hunters? The ownership and burial record shows Paulin Blanque as the owner of the tomb. The earliest burial was for Dame H. J. Stouse, age twenty-one, interred June 15, 1884. This would have been Delphine Macarty Lalaurie's great-granddaughter Marie Josephine Amable Ducros, daughter of Laure Forstall and Felix Ducros and wife of Henry Jules Stouse, who died on June 14, 1884. Twentieth-century burials in the tomb do not appear to be related to the Macarty family, indicating that it has been sold. (Photograph by the author, November 2007.)

Office ownership and burial record for the family tomb said to be Madame Lalaurie's resting place shows that it belonged to the family of Paulin Blanque. Paulin would have purchased this unusually large, six-vault tomb before having his mother's remains returned from Paris, and she is probably buried there as the newspapers attest. The record, however, lists neither Delphine Macarty Lalaurie nor any of her children, including Paulin Blanque, and the first interment on the page is for one of Delphine's great-granddaughters, who died in 1884.[74]

8

DENOUEMENT

The succession of Delphine Macarty, wife of Lalaurie, was opened in New Orleans' Fifth District Court on January 14, 1850, when her six adult children petitioned to be put into possession of their mother's estate.[1] By this time Borja López Forstall was forty-seven years old, the four Blanque siblings were in their mid-thirties, and Jean Louis Lalaurie was twenty-two. Both of Delphine's married daughters were "authorized and assisted" by their husbands. Pauline and Laure Blanque and Jeanne Blanque DeLassus were stated to be residents of France, and Borja López Forstall, Paulin Blanque, and Jean Louis Lalaurie were identified as residents of New Orleans.

A notary and two appraisers began the inventory of Delphine's estate on January 29, 1850. This list, which goes on for ten pages, included $1,060 in the Louisiana State Bank; promissory notes and drafts amounting to $58,580; stock in the Union Bank of Louisiana worth $12,000; and $6,480 worth of stock in the Levee Steam Cotton Press Company, together totaling $78,120. On the following day the appraisers itemized Delphine's real estate holdings. Included were several properties inherited from her brother: a three-story brick hotel on Conti Street valued at $25,000, four store buildings on Madison Street near the French Market worth $27,000, and thirty-eight vacant lots in Jefferson Parish, together worth $300. She owned three houses in the Faubourg Marigny and the Vieux Carré worth a total of $29,000, four store buildings on Levee (now North Peters) together worth $50,000, and a three-story brick store building on Chartres valued at $25,000. Also listed was the two-story brick townhouse on Royal Street where Delphine had once lived with Jean Blanque; in 1847 she had bought her half share from her brother's succession for $6,000, and it was now appraised at $22,000. Altogether, her real estate holdings were valued at $167,300. No slaves were included in the inventory. The total worth of the cash, promissory notes, stocks, and real estate was $245,420, almost $7 million in today's currency. Delphine had no creditors, meaning that each of the six heirs received assets valued at $40,903, now the equivalent of over $1 million.[2]

A declaration made in Paris on June 20, 1850, indicated that Delphine's only possessions in the French city were "furniture and personal effects" amounting to 12,567 francs; these presumably were sold and the proceeds added to the value of her estate.[3]

The New Orleans attorney Théodore Bailly Blanchard was heavily involved in the financial affairs of Delphine's adult children and became their primary adviser in matters relating to her succession. Blanchard had already assisted the family in the settlement of Louis Barthélémy Macarty's estate, and a few days after their mother's death, Pauline and Laure Blanque and Jeanne Blanque DeLassus had appeared before their Paris notary to authorize Blanchard to represent them before the Fifth District Court of New Orleans.[4]

On May 31, 1850, Pauline, Laure, Jeanne, and their half-brother Jean Louis (who had returned to France) again went before a Paris notary to empower Blanchard to "take the necessary measures for emancipation of the slaves Patsy and Elodie, pertaining to the succession of the aforesaid Dame Lalaurie." This act was subsequently verified by Paulin Blanque before a New Orleans notary. Blanchard was authorized to free not only Patsy and Elodie but also Oreste, who had already gained his liberty in 1849.[5]

Delphine had indeed owned a woman named Patsy, purchased in 1831 from a Kentucky slave dealer and described in the act of sale as being almost six feet tall and of "good moral character, not in the habit of running away." Elodie, who appears nowhere in Delphine's inventories or purchase records, might have been Patsy's daughter. As noted above, no slaves were listed in the inventory of Delphine's estate, but there is some evidence that Patsy was living in the Forstall household. Ownership of Patsy, Elodie, and Oreste could have been informally transferred to the Forstalls or other family members.[6] A search of all possible archival resources reveals no evidence that Patsy and Elodie were ever officially freed.[7]

.

On September 10, 1850, Pauline Blanque died at age forty in Biarritz, a seaside village on the Atlantic coast at the foot of the Pyrénées Mountains.[8] Biarritz had not yet become a fashionable resort at the time of Pauline's death. It was simply a health spa where invalids went to bathe in the ocean, which was believed to have therapeutic properties. During the 1840s Delphine and her family frequently vacationed in the Pyrénées, visiting various locations to "take the waters." If Pauline was the "crippled daughter" who in her youth was treated by Dr. Lalaurie, she might have been at Biarritz seeking relief for an orthopedic condition. As is always the case with French death records, the cause of Pauline's demise was not explained.

Théodore Bailly Blanchard was again authorized by Pauline's siblings to take charge of their sister's succession. Pauline had previously received a $5,000 donation from her uncle, Louis Barthélémy Macarty, which according to the Louisiana Supreme Court record had been "paid with interest by his executors since his death."[9] Pauline's one-sixth share of her mother's estate would have reverted to her brothers and sisters, and in subsequent notarial acts the parties were referred to as the "heirs of Delphine Macarty, wife of Lalaurie, and of Pauline Blanque."

On March 7, 1853, a team of auctioneers held an "unreserved and extensive sale of very valuable improved real estate [in New Orleans] and 38 squares of ground [in Jefferson Parish] . . . to affect a final partition between the heirs of the estate of the late Mrs. Lalaurie." The auction was held at noon in the rotunda of the St. Louis Hotel, with the stipulation that buyers were to make a down payment of "one-fourth cash," and were to register their purchases before the notary Adolphe Mazureau. The sales go on for sixty-five pages in Mazureau's record book.[10]

The settlement of Delphine's estate dragged on for years, and throughout the 1850s Borja López Forstall, Laure and Paulin Blanque, Jeanne Blanque DeLassus, and Jean Louis Lalaurie continued to sell off the New Orleans real estate inherited from their mother's succession.[11] The heirs also attempted to reopen the succession of their uncle Louis Barthélémy in order to recover some of the bequest made to his natural daughter

Louise.[12] In all of these transactions they were assisted by the ubiquitous Théodore Bailly Blanchard.

·

The original Macarty plantation house and its surrounding gardens had been retained by Louis Barthélémy Macarty until his death. John Mc-Donogh, a native of Baltimore who established a very successful business career in New Orleans, had bought the Macarty plantation at the sheriff's auction held in settlement of Louis Barthélémy's succession in 1847.[13]

In his will, McDonogh (who had no heirs) left most of his estate to the cities of New Orleans and Baltimore to be used for charitable purposes. He left an annuity to an asylum for the poor, financed a society for the relief of destitute orphan boys, and contributed funds to the American Colonization Society to ship freed slaves to Liberia. McDonogh's most cherished project, however, was "the establishment and support of free schools . . . wherein the poor . . . of both sexes and all classes and castes of color shall have admittance free of expense." McDonogh specified that his vast New Orleans land holdings were not to be sold, but were to "remain together as one estate" and rented to "good tenants." The proceeds were to be applied to "the purposes for which it is hereby intended and destined," primarily free education for every child.[14]

McDonogh died in 1850, and his estate was not settled until 1858. Contrary to his stated wish that his real estate be kept together and rented out, the City of New Orleans sold most of the McDonogh properties to individual buyers and used the $704,440 in profits to establish public schools.[15] The hundreds of acts related to the McDonogh succession occupy an entire volume of the notary Eusebe Bouny, who provided printed forms specifically for these transactions.

City surveyors subdivided the former Macarty Plantation into twenty streets with 795 building lots, which were sold for a total of $80,000.[16] Only a small portion of the Macarty property, including the original plantation house, was retained for a school and public square. In the summer of 1859 the *Daily Crescent* carried a long article titled "The Dismemberment of the Macarty Plantation." According to the *Crescent*, the process of destruction was going forward at a rapid pace, and "is withal a rather regretful thing to behold. The shady old plantation with its wealth of spreading trees, shrubbery, and flowers, is now all cut up into squares and picketed off in lots. . . . New streets . . . intersect the plantation. . . . The statues that used to adorn the central avenue through the garden are scattered about in the dirt, and whilst the birds continue to warble . . . from the shade of the old live-oaks and magnolias, the louder chorus of the carpenter's hammer and saw issues through the hedges."[17]

In 1867 the plantation house became the Macarty (sometimes spelled "McCarthy") School. The school, designated as being for "colored boys and girls," appears in city directories at 621 Pauline Street, and maps from the 1880s and 1890s show the "McCarthy School (Negro)" located in the square bounded by Chartres, Pauline, Jeanne (later Alvar), and Royal. The nearby Macarty Square was bounded by Burgundy, Pauline, Jeanne, and St. Claude. The streets are labeled "not paved." In 1927 the "McCarthy" School moved to the corner of North Claiborne and Lamarque, and the following year it moved to 1605 Caffin Avenue.[18] New Orleans rock-and-roll icon Antoine "Fats" Domino attended the Caffin Avenue "McCarthy" School from 1934 to 1938.[19] The old Macarty plantation house was torn down around 1927, and the space was later occupied by the Francis T. Nicholls (now Frederick Douglass) High School, which still stands. Macarty Square, with its Victory Arch built to commemorate World War I soldiers, is a center of what is now the Bywater neighborhood.

·

Delphine Macarty Lalaurie's surviving children lived out their days in New Orleans and Paris. Borja López, wife of Placide Forstall, spent the rest of her life in New Orleans. Placide earned a handsome living as an insurance broker. The Forstalls owned a fine home at the corner of Rampart and Ursulines, which was described in a later notarial act as "an agreeable family residence" with a service wing adjoining the main house and a "stable, brick well, cistern, shed, privy, &c." in back. The property was surrounded by "an ornamental garden containing fruit trees and flowers."[20] In this enclave Borja and her husband presided over their two sons and seven daughters and their many grandchildren.

One of the Forstall daughters, Laure, appears to have been a willful and disruptive girl, much as one imagines her grandmother Delphine to have been. In 1850 Archbishop Antoine Blanc received a letter from Annette Praz, headmistress of the St. Michael's Academy of the Sacred Heart of Jesus. This boarding school, located sixty miles above New Orleans at Convent, Louisiana, catered to the daughters of wealthy Catholic families. Praz asked the archbishop to "arrange with Madame Placide Forstall not to send Laure [age fourteen] back to school, as she gives a bad example." Three months later Praz wrote again, reminding Archbishop Blanc that the issue of Laure Forstall had not yet been resolved. She had heard that Laure was planning to return, and she asked Blanc to persuade Madame Forstall to keep her daughter at home, lest she be "obliged to send her away later." Within a few days Placide Forstall came to ask why the school no longer wished to have Laure, and the headmistress "explained Laure's conduct of last year and that they could not in conscience keep pupils who wronged others by their bad spirit and insubordination." Forstall promised that "if Laure does not give more satisfaction, he will withdraw her immediately."[21]

With the exception of the youngest daughter, Delphine, who remained single, all of the Forstall children eventually had successful careers and made good marriages. The sons, Anatole and Octave Forstall, were both cotton brokers and married girls from respectable families. The first daughter, Céleste, married Henry Rathbone, president of the Canal Bank. It was Céleste, Madame Lalaurie's granddaughter and goddaughter, to whom she wrote the affectionate letters from Paris in 1835 and 1836. The second daughter, Emma, married Emile DeBuys, a cotton broker.[22] The other Forstall girls also found well-to-do husbands, but it is the Rathbone and DeBuys names that have endured in New Orleans' elite society. Placide Forstall died in 1876 at age eighty. Borja survived her husband and died of pneumonia at her home on Rampart Street at the age of seventy-nine in 1884.[23]

Present-day descendants of the Forstall-Rathbone-DeBuys family argue that the accusations against Delphine could not have been true because their ancestors were successful merchants and professionals and married into other wealthy and socially prominent families. This, they say, would have been impossible if such a stigma had been attached to their name.[24] Fortune had indeed smiled on Borja and her descendants, but this was not the case with Paulin and Laure Blanque, Jeanne Blanque DeLassus, and Jean Louis Lalaurie, who led undistinguished or downright tragic lives and in some cases managed to lose the property inherited from their mother.

·

Paulin Blanque, a broker, married seventeen-year-old Felicité Amanda Andry on December 8, 1852. The marriage contract specified that the couple were to be separate in property.[25] When the heirs of Madame Lalaurie

Oil portrait of Jeanne Marie Céleste Forstall (born 1823), daughter of Placide Forstall and Borja López y Ángulo. A handwritten inscription on the mat identifies her as "Mrs. Henry A. Rathbone, neé Céleste Forstall, mother of Mrs. James DeBuys, neé Stella E. Rathbone, 'Nanine.'" This image, along with the portrait of Madame Lalaurie and other portraits of Forstall, DeBuys, and Rathbone family members, was published in Herman de Bachellé Seebold's *Old Louisiana Plantation Homes and Family Trees* (1941). The portraits were photographed by H. J. Harvey's Studio, probably in the 1930s. The location of the original painting is unknown. (Courtesy of John Ellis.)

divided her estate in 1853, Amanda paid $5,200 for a two-story brick house fronting on Hospital Street, built in the 1840s on what had been the back lot of the Lalaurie property. It was there that Amanda and Paulin made their home.[26] Two sons, Charles Macarty Blanque and François Placide George Blanque were the result of their union.[27]

In 1858 Amanda filed for a separation from bed and board on the grounds that Paulin had struck her, and that she had "frequently been menaced, humiliated, and her feelings [had been] lacerated by the offensive language of her husband." One of their quarrels was over Amanda's punishment of a young female slave; did Blanque see in his wife the same destructive tendencies that had caused his mother's downfall? Paulin was alleged to have stated in front of a witness that Amanda was "a bad woman," and that "it was she who should be flogged rather than the slave." The same witness testified that Paulin accused Amanda of "bringing men into his house . . . and making of it a bordello." When reminded that he was addressing "the mother of his children," he replied that she "had filled his house with bastards," and denied being the father of the child that Amanda was carrying at the time. A servant who had been employed in the household testified that Blanque would "throw his wife against the bed . . . and call her bitch and whore." Paulin Blanque did not contest these charges. The judge therefore ruled in favor of Amanda, and decreed that she would retain her dotal property and the house on Hospital Street.[28] The 1860 census shows Paulin Blanque renting a room on Ursulines near Rampart, around the corner from the Forstalls. In 1868, at age fifty-three, he died of lung cancer at the Forstall home and was interred in the Forstall family tomb.[29]

After separating from her husband, Amanda Andry Blanque gradually slipped into poverty. She had initially derived a good income from renting out the Hospital Street house. But when she used this property as security for two loans and failed to make the required payments, her creditors took their claims to court and the house was seized and sold at a sheriff's auction. Amanda lost a property valued at $6,000, plus the $1,000 yearly rent, for a debt of $4,800.[30]

In later years Amanda lived in a series of rented dwellings in the downtown Creole faubourgs of Tremé, Marigny, and what is now the Bywater, moving every few years. By 1882 she was listed in the city directory as a seamstress. Her grandson Charles Gabriel Blanque, who sometimes shared her home, died at Charity Hospital of "accidental morphine poisoning."

The census for 1910 lists seventy-year-old "Armanda" Blanque, described as "feebleminded," as an inmate at the Asylum of the Little Sisters of the Poor. She died there in 1913.[31]

Jean Louis Lalaurie, perhaps because of his surname, had the hardest time of all. He truly seems to have been a "lost soul." Shortly after appearing in New Orleans for the opening of his mother's succession, Jean Louis returned to Paris, leaving Théodore Bailly Blanchard in charge of his business affairs.[32] Jean Louis was out of the country until 1854, when he returned to New Orleans and was listed in the city directories as a broker.[33] He lived as a lodger in rented rooms and never married or (as far as we know) fathered any children.[34] Between 1866 and 1874, Jean Louis used some of the commercial real estate inherited from his mother as security for various loans, shady financial schemes, and risky stock speculations; these unwise business decisions resulted in lawsuits by his creditors. He ultimately lost his property, which was seized and sold at a series of sheriff's auctions.[35]

In 1870 Jean Louis Lalaurie became involved in a duel with his young kinsman Lucien DeBuys (brother-in-law of his niece Emma Forstall DeBuys) resulting from a quarrel during a performance of Charles Gounod's *Faust* at the French Opera House. According to the local newspapers, the difficulty arose from "an uncomplimentary remark accompanied by a blow." On the following Saturday morning Lalaurie and DeBuys had a "hostile meeting" at The Oaks, the traditional dueling place in City Park, where Lalaurie, the challenging party, received a "serious wound in the left breast near the heart" with a small sword.[36] The twentieth-century local-color writer Robert Tallant, an indefatigable purveyor of scandal and hyperbole, later claimed, in *The Romantic New Orleanians*, that it was Delphine's husband, still living in the city, who fought the duel "after an argument regarding a contralto's talents."[37]

In 1883 Jean Louis Lalaurie died at age fifty-five at the Hotel Dieu, a hospital operated by the Daughters of Charity; the cause of death was given as "cerebral softening."[38]

Laure Blanque and Jeanne Blanque DeLassus lived the rest of their lives in Paris. Jeanne had obtained a separation of property from Auguste DeLassus before the First District Court of New Orleans in 1846, possibly because of his irresponsible handling of her family's money.[39] Jeanne and her husband were in Paris at the time of her mother's death in 1849. Jeanne stayed, and DeLassus returned to New Orleans to represent Jeanne's interests at the opening of Delphine's succession in January 1850. DeLassus eventually relocated to Missouri, where he died in 1888.[40] Laure and Jeanne moved from the center of Paris to the 17th arrondissement, at that time a rural district. Laure died, still unmarried, at age sixty-eight on May 1, 1881. Jeanne died in 1900 at the age of eighty-five.[41]

·

Louise Macarty, the daughter of Louis Barthélémy Macarty with his concubine Eugénie Adelaide "Pancine" Gomez, grew to adulthood in Paris, and in 1860 she became the wife of Henri Ferdinand Berthod.[42] In January 1874 Louise Macarty Berthod traveled alone to New Orleans, where she used the property on Royal Street, donated to her in 1841 by her father, as collateral for a $3,000 loan. The loan was due in one year, and when Louise returned to France without making the required payment, the building was seized and sold at public auction by the sheriff of Orleans Parish.[43]

·

The Macartys of mixed race—the concubines and natural children of Delphine's father, uncles, and cousins—remained in New Orleans, where they were part of the well-to-do Afro-Creole community residing in close proximity to Delphine's children and grandchildren. The free women of color who had been the domestic partners of the Macarty men might have had behind-the-scenes assistance, but they had purchased land and slaves in their own names rather than acquiring property as donations from their white benefactors. Most of these women, Sophie Mousante, Eulalie Mandeville, Totote Destrés, Helöise Croy, Henriette Prieto, and Céleste Perrault, survived their male partners and spent their later years in comfortable economic circumstances.[44]

Only CéCé Carpentier died young, at age thirty-eight. Ironically, her death occurred on April 11, 1834, the day after the fire at the Lalaurie mansion. According to a letter from Jean Boze to Henri de Ste-Gême, after the death of her "protector," Jean Baptiste Barthélémy Macarty, CéCé had used her resources to make an extended trip to Paris. The cold, damp climate there undermined her health, and she returned to New Orleans to be cared for by her family and friends. She died two months later.[45]

Creole cottage occupied between 1808 and 1879 by Eulalie Mandeville and Eugène Macarty and their children. The drawing is described as "a house on the corner of Dauphine and Barracks streets, constructed of wood and brick, with a tile roof, having six rooms, a large gallery, a kitchen with four rooms for servants, and a fine yard with several fruit trees, situated on a lot measuring 60 by 120 feet." The site of the Mandeville-Macarty house is now Cabrini Park, used by neighborhood residents as a dog run. (Detail, "Plan of 1 Lot of Ground with Buildings in 2nd District," Plan Book 6, folio 87, drawn by the free man of color Pierre Crocker, ca. 1820, Courtesy of the Notarial Archives Research Center.)

Three Creole cottages on Burgundy Street between Toulouse and St. Louis. The cottages were owned by Henriette Prieto, domestic partner of Jean Baptiste Barthélémy Macarty, and their adult children between 1809 and 1868. (Photograph by the author, October 2007.)

The children of these free women of color, all of whom had the surname Macarty, married or formed domestic relationships and started families of their own. Aided by their fathers, who oversaw their education and helped establish them in business, several of the non-white Macarty men became successful entrepreneurs. Two of the very light-complexioned members of the family eventually abandoned New Orleans to begin new lives as white people.

Delphine Emesie Macarty was the natural daughter of Delphine's father with Sophie Mousante. Emesie was evidently so Caucasian in appearance that sometimes she was not identified in notarial records as a woman of color. She became the concubine of the white merchant Benjamin Hart, a native of New York.[46] Sometime in the late 1840s the couple and their children settled in Philadelphia, where they were designated as white in every census between 1850 and 1880. Emesie, going by the name Delphine Hart, became a music teacher after Hart died.[47] Sophie Mousante may have gone to Philadelphia with her daughter's family; she disappeared from the New Orleans city directories after 1846 and there is no record of her death in New Orleans.[48]

Armand Henri Macarty was the natural son of Delphine's cousin Jean Baptiste Barthélémy Macarty with CéCé Carpentier. He and his brother Gustav had been educated by their father at northern colleges. Armand lived for a time in Cuba and established himself as a successful businessman. In 1849 he married a white New England woman, Matilda Eaton Post, at the Church of the Divine Unity in New York City.[49] The couple returned to Cuba, where two of their three daughters were born. In 1860 the family, all designated as white, was enumerated in the census for New York City; Armand was listed as a merchant owning real estate valued at $25,000 and $10,000 worth of personal property. Armand Macarty died in 1870, and his widow and adult daughters settled on Staten Island.[50] A 1905 genealogical account of the Post family by Marie Caroline de Trobriand Post referred to "Count Armand de Macarty," who, after marrying Matilda Eaton Post was "obliged by his business interests" to return to Matanzas, Cuba. Another such account was written in 1930 by a daughter of Armand Macarty and Matilda Post. These authors obviously believed their ancestor to be descended from white Louisiana-French aristocrats.[51]

Drauzin Barthélémy Macarty, natural son of Jean Baptiste Barthélémy Macarty and Henriette Prieto, became the patriarch of the racially mixed branch of the Macarty family in New Orleans, watching over the social and business interests of his siblings and cousins. Drauzin was a successful real estate dealer, commodity broker, and merchant of "fancy dry-goods." When he died in 1870, he was one of the wealthiest men of color in the city.[52] The natural sons of Eugène Macarty and Eulalie Mandeville also became prosperous businessmen: Barthélémy Macarty was a merchant in Santiago de Cuba, and Pierre Villarceaux, Théodule, and Eugène Macarty Jr. were engaged in real estate and commodity trading in New Orleans.[53] Patricio Macarty, natural son of Augustin Macarty and Céleste Perrault, left New Orleans to establish a general store in Pensacola, Florida.[54]

The only one of the Macartys of color to attain lasting fame was the musician Eugène Victor Macarty, natural son of Eugène Macarty and Helöise Croy. Eugène Victor (also referred to as Victor Eugène) became a music teacher, composer, and performer, described on the cover of his published sheet music as the "pianist for the fashionable soirées of New Orleans." His musical performances at the Théâtre d'Orléans were announced in the local newspapers. He shared his home with his wife, children, and his mother, Helöise Croy.[55]

The secure position of the Macartys of mixed race began to erode after the Civil War. Reconstruction, the process by which Louisiana was reintegrated into the Union between 1863 and 1877, offered people of color a hope for the future that proved to be false. The Louisiana constitution of 1868 gave those who had been free and those who had been enslaved before the war unobstructed access to public conveyances, places of business, and schools. Men of African descent were granted the right to vote, serve on juries, and hold public office. Interracial marriage was legalized in 1870. These radical social reforms were bitterly opposed by white New Orleanians, and Creoles and Americans were united against "carpetbag government" and "Negro rule." New laws supported ever more repressive Jim Crow segregation and racism, again outlawing interracial marriage, disenfranchising voters of African descent, and making many public venues off limits to people of color. The Louisiana Legislative Code of 1890 classified persons with "any appreciable amount" of African ancestry as Negro, even those who appeared to be Caucasian.[56]

In 1869 Eugène Victor Macarty was the victim of racial discrimination. While attending a performance of Rossini's *The Barber of Seville* at the French Opera House, he was asked to leave his seat in the *parquette* section reserved for white patrons. The *Daily Crescent* described Macarty as "a colored man . . . very light in complexion, very polished and elegant

Cover of "Fleurs de Salon, 2 Favorite Polkas" ("A'Alzea" and "La Caprifolia"), composed by Victor Eugène Macarthy (Macarty). Notice that the two pieces are dedicated to "M^ells Anaïs Boudousquie and Delphine Forstall." The second young lady was Madame Lalaurie's granddaughter, the daughter of Borja López and Placide Forstall. (Marcus Christian Collection, sheet music, accession no. 11, courtesy of Louisiana and Special Collections, Earl K. Long Library, University of New Orleans.)

in his style of dress, and withal somewhat pompous in his manners." When the manager of the opera house came to order him out and return the price of his ticket, Macarty became indignant and "used some rather uncomplimentary language" toward the gentleman, and threatened him with "corrections by slaps in the face and kicks *a posteriori*." An article in the next day's *Crescent* commented that Macarty intended to "make a test case of it." But, blustered the writer, "Let the bogus assembly pile act upon act . . . they will never force the union they would compel between the two races. Civil equality bills will not seat Macarty or any of his color in places under the control of white men."[57] Eugène Victor Macarty initiated a suit for $1,500 damages against the French Opera House in the United States Court for the Eastern District of Louisiana. The outcome is unknown.[58]

It may have been this humiliating incident that inspired Eugène Victor

Macarty to become involved in politics. He was a member of the Radical Republican Club composed of upper-class men of color who sought to achieve the same rights and privileges as white citizens. He held various positions in New Orleans city government, and from 1870 to 1872 he served in the Louisiana House of Representatives as the delegate from the 6th Ward of Orleans Parish.[59] He died in 1881.[60]

·

Thus ends the chronicle of the Macarty clan, the numerous white and non-white progeny of Jean Jacques and Barthélémy Daniel de Macarty, two French-Irish military men who arrived in New Orleans during its earliest years. We have traced the Macartys from the founding of the Louisiana colony in the eighteenth century through the turn of the twentieth century, concentrating on the most notorious member of the family, Delphine Macarty Lalaurie. Some of the descendants of Madame Lalaurie and her relatives on both sides of the color line have continued to live in New Orleans, while others have scattered to unknown destinations. In the final chapter, the story will shift focus to the famous "Haunted House" on Royal Street.

9

THE "HAUNTED HOUSE"

During the days following the fire of April 10, 1834, the *Louisiana Courier*, the *New Orleans Bee*, and the *Louisiana Advertiser* described the attack on the Lalaurie mansion by the angry populace. Not only did the rioters smash furniture, china, crystal, and works of art, they wrecked the floors, stairs, and wainscoting, broke windows, dismantled the iron balconies, and continued their assault on the roof and walls until "nearly the whole of the edifice had been pulled down." Jean Boze wrote to Henri de Ste-Gême that the beautiful residence had been so damaged that the Lalaurie family could no longer live there. When Harriet Martineau visited New Orleans in 1836, she saw the house still standing in its derelict state, with its broken windows and partially demolished walls.[1]

In 1837, Madame Lalaurie's son-in-law and business agent Placide Forstall sold what was left of the Lalaurie mansion to Pierre Edouard Trastour for $14,000, less than half what she had paid for it in 1831. Three months later, Trastour sold the ruined house for the same price to Charles Caffin, who took out a mortgage of $16,700 for renovation and enlargement. It is ironic that these sales were enacted before the notaries Amédée Ducatel and Felix Grima. Ducatel was one of the men who helped rescue the slaves from the fire, and Grima was the judge of the criminal court during the years when Delphine was under investigation.[2]

Owing to the major reconstruction undertaken by Caffin, the famous

"Haunted House" in the Vieux Carré is very different in appearance from the site of the shocking events of 1834. It was probably Caffin who added the flat-roofed third story topped by a belvedere (also referred to as an observatory or cupola), increasing the size of the house and giving it a more severe and fortress-like appearance than it had originally. Historians associated with the Tulane University School of Architecture's survey of buildings in the Vieux Carré noted that the "impressive mansion known as the Lalaurie or Haunted House actually is not the same building that the infamous Madame Lalaurie inhabited. . . . When the fire burned and the mob completed the destruction during [her] ownership . . . there was probably little left. It was rebuilt around 1837–38, and assumed the appearance that it has today."[3]

·

After passing out of the hands of Delphine and her family, the Lalaurie mansion served various institutional or commercial functions and later was divided into rental apartments. Henry Castellanos wrote in *New Orleans as It Was* that "No spirits wander through its wide halls . . . but in lieu thereof there rests a curse . . . that follows everyone who has ever attempted to make it a permanent habitation . . . every venture has proved a ruinous failure."[4] It is indeed true that from the 1830s until the present, many of the institutions and tenants that tried to occupy the "Haunted House" have experienced financial insolvency or bad luck.

In 1845, having renovated and enlarged the house, Charles Caffin leased it to the Franklin High School. This was, according to an announcement in the *Courier*, an "institution for the education of young gentlemen" that offered languages, mathematics, history, geography, and science. After this first announcement, advertisements for the school disappeared from the newspapers, and it was never listed in the city directories, indicating that the school shut its doors shortly after opening. Caffin was left with an untenanted building.[5]

In 1862 Charles Caffin sold the house, now designated as 282 Royal Street, to a music teacher named Amelia Zacherie Saul Cammack for $17,000.[6] Within five years Cammack wanted out. An 1867 auction notice described her "palatial residence" as "a large three-story building with handsome exterior decorations containing 21 rooms, 8 closets, and 2 fine stores [with] an iron front gate and marble steps, observatory on roof, and gas throughout; admirably adapted for a school, an asylum, a first class boarding house, or a spacious residence."[7] The turbulent years of the Civil War and the occupation of New Orleans by Union troops intervened, and it was only in 1869 that Cammack sold the house for $10,000 to Joseph Barnes.[8]

Barnes, a tobacco merchant, used the former Lalaurie mansion as his business establishment until 1872, when he leased it to the City of New Orleans for a public high school for girls. On three occasions Barnes offered the building as collateral when he borrowed money from Barthé-lémy Beobay, a butcher operating a stall in the Tremé Market. In 1873, when Barnes defaulted on these promissory notes, Beobay instituted a lawsuit before the Sixth District Court. The property was seized by the court and sold at a sheriff's auction, where Beobay acquired it for $6,000.[9]

Barthélémy Beobay continued the lease arrangement with the city's public school system. The institution, which served the downtown neighborhoods below Canal Street, was known as the Lower Girls' High School. The Louisiana constitution of 1868 had provided for the establishment of at least one free public school in each parish, open to children ages six to eighteen regardless of race or previous condition of servitude.[10] The controversy over these racially mixed schools erupted in December 1874. The story made the front pages of New Orleans' English-language newspapers, the *Times* and the *Daily Picayune*.

The trouble started uptown on December 14, when three young women of African descent, having completed their primary schooling, arrived to take the entrance examination for admission to the Upper Girls' High School that served the mostly Anglo-American neighborhoods above Canal Street. The white students staged a noisy protest, and the principal persuaded the black girls to leave on the grounds that their names had not been submitted by the required deadline. Three days later a gang of white youths from the Central Boys' High School began visiting other public schools, including the Lower Girls' High School in the former Lalaurie mansion, with the intention of removing any students of African ancestry who were already enrolled or were there to take the entrance examination. In contrast to the uptown schools, the Lower Girls' High School in the Vieux Carré had accommodated students of both races for several years without any disturbances. When the white high school boys, by then accompanied by a number of white men, arrived at the Lower Girls' High School, they found twenty African American girls and forced them out. Neither the superintendent of schools nor the chief of police made any move to stop the attacks on these institutions, and the *Daily Picayune* heartily congratulated the "young regulators" on having accomplished their purpose with such "admirable firmness and propriety."[11]

George Washington Cable, an ardent champion of civil rights for people of color, wrote about this ugly racial confrontation in his 1889 essay, "The Haunted House in Royal Street." Rather than attributing the removal of the black students to the high school boys, Cable blamed the White League, a segregationist organization similar to the Ku Klux Klan.[12]

Cable's research assistant Dora Richards Miller, a former teacher at the Lower Girls' High School, wrote that despite the terrible things that had happened there, "There was one day in the history of this old house when it showed a gay and gallant aspect. On the Mardi Gras day of the Centennial Year 1876, when the procession of Rex was to pass by, the principal of the Lower Girls' High School, wishing to have something cheerful about the place . . . bought a great lot of tiny U.S. flags and decorated the whole front of the iron balcony. In and out of the somber iron-work they fluttered all that fair day like bright leaves."[13] In 1878 the Lower Girls' High School moved to another location, and the following year it closed altogether.[14]

As background for his account of the protest against racially integrated schools, Cable told the story of Madame Lalaurie, the slaves, and the fire, and included a detailed description of the Lalaurie mansion. Cable apparently gained entry to the house shortly after the school had vacated the premises. In the late 1880s, when Dora Richards Miller and J. W. Guthrie were working for Cable, they were refused admittance by the landlord (Beobay), who said that "over 300 visitors had called last winter" and he was tired of being bothered.[15]

Cable wrote of a "a large, solid, rectangular pile . . . [built] of brick, covered with stucco [painted] gray. An uncovered gallery as wide as the sidewalk makes a deep arcade around its two street sides. . . . Every one of its big window-shutters was closed, and by the very intensity of their rusty silence spoke a hostile impenetrability." The entrance, under the surrounding gallery, was on Royal Street. Behind "a pair of great gates of open ornamental ironwork," the entryway was embellished with "urns and flowers, birds and fonts," and a "centerpiece of Phoebus in his chariot." Within the deep recess was a wide door opening onto a marble hallway, from which rose "an iron-railed, winding stair" that led to the large drawing-rooms above. All of the interior doors had carved panels. The walls were topped by a frieze of "angels with palm branches and folded wings, stars, and wreaths . . . interrupted only by high, wide windows . . . between fluted Corinthian columns. The lofty ceilings, too, were beautiful with raised garlandry," and from them hung "old crystal chandeliers." Since all accounts of the 1834 fire and the ensuing riot say that the house was severely damaged inside and out, these architectural details represent the later renovation.

Even though the house that Cable described was vastly different from the two-story dwelling originally finished for Madame Lalaurie in 1831, he supplied creepy details that bring to mind the story of slaves confined in tiny, low-ceilinged rooms with iron bars and oversized locks, and of the terrified black child running up the outside stairs to the roof, pursued by her crazed mistress with the cowhide whip. The house, wrote Cable, had three stories and an attic. From the rear, the upper stories were "masked by long, green-latticed . . . galleries," which communicated with each other by staircases." Below was "a small, damp, paved court," which was "quite hidden from outer view." From the main house extended the service wing, once the kitchen and slave quarters. It was "a long, narrow annex four stories high, with galleries . . . along the entire length of each floor. . . . Each story [is divided into] a number of small square rooms, with a single high window and a door [opening] upon the latticed gallery." Here Cable saw "locks seven inches across," and "windows with sturdy iron gratings and solid iron shutters." On the fourth floor of the former slave quarters "the doorway communicating with the main house" was closed off by "two pairs of full length batten shutters" secured by "iron hooks eighteen inches long." The attic of the main house was "cut up into little closets," and here Cable found, "close up under the roof . . . all the big iron keys of those big iron locks." A rickety staircase led from the attic to the roof, topped by a belvedere, and Cable noted how the roof "dropped away in eight different slopes."[16]

Tales of the fire and the tortured slaves lingered in the popular imagination. After the publication of Cable's "The Haunted House in Royal Street," late-nineteenth-century tourist guidebooks and newspaper articles fostered the notion that the house was infested with malevolent spirits. These sources described the ghost of the little girl, who "committed suicide by leaping from the roof to the courtyard . . . to escape from her mistress," appearing near the belvedere on the roof. They reported that "people whispered in awed tones" of hearing "weird noises in the deserted building . . . muffled groans of people in dire distress, and . . . the clanking of chains and a noise as if heavy shuffling feet were slowly dragging along the echoing corridors and empty rooms of the abandoned premises."[17]

After the Lower Girls' High School moved out, the former Lalaurie mansion, still owned by Barthélémy Beobay, housed the New Orleans Conservatory of Music. According to an 1883 article in the *Daily Picayune*, "the building is admirably adapted for its purpose. It is an enormous house, containing something like forty-five rooms at once picturesque and convenient. The parlors are of great size, and finished with the most elaborate carvings. . . . The director of the conservatory, and a number of the professors with their families, reside in the building . . . and arrangements have been made for a number of boarders." The school was said to be "modeled after the best European establishments, and the professors for the voice and for the various instruments have been so carefully chosen, that success seems inevitable." Several hundred guests attended the opening performance and reception. A later article reported that all went well until, on the day when a grand concert was planned, "some scurrilous publication" attacked the character of the director. By evening "every one who had been engaged to play, sing, or attend" had heard this gossip, and all had excused themselves. Although the story was false, the director was thenceforth a ruined man, and the conservatory was closed.[18]

Other tenants came and went at the grim and forbidding house on Royal Street. According to Marie Points' 1892 article, "The Haunted House—Its Interesting History and Strange Romance," a furniture store "flourished on the ground floor for a few months," and "at another time a barber shop hung out its painted pole, but those were only for a while; the work of decay was progressing."[19] A search of city directories shows neither of these businesses at the address of the Lalaurie house.

Jeanne Delavigne elaborated on the alleged furniture store in her sensationalistic 1946 "The Haunted House of the Rue Royale" from *Ghost Stories of Old New Orleans*. Here she created an imaginary scenario of chairs and sofas "splattered with filth, [their] upholstering torn and spoiled. The merchant moved hurriedly before any more of his stock fell prey to ghostly vandals."[20] The Web site *New Orleans Paranormal Research Society Ghostly Gallery—The Haunted Mansion* offers an even more outlandish tale of the ill-fated furniture store: "Shortly after the store had opened for business, the owner entered the shop one morning to find that the entire inventory had been covered in urine, feces, and blood. Believing he had been vandalized, he had the mess cleaned up and ordered a new inventory. When he experienced the same thing a second time, he decided to wait in the building with a shotgun. In the morning, the inventory had been destroyed again, but no vandals had entered the building. He soon moved the business."[21]

During the 1880s and early 1890s, Barthélémy Beobay accepted any tenants he could find, many of them Italian and Sicilian fruit and vegetable vendors at the French Market. He also rented an apartment to an old man named Joseph Edouard Vignie, a seemingly impoverished member of a "respectable, ancient family of this city." For three years Vignie, his sister "Miss Aimée," and a servant lived a secluded life on an upper floor of the decaying mansion. Then, on February 3, 1892, Joseph Vignie died, and relatives, along with their attorneys, crowded into the rented rooms to inventory his property. The *New Orleans States* and the *Daily Picayune* described the scene: "The surprise of the searchers was intense when they found, concealed in armoires, in trunks, and in odd hiding places, the sum of $2,500 in gold," plus bank books indicating that "Mr. Vignie had deposited to his account a sum aggregating about $6,500." Also found in Vignie's rooms were "grand old pieces of furniture, antique sofas, cabinets and libraries, rare and costly pictures, bric-a brac and bronzes, and old swords and family relics enough to fill a museum." All of these treasures were sold at public auction.[22]

In 1893, Barthélémy Beobay sold the property for $5,800 to an Italian immigrant named Fortunato Greco. Greco, whose grocery store was located nearby on Decatur Street, was listed in the city directory as a purveyor of "wines, liquors, Italian produce, pasta, cheese, olive oil, etc."[23] According to a *New Orleans Times-Democrat* article, the building's reputation for being "inhabited by spooks" had made it "a white elephant to its owner," and had "yielded practically no revenue whatever." No sooner had Greco taken possession than "simple-minded people" began loitering around the premises, "awaiting sight of some nocturnal visitor." Deciding to exploit their curiosity, he posted "large flaming placards" announcing that there were no ghosts in the so-called "Haunted House," and inviting the curious to "come and be convinced. Admission ten cents." Greco decorated the building with flags and bunting and set up a concession stand. As the newspaper reported, "The place was visited by great crowds . . . the shrewd Italian collecting a large sum from the superstitious . . . by his cleverly devised scheme. For a small fee they whetted their appetite for the morbid, and he lined his pockets with their dimes."[24] Between 1895 and 1909, Greco operated a saloon called the "Haunted Exchange" on the ground floor, and made his residence in one of the upper apartments. After the New Orleans numbering system changed in 1894, the Lalaurie house was designated as 1140 Royal Street, the address that it has today.[25]

By the late 1800s, the Vieux Carré had become a slum occupied by the waves of impoverished Italian and Sicilian immigrants who poured into New Orleans, and its decline continued until the mid-twentieth century. Its elegant old buildings, including the Lalaurie mansion, were converted to multi-family tenements. As Henry Castellanos so indelicately phrased it in 1895, "the fumes of the malodorous filth that emanated from its interior proclaimed it what it really is—a house accursed."[26] Jeanne Delavigne later wrote in "The Haunted House of the Rue Royale" that "The forty rooms of the Lalaurie mansion meant shelter for dozens. So [the Italians] swarmed into it, painting its stately carved front door red, its delicate terra cotta friezes red, and its mahogany stairs and marble floors red. They wrecked the remains of the crystal chandeliers, they smashed the carved marble fireplaces in the lower lounge and the billiard room, they filled the beautiful courtyard with junk and rags and garbage and broken wood. And then they began to complain to the landlord that ghosts were besieging them. . . . Even the man who kept a saloon on the ground floor began to say the place was haunted."[27] Fortunato Greco kept the building until 1916, when he sold it to the Lafayette Realty Company for $5,000.[28]

After that the former Lalaurie mansion passed through several owners in quick succession.[29] Every inch of space was rented to tenants. A 1920 article from the New Orleans States described families crammed into the parlors, dining room, and bedchambers of the main residence, the children who romped and played in the halls and stairways, and the single men who occupied the tiny cubicles of the former slave quarters. The whole place was "filthy." The ground floor was "a mass of ruin," with one room being used as a stable. Tenants interviewed by the reporter were well aware of the building's reputation, and some reported hearing noises and seeing apparitions, but claimed that they were not afraid.[30]

During this time, the children of an Italian family living in one of the rooms "used to make spending money by charging a nickle to see the ghosts. The brothers would drag chains in the attic and go from window to window on one of the upper floors dressed in sheets. The girl would stand on the street telling passersby that the house was haunted, and collect money from those who wanted to go into the courtyard for a closer look."[31]

The city directory indicates that in 1922 William Jennings Warrington began operating a "lunch house" at 1140 Royal. In 1923 Warrington purchased the building for $15,000, and in 1924 he opened the Warrington House, a social service agency for homeless boys and men.[32] It was Warrington who supplied much of the misinformation about Madame Lalaurie for John P. Coleman's 1924 *New Orleans States* article, "The Famous Haunted House in Royal Street." Coleman noted that "the old mansion . . . has recently been brought up to date . . . by the philanthropic organization (with Mr. W. J. Warrington as its active spirit) which is now conducting the place as a home for those in need and without a home." Warrington, according to Coleman, had spent over $17,000 to "restore the damage that had been done by those who had exploited [the house] as a rallying place for spooks and a refuge for the most depraved characters to be found in any city in the country."[33] Warrington later told *New Orleans Morning Tribune* journalist Charles Richards that "Negroes . . . were paid to clank chains there many years ago to heighten interest in the old place."[34]

In 1932 William Warrington sold the building to the Grand Consistory of Louisiana, an organization of thirty-second degree Masons of the Ancient and Accepted Scottish Rite. Warrington took a great financial loss when the property was transferred for only $4,950. With this transaction, in the midst of the Great Depression, the price had hit rock bottom. The sale was made with the stipulation that Warrington House held the lease and that the "purchaser obligates himself, in case he desires said tenants to vacate the premises, to give them sixty days notice." The Grand Consistory never occupied the building, and Warrington House continued to serve the needy there until 1942.[35]

In that year the Lalaurie mansion changed hands again, when the Grand Consistory sold it to the Guarantee Savings and Homestead Association for $9,000; on the same day, Guarantee Savings and Homestead turned it over to Mary Howell Laycock for a mere $5,500. At this point the rooms were partitioned off into twenty tiny rental apartments. When Mrs. Laycock sold the building to Malcolm and Edward de la Houssaye in 1946, the price had jumped to $35,000. The de la Houssaye brothers, both attorneys, lived in the Lalaurie house, along with other tenants, and had their law offices next door. The city directories for 1942–60 show that renters came and went, and there were many vacancies.[36]

The Lalaurie mansion in 1937, during its incarnation as the Warrington House. (Historic American Building Survey, LA-176012, Division of Prints and Photographs, Library of Congress.)

Malcolm and Edward de la Houssaye transferred the house to Frank Occhipinti for $85,000 in 1964. Occhipinti announced that he intended to carry out an $80,000 restoration of the former Lalaurie mansion and turn it into a tourist attraction. This plan did not come to fruition, and city directories of the later 1960s show that only about half of the apartments were occupied and there were no businesses on the ground floor.[37] After taking out several mortgages with the Security Homestead Association, Occhipinti sold the building in 1969 to the New Orleans radiologist and art collector Dr. Harry Russell Albright for $230,000.[38] Shortly after this sale was finalized, a *Times-Picayune* article, headlined "Delphine's Old Mansion Sold," once again rehashed the story of Madame Lalaurie, the fire, and the tortured slaves.[39]

Dr. Albright gradually reversed the damage that had been done to the main residence and the former service wing. General contractor Patrick Ahern and his crew restored the decorative crown molding and ceiling medallions that were ruined when the large interior spaces were divided into smaller rooms. Ahern remembered Dr. Albright as "a real neighborhood guy" who would "go out in the morning and hose off the sidewalk, talk to everybody, walk his little dog. People loved him." He enjoyed entertaining friends and generously made the building available to arts and civic groups to hold fund-raising events.[40]

A *Times-Picayune* story indicates that Dr. Albright tried to sell the Lalaurie mansion in 1988. The article announced that "the renowned Lalaurie House in the French Quarter is up for sale. Asking price: a cool $1.9 million." The reporter noted that a "flashy four-page real estate flier describing the imposing nineteenth-century French Empire mansion . . . fails to mention the woman for whom the house is known locally or the folk tales that attribute its alleged haunting to her eccentricities." And once again the press resurrected the stories of "shadowy figures flitting from window to doorway, hoarse voices, the clanking of chains, and the snap of a stinging whiplash," and the house was not sold.[41]

In 2000 Dr. Albright finally transferred ownership of the property to James Monroe, a Colorado investor, for $1,700,000. After that, the house sat empty except for occasional visits by Monroe and his family.[42]

Dr. Albright reported no paranormal experiences while living in the house, but several years after selling to Monroe he indeed experienced the tragedy that plagued many of its owners. On a Sunday evening in January 2005, Albright was having dinner at Galatoire's famous French Quarter restaurant, which was crowded with locals and visitors in town for the Sugar Bowl game at the Louisiana Superdome. It was a lively scene, with patrons socializing and table-hopping while lobbing candies and Carnival throws at each other. As Dr. Albright left the restaurant, he tossed a mint onto the table of a group from Dallas. One young man, Anthony Creme, took offense. He followed Albright out onto the sidewalk and attacked him from behind, causing the elderly man to strike his head on the pavement. Afterwards, according to witnesses, Creme returned to his table and nonchalantly continued his meal until police arrived to arrest him. The Orleans Parish District Attorney reported that Dr. Albright was in a coma for three weeks, suffered "permanent brain damage, and will require assisted-living arrangements for the rest of his life." Creme was charged with second-degree battery, which carried an eight-year prison sentence, but the charges were eventually dropped after the parties reached a financial settlement.[43] Those who are acquainted with Dr. Albright say that he is now severely impaired, physically and mentally, as a result of the attack.

In 2006 the motion picture star Nicolas Cage bought the Lalaurie mansion for $3,450,000, adding it to his collection of homes in New Orleans and other American and European cities.[44] According to Cage's property manager, Tommy Williams, the actor "loved this house more than any of the others," and enjoyed visiting there with his wife and young son.[45]

Like many of the previous owners, Cage experienced financial difficulties. His penchant for extravagant spending, a run of unsuccessful films, and the international monetary crisis of 2008–2009 resulted in a staggering accumulation of debt and millions of dollars in unpaid taxes. In 2008

The Lalaurie mansion decorated for Halloween 2009. A costumed mannequin with yellow eyes and scarlet lips represents Madame Lalaurie standing in the front entrance. (Photograph by the author.)

Cage offered 1140 Royal Street for sale for $3,999,000, and reduced the price to $3,550,000 the following year. Sothebys International Realty advertised the property as having "approximately 10,284 square feet, six bedrooms, six full and two half bathrooms, central air and heat, garage parking, galleries, and widow's walk." According to the Sothebys' Web site, the house, "formerly the Lalaurie Mansion, is known for its ghostly history."[46]

In November 2009, Nicolas Cage lost the Lalaurie mansion and his other house in New Orleans' Garden District to foreclosure. On November 12, both properties were sold at a sheriff's auction in the lobby of the Civil District Court building. The mortgage holder, Regions Bank of Birmingham, Alabama, purchased both houses for a collective 4.5 million dollars, two-thirds their appraised value. There were no other bids.[47] That afternoon the New Orleans Police Department blocked off Governor Nicholls Street to allow for the removal of Cage's belongings into a fleet of moving vans, a process that took several days.

On July 30, 2010, title to the Lalaurie mansion was transferred by Regions Bank to WhaleNola LLC for $2,100,000.[48] The buyer, Michael Whalen, is a successful Texas businessman who intends to use the house as his private residence. In 2011, as this book is going to press, Whalen is making extensive renovations to the building, and the site bustles with activity in preparation for its next incarnation.

The Lalaurie mansion is sold at auction by the sheriff of Orleans Parish in the lobby of the Civil District Court building, November 12, 2009. (Photograph by the author.)

CONCLUSION

Was Delphine Macarty Lalaurie really the notorious woman who tortured her slaves, or was she, as her defenders staunchly maintain, the innocent victim of malicious slander?

If a record of an indictment by the grand jury or a criminal court proceeding against Madame Lalaurie ever existed, it has not survived. If she wrote letters or kept a journal in which she admitted her offenses or protested that she had been wrongly accused, they have not come to light. I could make only a tentative identification of her enslaved victims. The one document that might qualify as the proverbial "smoking gun" is the receipt from the attorney John Randolph Grymes, indicating that on June 22, 1829, Madame Lalaurie paid him a fee of three hundred dollars for her defense in the "prosecution of the State against her in the Criminal Court."[1]

The evidence against the lady is nevertheless strong. The testimony of numerous credible witnesses has persuaded me that the story of the fire, the abused slaves, and the attack on the Lalaurie mansion by the mob is fundamentally true, and that Madame Lalaurie was indeed guilty of the crimes of which she is accused.

The reports published in the *Courier*, the *Bee*, and the *Advertiser* from April 10 through April 15, 1834, are the primary source for what would become the legend of Madame Lalaurie and the "Haunted House." These articles provided details on the outbreak of the fire, the citizens who volunteered assistance, the rumors of abuse, concern over the whereabouts of the slaves, the rude response by Dr. Lalaurie, the forced entry into the burning service wing, and the seven "wretched negroes" found there starved, tortured, and chained. The editors of the *Courier* and the *Bee*, J. C. de St. Rome and Jérôme Bayon, went in person to the Cabildo and saw the emaciated and mutilated slaves and the "instruments of torture" that were applied to their bodies. John Gibson, the American editor of the *Advertiser*, did not claim to have been present at the fire or to have seen the victims, and his statements were brief but seemingly factual. The *Courier*, the *Bee*, and the *Advertiser* also gave detailed reports of the ensuing melee and the partial destruction of the house.[2]

Even more compelling than the newspaper stories is the deposition given by Judge Jacques François Canonge before Judge Gallien Préval of the Parish Court, which was published in the *Bee* on April 12. Judge Canonge was present at the fire and, after getting the brush-off from both Lalauries, led the attempt to rescue the slaves. It was Canonge, along with several other volunteers, who discovered the "two negresses," one of whom was "wearing an iron collar, very large and heavy, and was chained with heavy irons by the feet." Canonge also described the old woman, mentioned by the *Courier* and the *Bee*, with a "deep wound on her head," who was so feeble that she was unable to walk.[3]

The letters of Jean Boze to Henri de Ste-Gême are also extremely significant because Boze was, from 1830 through the time of the fire, a neighbor of the Lalaurie house. The Boze–Ste-Gême correspondence, written in French in a nearly illegible hand, available only at the Historic New Orleans Collection, and unknown outside of a small circle of researchers, offers some of the most damning testimony against Madame Lalaurie. The letters support the statements of the *Courier* and the *Bee* that the lady had "long been celebrated in New Orleans for such atrocities, which drew upon her . . . the reprimand of the authorities." As early as December 1828 Boze had reported to Ste-Gême that the whispered tales of Madame Lalaurie's cruelty to her bondspeople had been verified, and that those who came to investigate had found the slaves "incarcerated," provided with "only the bare necessities," and "still all bloody" from flogging. On July 20, 1829, Boze wrote that she had been absolved of these charges, corroborating the evidence of John Grymes' June 22 receipt for defending her in the criminal court. The Lalaurie family moved into the mansion on Royal Street in late 1831. Boze was living in an upstairs room less than a block away, and from this vantage point he kept an eye on what went on there. In 1832 Boze wrote that Madame Lalaurie had again been called before the criminal court on charges of slave abuse, but had cleared herself of the accusation by "paying a sum of money." Boze's letters to Ste-Gême after the fire are similar to the accounts given by the newspapers. He described Judge Canonge's arrival on the scene and the "riot and fracas" that accompanied the destruction of the house by the angry throng. He again complained that Madame Lalaurie's misdeeds had "involved her in a criminal procedure, but with her fortune, she was always able to succeed in extricating herself."[4]

The report submitted to the French Minister of Foreign Affairs by Armand Saillard, French Consul to New Orleans, also corroborates the 1834 newspaper articles. This document, written in French, was not published until 1981 and is not widely known. Like the editors of the *Courier* and the *Bee*, Saillard had gone to the Cabildo to see the abused slaves on the day of the fire. He described their "dislocated heads, legs torn by the chains, [and] bodies streaked [with blood] from head to foot from whiplashes and sharp instruments." Saillard also stated that, at an earlier date, Madame Lalaurie had been denounced for cruelty by one of her relatives and called before the criminal court to answer to this charge, but she "raised her hand," swore that she had not mistreated her slaves, and her case was dismissed.[5]

Other eyewitness descriptions that were given years after the fire are also meaningful. The notary Amédée Ducatel said in an interview that he was one of the men who broke into the service wing to liberate the imprisoned slaves.[6] The jurist and historian Charles Gayarré told Grace King that he had seen the half-dead victims carried out of the building on stretchers and laid under the arches of the Cabildo, and had witnessed the subsequent attack on the Lalaurie mansion.[7]

Harriet Martineau's travel memoir, *Retrospect of Western Travel*, does not qualify as an eyewitness account, but it nevertheless provides some valid information. Martineau was in New Orleans only two years after the fire, while the Lalaurie mansion still stood in ruins, and received her information from local people who had direct knowledge of the events. In addition to the already-familiar description of Madame Lalaurie's abused slaves, Martineau's friends told her the story of the little enslaved girl chased from the roof, and of the lady's escape in the carriage driven by her loyal coachman.[8]

Fredrika Bremer, who visited New Orleans in 1851, is also not an eye-witness, but her narrative in *Homes of the New World* supports the other testimony. According to Bremer's informants, even before the Lalauries moved to their new home on Royal Street, the lady's treatment of the slaves on her downriver plantation had "roused her neighbors in arms against her," and they had threatened to make her "amenable to law" if such behavior continued.[9] This, like Boze's 1829 letter, might refer to the criminal charge against Madame Lalaurie in June of that year, when she was defended by John Grymes.

A final, and extremely telling, piece of evidence is the August 15, 1842, letter from Madame Lalaurie's son Paulin Blanque. Paulin wrote to his brother-in-law Auguste DeLassus that his mother had conceived the idea of returning to New Orleans to put her business affairs in order. He solic-ited the aid of DeLassus and other family members in dissuading her from this "insane project." Referring to "the sad memories of the catastrophe of 1834," Paulin confided that the scandal had followed them everywhere, and he feared that his mother's reappearance in New Orleans would have disagreeable repercussions for the whole family. He announced that if she persisted in this scheme, his uncle Louis Barthélémy would surely disapprove, he and his sisters would not go with her, and that neither of her married daughters would welcome her into their homes. Although Paulin's reference to the "catastrophe of 1834" does not explicitly indict his mother for torturing her slaves, the letter confirms that something truly dreadful had happened in New Orleans, resulting in her permanent banishment from the city.[10]

In addition to this testimony, we know from the St. Louis Cathedral funeral records that at least twenty of Delphine's slaves died between 1816 and 1833. Most of them were children and seemingly healthy young women. Three enslaved women and four teenagers were sold to a family friend and later sold back to Madame Lalaurie by another friend; all but one of them subsequently died. The fate of Bonne, a negress from Saint-Domingue who was described in her act of sale as a habitual runaway, arouses particular suspicion. Bonne and her four children all perished in the Lalaurie household. There may have been more deaths that were not entered into the sacramental registers of the Catholic Church.

Nineteen enslaved men and women completely vanished from the archival record after the fire of 1834. Of the bondspeople that Delphine Macarty Lalaurie acquired before her marriage to Dr. Louis Lalaurie, those who disappeared are the old woman Françoise; Arnante, a cook, laundress, and domestic; the elderly gardeners Thom and George; William, a middle-aged man who was also a gardener; Rosette, a laundress; Nancy, mother of the mulattos Ben and Nicolas; Louis and Lubin, carters and laborers; Pauline, a gift from Delphine's father; and John, the young manservant purchased the day before her wedding. Of the "American Negroes" bought after her marriage to Lalaurie, there is no further documentation for Amos, Cyrus, Jack, Mary, Matilda, Rochin, and Samson. Delphine's children authorized the manumission of Patsy and another slave called Elodie, possibly Patsy's daughter, but there is no record of their ever being freed.

As stated earlier, there are reasonable explanations for why a few individuals might be unaccounted for—they died of natural causes, they ran away, they were living in the homes of other family members—but it seems unlikely that so many people would have officially ceased to exist. Given the appalling condition of the seven slaves carried out of the burning service wing on the day of the fire, it is reasonable to assume that some of the missing, and some of the twenty known to have died, were Madame Lalaurie's victims, the ones said to have perished from starvation and abuse before the fire and those who either died after being rescued or were too disabled by their ordeal to be sold. The *Advertiser* of April 14, 1834, claimed that one person had died, and that human remains were disinterred from the courtyard. Jean Boze wrote in May 1834 that Madame Lalaurie had "killed her slaves without pity." In 1836 Martineau heard from her informants that two of the slaves died on the day of the fire, and "The rest, maimed and helpless, are pensioners of the city."[11]

.

From the day of the fire until the end of the nineteenth century, every reiteration of the legend assumed that Madame Lalaurie was guilty. During the first half of the twentieth century, Lyle Saxon, Herbert Asbury, and especially Jeanne Delavigne, in her chapter "The Haunted House of the Rue Royale" from *Ghost Stories of Old New Orleans*, embellished the tale with even more revolting details.[12]

At the same time, local historians Grace King and Stanley Clisby Arthur, along with journalists John C. Coleman, Meigs Frost, Charles Richards, and Bob Brown, put forward arguments in defense of Madame Lalaurie. In these efforts they were encouraged by her descendants and their friends, who made indignant denials, proposed improbable explanations, and provided inaccurate information. Some maintained that the lady was completely innocent, and that the stories about her were flagrant lies: that her disgruntled cousin Barthélémy Montreuil spread vicious gossip about her because she had cheated him out of the family fortune; that the American press was motivated by prejudice and spite to destroy her reputation; that the Creole newspaper editors, or even Judge Canonge, had a personal grudge against her or envied her wealth and social position. Others conceded that she disciplined her servants harshly, but offered excuses for her actions: that her parents were killed by slaves during the revolution in Saint-Domingue or her mother was killed by Saint-Dominguen slaves in Louisiana; that she objected to the family fortune being lavished on the free colored concubines and natural children of her Macarty kinsmen.[13]

Some scholars and non-scholars continue to support these hypotheses and invent new ones, but most can be refuted.[14] Barthélémy Montreuil may indeed be the person who denounced Delphine to the authorities, but in no way had he had been deprived of his inheritance. The coverage of the Lalaurie incident in the American press was less harsh than that of the Creole newspapers. The idea that the editors of the *Courier* and the *Bee* invented such a calumny against a fellow Creole is nonsense, and the assertion that the highly respected Judge Canonge gave a false statement is even less believable. Neither of Delphine's parents were killed by slaves. There is no proof that Delphine was hostile to the non-white domestic partners and children of her father, uncles, or cousins. She appears to have had an amicable relationship with her father's biracial natural daughter, and her lawsuits against her uncle Eugène's free colored concubine and her brother's white natural daughter were strictly about money.

One element of the Lalaurie legend, the possible complicity of Dr. Lalaurie in the torture of the slaves, cannot be so easily dismissed. Delphine was reportedly a slender and gracefully built woman. Several early-nineteenth-century observers noted that Creole women were "habitually cruel to their slaves," but that in most cases the abusive mistress did not carry out the punishment by herself.[15] Martineau implied that Madame Lalaurie wielded the whip, but without the assistance of a larger and stronger person, she could not have subdued adult male and female slaves, affixed the chains and the heavy iron collars, bound the victims in constrained postures, suspended them by the neck with their arms and legs stretched, and thrown them into locked cells. Some writers conjecture that it was her enslaved coachman, Bastien, who acted as her household spy and partner in crime.[16] Others propose that she tortured her bondspeople in collusion with her husband. The unlikely notion that Dr. Lalaurie was performing medical experiments on the slaves has gained credence in recent years.[17]

Nobody can know the negotiations that went on between Delphine and her husband or exactly who did what to whom in the privacy of the Lalaurie household. The 1834 newspaper articles never implicated Dr. Lalaurie in the torture, and Harriet Martineau exonerated him from blame. On the other hand, the French Consul Armand Saillard reported that Madame Lalaurie acted "with the agreement of her husband," and George Washington Cable later wrote that Lalaurie was "as deep in the same mire as passive complicity could carry him."[18]

I personally doubt that Louis Lalaurie condoned or participated in the torture of the slaves. Maybe his abhorrence of Delphine's actions, plus fear that he might become a co-defendant in the criminal procedures against her, prompted him to stay away from home most of the time. Maybe it was indeed the coachman Bastien (or some other accomplice) who carried out her orders. Still, Lalaurie must have been aware of the situation. His refusal to cooperate with Judge Canonge and the other rescuers indicates that he knew there were starved and mutilated slaves confined in the service wing, and that their discovery would be disastrous for him and his wife. He is not blameless.

·

Having reached the conclusion that Madame Lalaurie is guilty, and that her husband was at least cognizant of her crimes, let us now examine the cultural milieu of the time, which might have persuaded her that starving and torturing her slaves was acceptable behavior.

Until the day of the fire, Delphine Macarty Lalaurie had passed her entire life in a society in which most people of means owned slaves. In New Orleans, enslaved domestics, vendors, and skilled artisans enjoyed a fair amount of autonomy, but such privileges were not extended to the hard-working plantation field hands in the rural parishes. Many people treated their bondspeople with fairness and compassion, but the behavior of some slave owners toward the "passive beings" over whom they legally had almost absolute power ranged from petty harassment to outright brutality, torture, and murder. The loss of their valuable human property was no deterrent to these vicious masters. Even though the French, Spanish, and American laws governing Louisiana forbade extreme cruelty to slaves, it was understood that some form of physical punishment was necessary as a means of control. Little social stigma resulted from the casual bullying that took place in almost every household, and even masters and mistresses who starved, whipped, shackled, imprisoned, maimed, or killed their slaves usually went unpunished when called before the courts.

Some slaveholders acted more from fear than malevolence. Louisianians had an obsessive dread of slave insurrection. The citizens were well aware of the many conspiracies and rebellions that had taken place throughout the southern United States and the Caribbean. The most terrifying of these was the major slave revolt in Saint-Domingue, which began in 1791 and ended in 1804 with the creation of the Republic of Haiti. Although the theories regarding the death of Delphine's parents at the hands of slaves from Saint-Domingue are without foundation, the pervasive fear of insurrection was very real. Delphine's uncle was murdered by his own slaves in 1771. A number of attempted revolts occurred in Louisiana in the late eighteenth and early nineteenth centuries, resulting in extreme paranoia. Many slave owners felt it necessary to exercise strict supervision over their bondspeople and punish those suspected of subversion.

As a member of a slaveholding society, Delphine would have believed that correction of her slaves was entirely justified. She might have disciplined them for any number of offenses, either real or imagined: impertinence, failure to perform their duties or bring home their wages or the money earned from vending, engaging in rebellious plots, or running away. Maybe she suspected some of the women of being too familiar with her husband.

The journalist John C. Coleman argued in defense of Madame Lalaurie that the accusation of "torture" had been greatly exaggerated; that she may have meted out "chastisement with a whip, a reduced allowance of food, and confinement," but she engaged in "no punishment that was not usually administered to recalcitrant slaves of that day."[19] Delphine probably considered such management of her bondspeople to be nothing out of the ordinary, and even years after the fire and the frantic dash out the Bayou Road, she was still wondering what all the fuss was about. As her son Paulin Blanque wrote to his brother-in-law in 1842, "I truly believe that my mother never had any idea concerning the cause of her departure from New Orleans."[20]

In addition to cultural factors that would have caused Delphine Macarty Lalaurie to think that harsh treatment of her slaves was normal, there are aspects of her character and personal life that also might have contributed to her propensity for cruelty. Delphine was born in 1787, during the late Spanish colonial period. One can imagine her as a willful and unruly girl. She was raised on the family plantation below the city, scene of bathing parties, card games, and horse races, indulged by her parents, and surrounded by her many aunts, uncles, cousins, family friends, and the ever-present house servants and field slaves.

When barely in her teens, Delphine became involved in a scandalous love affair with an official of the Spanish Crown, Ramon López y Ángulo, and their haste to wed resulted in his being dismissed from his position and sent back to Spain in disgrace. Shortly after López finally extricated himself from this distressing situation and was appointed Spanish consul to New Orleans, the unfortunate man died when the ship carrying him to Louisiana ran aground near Havana. Delphine's marriage to the powerful and unscrupulous Jean Blanque would have rendered her more disciplined and calculating and honed her social and business skills. After Blanque's death she established herself as a wealthy and independent widow, free from the control of a father or husband. Then, from the lofty position that she had attained, she fell for a young and opportunistic Frenchman fresh out of medical school, who was far beneath her in economic and social standing.

Dr. Louis Lalaurie was youthful, ambitious, and was under continual pressure from his family back in France to make an advantageous marriage with a woman of wealth. The widowed Delphine suited his needs—no matter that she was a grandmother almost twice his age. Louis Lalaurie courted the lady—or she courted him—and they conceived a child. Shortly after the birth of their son Jean Louis on August 13, 1827, Lalaurie left New Orleans for unexplained reasons, and only returned to marry Delphine on January 12, 1828.

Jean Boze wrote to Henri de Ste-Gême in December 1828, the year of Delphine's marriage to Dr. Lalaurie, that the mismatched couple did not have a happy household. They fought constantly, and Boze predicted that they would one day "abandon each other completely."[21] Delphine's stormy relationship with her third husband might have been the culminating factor that led her to commit the atrocities of which she is accused.

Reading between the lines of letters and archival documents, one intuits that Dr. Lalaurie soon regretted having become involved with this rich but eccentric lady. Desperate to get away from her, he claimed that his medical practice required his absence from home, and retreated to Plaquemines Parish. Perhaps he found a more agreeable female companion there. In 1832 Delphine petitioned the First Judicial District Court for a separation from bed and board. Lalaurie's neglect and outright antipathy toward her could have pushed the already-unstable woman over the edge. Her young husband had slipped beyond her control, but she still had dominion over her human property. One can imagine her—jealous, disconsolate, abandoned, aware of her advancing age—venting her frustration and rage on the slaves.

Delphine undoubtedly suffered from some form of mental illness that resulted in extreme mood swings, from a captivating amiability to violent fits of temper and murderous deeds. This is borne out by the observations of New Orleanians who were her contemporaries. The notary Amédée Ducatel, one of the men who helped recover the slaves from the fire, later told an interviewer that Madame Lalaurie "was a beautiful, charming woman with a bright disposition and a great favorite in society. She was very wealthy. No one would ever have supposed, judging from her manners and her sweet conversation, that she could be guilty as charged." Charles Gayarré, who had seen the victims on the day of the fire and knew that Madame Lalaurie was guilty, later met her in Paris and described her to Grace King as a "beautiful, gentle woman, reputed to be very kind to her servants there."[22]

Nineteenth-century writers who had not been personally acquainted with Madame Lalaurie also commented on her apparent madness. Harriet Martineau heard during her 1836 visit to New Orleans that Delphine's unmarried daughters were "thought to be spiritless and unhappy-looking," and that Delphine punished them when they tried to convey food to the starving slaves. In 1889 George Washington Cable noted in "The Haunted House in Royal Street" that "a high temper . . . had led her into a slough of misdoing to a depth beyond all her expectation." Marie Points, writing for the *Daily Picayune* in 1892, described the lady's "well-known eccentricity and her high, ungovernable temper, which at times . . . almost bordered upon insanity."[23]

In 1895 Henry Castellanos expressed his opinion of Madame Lalaurie's character in *New Orleans as It Was*, where he reported that he had been "positively assured" by persons who knew her that "at the very time when she was engaged in those atrocious acts, her religious duties . . . were never neglected and her purse was open to the hungry, the afflicted, and the sick . . . her heart at one time softening to excess at the sight of human suffering, while at another it turned obdurate and hard as adamant." Castellanos went on to observe that "There is a class of females . . . the idiosyncrasies of whose natures are at times so strange and illogical as to defy the test of close analyzation, and to that class Madame Lalaurie, with her sudden contrasts of levity and sternness, melting love and ferocity, formed no exception." Her "spirit of cruelty" was not the result of "a general detestation of the African race"; many of her servants were "devotedly attached to her, and the affection seems to have been as warmly returned." Rather it was "a morbid, insatiate thirst for revenge on those who had incurred her enmity. Our lunatic asylums . . . are filled with similar cases, all traceable to similar causes."[24]

The family letters to which I have had access also reveal the two sides of Madame Lalaurie's personality. Her affectionate letters to young Céleste Forstall in 1835 and 1836 show her as a loving grandmother. In 1836, her daughter Jeanne Blanque DeLassus wrote of the "tenderness [with which] I love [Maman]. She was, and is, always so good to me." In 1838 Paulin Blanque was recovering from an illness and wrote of his mother's "kindness without equal." In 1842, even while badgering Auguste DeLassus about the payments he had failed to send, Delphine expressed love for the absent grandchildren whom she longed to "kiss and press to my heart." But other letters indicate that her adult children were afraid of her and made every effort not to arouse her wrath. Her daughter Pauline wrote that they were careful to "avoid anything that might excite Maman's bad mood," and her son Paulin complained of his mother's "fits of bad humor" and her "indomitable nature."[25]

·

We have seen that there were other vicious slaveholders in Louisiana, that women were said to be the worst offenders, that many perpetrators were never reported, and that those who were called before the courts were seldom convicted. Why has Delphine Macarty Lalaurie gone down in history as the very epitome of cruelty? Why was she, and not others who committed similar crimes, denounced to the authorities? Why were the citizens angry enough to attack her home when she escaped punishment after the fire? The answer is that Madame Lalaurie's transgressions were so extreme that, even in such a society, she had crossed a line that could not be tolerated. The fire exposed her starved and tortured slaves to public view. Her fellow New Orleanians not only heard rumors about the abuse, two thousand of them actually *saw* the victims and knew that she had been willing to let them perish in the flames rather than risk discovery by the rescuers. They exulted in this opportunity to bring her down.

The impulse of the strong to torment the weak is universal. Children bully their classmates, parents abuse their children, husbands beat their wives, caregivers tyrannize the sick and elderly, policemen rough up criminal suspects, prison guards torture inmates. Before the abolition of slavery, there were masters and mistresses who brutalized their slaves.

As ardent abolitionists, both Harriet Martineau and Fredrika Bremer seized upon the Lalaurie incident to illustrate the extremes to which the evils of slavery could be carried. The New Orleanians who acquainted Martineau with the story begged her not to publish it, because it would be so prejudicial to the public perception of slavery in Louisiana. And while Martineau conceded that Madame Lalaurie was probably insane, she concluded that "the insanity could have taken such a direction, and perpetrated such deeds, nowhere but in a slave [holding] country." Bremer marveled at the hypocrisy of Americans who could "defend slavery as a patriarchal institution . . . compatible with the laws of a free people." Later on George Washington Cable, also an advocate for the civil rights of people of color, wrote in "The Haunted House in Royal Street" that even if most slave owners did not mistreat their bondspeople, the institution of slavery "is answerable for whatever can happen more easily with it than without it."[26]

I believe that Delphine Macarty Lalaurie's cultural background, her unhappy relationship with her third husband, and her erratic and undoubtedly deranged personality resulted in the violent outbursts of temper that led her to commit hideous deeds. Had she lived in another time and another place, her fury would have found some other outlet. Because she lived in early-nineteenth-century New Orleans, she tortured the slaves over whom she had power, and until the day of the fire, she got away with it.

EPILOGUE

The Lalaurie mansion, sometimes referred to as "the most haunted house in America," has naturally attracted the attention of psychics, ghost hunters, and paranormal researchers. Few have been allowed inside since the building became a private home, but those standing on the sidewalk report sensations of dizziness, nausea, chills, headaches, and a feeling of pressure. Some have seen brilliant orbs and luminous streaks of energy appearing above the house.[1]

I personally have no extrasensory powers, and to me there is nothing remotely frightening about this ancient gray building located on a busy corner thronged with tourists in a holiday mood. On the one occasion when I was allowed inside the unoccupied Lalaurie mansion, I had absolutely no sense of a spectral presence. It was just an elegant, but empty, house. The high-ceilinged rooms are beautifully proportioned, and the winding center staircase, the crystal chandeliers, the carved wooden doors, the plaster ceiling medallions, even the representations of Phoebus in his chariot and the frieze of angels holding palm branches, are exactly as George Washington Cable depicted them in the 1880s. Cable also described the former slave quarters in the service wing, with its "small square rooms," "sturdy iron gratings" and "locks seven inches across." These grim cells have now been renovated into pleasant guest suites and evoke no feeling of horror.

"Orbs" appearing over the Lalaurie mansion, Governor Nicholls Street side. Mary Millan, who conducts tours under the name "Bloody Mary," often captures such images "after requesting spirits to come forth for photos." Millan reports that she and the tour participants have seen "apparitions and ghost orbs," accompanied by "physical reactions such as choking sensations, tingling, and cold spots." One tourist fainted when "overcome with energy," and since that experience Millan has put her tour groups in a "circle of protective spiritual energy." (Photograph by Mary Millan.)

Despite my lack of sensitivity to ghostly phenomena, I was interested in the reactions of some friends who are professional psychics. On Good Friday, April 10, 2009, the 175th anniversary of the fire, I invited Mary Millan, Karen Jeffries, and Juliet Pazera to meet me at the Lalaurie house to "channel" any entities that inhabit the space. All of the psychic women were familiar with the legend of Madame Lalaurie and the "Haunted House," but they did not know the particulars of my research on the Lalaurie slaves.

We gathered on the sidewalk on Governor Nicholls Street at ten in the morning, about the time that the crowd would have assembled to see the slaves carried out. Mary Millan, who is also a priestess of Voudou, began with a traditional ritual to open the way for the spirits, ringing a tiny bell, shaking an *assan*—the ceremonial gourd rattle strung with beads, drawing *vévé* symbols on the sidewalk, fumigating the area with cigar smoke,

Streaks of "energy" appearing over the Lalaurie mansion, Governor Nicholls Street side. Mary Millan, proprietor of Bloody Mary's Tours, took this picture on the night of April 10, 2009, after performing a ceremony to open the way for the spirits that morning.

The three psychics—Mary Millan, Karen Jeffries, and Juliet Pazera—performing the ceremony to open the way for the spirits across from the Lalaurie mansion, Good Friday, April 10, 2009, the 175th anniversary of the fire. (Photograph by the author.)

and pouring out libations of wine. During our time at the site, we did not converse. Each woman went into a trance state and jotted down her impressions. The quotes below are from their notes.

After Millan performed the "opening" ritual, the site seemed to the psychics to be thronged with spiritual entities. Madame Lalaurie's presence was perceived as a controlling force. Juliet Pazera observed that her "spirit is huge and pervades the whole block, she has her eye on everything." She is "flattered that people keep her story alive. She likes being remembered, even in a negative way. She thrives on activity, even the tour groups that come every night. Their fears feed her spirit."

The psychic investigators were drawn to the back left corner of the service wing and the courtyard. They noticed a "rank" odor of decomposition, and sensed a "dark, heavy energy" and the presence of smoke and flames.

Mary Millan made contact with the spirits of several enslaved persons, especially a man who identified himself as an "overseer" of the other slaves. These entities conveyed that "There were some good days and some bad ones, yet doubt and fear throughout it all. If we escaped the fate of those so low, the next day it could have been us, the threat was always near. Madame was masked well; her party face was quite different from the one that lay behind it. She had her way to tease you. Fear was her friend." But, said the man, "I saw through her—may she burn in hell." Dr. Lalaurie was aware of what was going on in the house: "He knew all—he watched." He was "not hot-tempered like Madame. She could lash out or lavish you with kindness. He was cold and dispassionate; he ignored most of us except to give a command."

Karen Jeffries visualized the gallery "filled with slaves, wailing, their hands in the air reaching up to heaven. They are crying and praying for help. The pain is terrible. They will never live through this." She asked if anyone would like to speak, and a "very strong, tall, and lean man" came forward: "My name is Marquette. I was brought here because of my strength. I worked hard for [Madame Lalaurie], and then she punished me for no reason. She chained me, whipped me, broke me. Then she hurt my loved one and our children. The mistress is polish and beauty on the outside but evil on the inside. She is like the sleek panther, grabs her prey, pounces and kills. She enjoys the kill and watches the twisting and writhing of the victim." When urged by Jeffries to leave this painful place, the man "threw his fists up to the sky and shouted NO!" He vowed that he would "see that [Madame Lalaurie] pays for the cruelty and suffering [that she inflicted], and that she would burn in the fires of eternity."

Jeffries also communicated with "a kitchen slave who was rather large and round, sitting at a table with her hands covered in flour as she patted out dough for biscuits." The woman said that "I just keeps my mouth shut" so she won't be noticed. "Madame has slapped me, but I cook good so she don't hurt me much."

Juliet Pazera felt drawn to the front of the house on Royal Street. She sensed "disembodied spirits; most of them are trapped inside the house. They gather toward the front; they are afraid to be near the courtyard. The prevalent feeling is one of heaviness and despair." Pazera became aware of an old enslaved man "crouched down in fear" near the front door. She also perceived the spirits of two children and a woman. The children "died in the house." The woman "does not let the children out of her sight, she feels that she neglected them during life and that she must protect them in the other world."[2]

None of the spirits encountered by the psychic women could be definitely identified as Madame Lalaurie's property. One does, however, think of Bastien, her favored coachman, who was said to have lorded it over the other servants; George, a gardener, who would have been seventy-eight at the time of the fire; the cook, possibly Arnante, who claimed responsibility for setting the fire in the kitchen; and Bonne and her children Florence, Juliette, Jules and Leontine, who all died between 1831 and 1833.

.

As long as the Lalaurie mansion stands in the Vieux Carré, and popular historians, journalists, tour guides, and the creators of Web sites continue to tell its story, some people will believe that the house is "haunted" and others will scoff at the idea. Those who have psychic powers will sense the presence of Madame Lalaurie and the tortured slaves, and others, like myself, will feel only interest and curiosity.

ACKNOWLEDGMENTS

I began my love affair with New Orleans in 1978, visiting first as a tourist, then as a passionate aficionado of the city's unique culture—the music, food, architecture, celebrations, Afro-Catholic spirituality, and especially the people. After 1995 I went there with a more focused purpose, completing my two previous books, *Spiritual Merchants* and *A New Orleans Voudou Priestess: The Legend and Reality of Marie Laveau*. In the beautiful spring of 2005, I commenced researching Madame Delphine Macarty Lalaurie; that fall came Hurricane Katrina and the flooding that nearly destroyed the city. Thanks to the wise planning of the custodians of New Orleans' remarkable archival collections, few of these resources were lost, although many institutions remained closed for months.

I resumed my work the following year and since then have made frequent research trips to New Orleans. On any day that the archives and libraries were open, I was there, poring over original handwritten eighteenth- and nineteenth-century French and Spanish documents or squinting at a microfilm reader. Evenings and Sundays I was out with my friends at restaurants, music clubs, and second-line parades. These intervals of intense work and play in my favorite place in the world have been extraordinarily happy and fulfilling.

So many people facilitated the completion of this book. First, I thank the staff at University Press of Florida, particularly director Meredith Morris-Babb and former editor in chief John Byram for continuing to encourage and believe in me. Nevil Parker, my project editor, facilitated the publication process, and copy editor Jonathan Lawrence corrected my mistakes. Two excellent scholars read the draft of the manuscript and saved me from many errors through their generous willingness to answer queries and discuss points of interpretation. I am tremendously grateful to Elizabeth Shown Mills, historian, genealogist, and expert on Louisiana's free people of color, and to Dr. Nathalie Dessens, professor of American History at the Université Toulouse-Le Mirail and expert on the Jean Boze-Henri de Ste-Gême correspondence now housed at the Historic New Orleans Collection.

As always, I thank the archivists and librarians of New Orleans who helped me while I was in residence and answered my desperate long-distance requests for photocopies of documents and scans of visual images when I was back home in the District of Columbia. At the Archives of the Archdiocese of New Orleans, archivists Charles Nolan and Emilie Leumas allowed me access to the sacramental registers, and Janet Adams and Jack Belsom located the volumes that I needed. In addition, Jack picked me up on his way to work, saving me the long bus trip to the archives. Alana Mendoza of the New Orleans Archdiocesan Cemeteries office found the ownership and burial record for the tomb alleged to be that of Madame Lalaurie. The staff at the Notarial Archives Research Center was also wonderful. I thank archivists Ann Wakefield and Yvonne Loiseau, and assistants Isabel Altamirano, Kara Brockman, Juliet Pazera, and Sybil Thomas. It was a great pleasure to work with Irene Wainwright and Gregory Osborn of the Louisiana Division, New Orleans Public Library. At The Historic New Orleans Collection Williams Research Center, Siva Blake, Mary Louise Eichhorn, Daniel Hammer, and Sally Strassi were very patient with my requests for documents, maps, and pictorial images. Kathryn Page, archivist of the Louisiana State Museum Historical Center, allowed me to photocopy many pages from the Pontalba family letters. Florence Jumonville, Chair of the Louisiana and Special Collections Department, and James Clifford, Library Associate, at the Earl K. Long Library, University of New Orleans, made photocopies of Louisiana Supreme Court documents and scans of materials from the Marcus Christian Collection. Leon Miller, Special Collections Manuscripts Librarian at the Howard-Tilton Memorial Library, Tulane University, allowed me access to the George Washington Cable Papers and the DeBuys Family Papers.

Dr. Gilbert Din, authority on Spanish colonial Louisiana, helped me resolve questions about Madame Lalaurie's first marriage to a Spanish government official. Dr. Judith Schafer, expert on nineteenth-century Louisiana civil law, patiently answered my many questions. Dr. Robert Paquette, researcher of the 1811 Louisiana slave uprising, helped me sort out the historical facts. Historian Mary Gehman led me to several important sources. Meredith Shedd-Driskel, curator of rare books at the Law Library, Library of Congress, photocopied many pages of the 1808 *Digest of the Civil Laws* for the Territory of Orleans and the 1825 *Civil Code* for the State of Louisiana. Judith Chelnick of the Division of Medical Sciences, National Museum of American History, Smithsonian Institution, helped me find information on early nineteenth-century orthopedic practices. Christopher Gordon, archivist at the Missouri History Museum, provided photocopies of the Lalaurie family letters from the DeLassus–St. Vrain Collection.

I was extremely fortunate to secure the cooperation of several Macarty descendants. John Ellis and Mac McCall are directly descended from Delphine Macarty Lalaurie's eldest daughter through the Forstall-Rathbone-DeBuys line, and I appreciate that neither of them objected to my writing about their notorious ancestor. John was especially helpful in allowing me to make electronic scans of family photographs. Sonja MacCarthy, descended from Delphine's uncle Eugène Macarty and the free woman of color Helöise Croy, generously shared her research on the Macartys of mixed race. I had informative conversations with Patrick Ahern, the building contractor who helped to restore the Lalaurie mansion in the 1980s, and with Tommy Williams, manager of the property for its former owner, the actor Nicolas Cage. In France, Gisele Bourdier found and copied several useful documents. I thank the psychics Cari Roy, Karen Jeffries, Juliet Pazera, and Mary Millan for accompanying me to the Lalaurie mansion and sharing their impressions.

I was honored to receive a Publication Initiative Grant from the Louisiana Endowment for the Humanities. The grant helped cover expenses for travel to New Orleans, photocopying archival materials, acquiring illustrations, hiring translators for the most difficult of the handwritten Spanish and French documents, and engaging a research assistant in Paris.

Nilda Aponte tackled the nearly indecipherable eighteenth-century Spanish colonial records, with handwriting replete with flourishes, curlicues, archaic legal terms, and unfamiliar abbreviations. Gail Moreau-Desharnais worked with the equally challenging nineteenth-century French letters from the DeLassus–St. Vrain Collection and the Ste-Gême

Family Papers. Jérôme Malhache, a professional researcher and genealogist, scoured the archives of Paris and Dr. Louis Lalaurie's hometown of Villeneuve-sur-Lot for evidence of Madame Lalaurie's life after she fled New Orleans. I could not have written this book without the help of Nilda, Gail, and Jérôme.

Finally, I thank my beloved husband, Douglas Wonderlic, who has been my best friend since 1981, accompanied me on research trips, read every draft, and put up with my fanatical work schedule for the past fifteen years.

NOTES

Abbreviations

AANO	Archives of the Archdiocese of New Orleans
ADL	Archives Départementales du Lot-et-Garonne, Agen, France
AGI	Archivo General de Indias, microfilm, The Historic New Orleans Collection, and photostats, Manuscript Division, Library of Congress, Washington, D.C.
LC	Library of Congress Manuscript Division, Washington, D.C.
LHC	Louisiana State Museum Historical Center, New Orleans
LSA	Louisiana State Archives, Baton Rouge
MHM	Missouri History Museum, St. Louis
NARA	National Archives and Records Administration, Washington, D.C.
NARC	Notarial Archives Research Center, New Orleans
NOPL	City Archives, Louisiana Division, New Orleans Public Library
SCHA	Supreme Court Historical Archives, Louisiana and Special Collections, Earl K. Long Library, University of New Orleans
SLC/S-FPC	St. Louis Cathedral baptismal, marriage, and funeral registers for Slaves and Free Persons of Color, Archives of the Archdiocese of New Orleans
SLC/WP	St. Louis Cathedral baptismal, marriage, and funeral registers for White Persons, Archives of the Archdiocese of New Orleans
THNOC	The Historic New Orleans Collection, Williams Research Center

.

Translations of French and Spanish documents are by the author unless otherwise noted. All newspapers cited are from New Orleans unless another city is specified.

Preface

1. An exception is "Finding Madame Lalaurie," written in 2006 by Christopher Gordon, archivist at the Missouri History Museum, for *Le Journal*, a publication of the Center for French Colonial Studies. Gordon's short article is based on the Lalaurie letters in the DeLassus–St. Vrain Collection, MHM. Victoria Love and Lorelei Shannon also used some of the Lalaurie letters from the DeLassus–St. Vrain Collection in their 2011 book, *Mad Madame Lalaurie*.

Definition of Terms

1. Tregle, "Creoles and Americans," 132–33, 173, 181; Domínguez, *White by Definition*, 93–181; Gayarré, *The Creoles of History*.

Introduction

1. Stories of the fire come from newspaper accounts of April 10–15, 1834, in the *New Orleans Bee, Louisiana Courier,* and *Louisiana Advertiser*. These sources are quoted at length in chapter 6.

2. Martineau, *Retrospect of Western Travel*, 263–67.

3. Bremer, *Homes of the New World*, 243–45.

4. Cable, "Haunted House in Royal Street," 192–232. Cable's notes and his correspondence with J. W. Guthrie and Dora Richards Miller are preserved in the George Washington Cable Papers, Special Collections, Howard-Tilton Memorial Library, Tulane University. For Cable's professional relationship with Miller, see Turner, *George W. Cable*, 239–42.

5. Points, "The Haunted House," *Daily Picayune*, March 13, 1892, p. 16, cols. 1–5. Also see "Ghosts Put to a Practical Use," *Times-Democrat*, June 4, 1893, p. 9, col. 2; and "A Miser's Snug Fortune Revives Interest in the Famous Haunted House," *Daily States*, February 28, 1892, p. 1, col. 5.

6. Castellanos, *New Orleans as It Was*, 52–62.

7. *Picayune's Guide to New Orleans* (1897), 20.

8. Rathbone and Lawrence Richard DeBuys were descended from Delphine Macarty through her eldest daughter, Borja López y Ángulo, who married Placide Forstall. Their daughter Céleste Forstall married Henry Rathbone. Stella Rathbone, daughter of Céleste Forstall and Henry Rathbone, married James DeBuys, and they became the parents of Rathbone and Lawrence Richard DeBuys. "Last Rites Set for Dr. DeBuys," *Times-Picayune*, June 21, 1957, p. 1, col. 4; "N.O. Architect Taken by Death," *Times-Picayune*, June 28, 1960, p. 1, col. 5.

9. Coleman, "The Famous Haunted House in Royal Street," *States*, November 2, 1924, p. 10, cols. 1–6.

10. Frost, "Was Madame Lalaurie ... Victim of Foul Plot?" *Times-Picayune*, February 4, 1934, Sunday Magazine, p. 3.

11. Richards, "Madame Lalurie [*sic*] Legend Just Fiction," DeBuys Family Papers, Manuscripts Collection M434, Special Collections, Howard-Tilton Library, Tulane University. The photocopied clipping is labeled *New Orleans Morning Tribune*, August 10, 1936, but the article does not appear in the *Morning Tribute* for this date. Richards described Corinne DeBuys as "a cultural leader of the city, seven years secretary-treasurer of the Philharmonic Society, interior decorator, world traveler, and linguist."

12. Brown, "Proof That Madame Lalaurie ... Rests Here," *New Orleans States*, January 27, 1941, p. 3, cols. 3–5, and p. 5, cols. 4–6. Miriam DeBuys is quoted throughout the article.

13. Tinker, "Cable and the Creoles," 324. The quote about Cable's "colored blood" is unattributed.

14. King, *Creole Families of New Orleans*, 357–91; Arthur, *Old New Orleans*, 147–51; Seebold, *Old Louisiana Plantation Homes*, 158–74. Miriam DeBuys furnished photographs of portraits of family members and a painting of Grace King to Herman Seebold and furnished a photograph of the portrait of Madame Lalaurie to Stanley Arthur.

15. Saxon, *Fabulous New Orleans*, 202–17; Asbury, *The French Quarter*, 247–52.

16. Delavigne, "Haunted House of the Rue Royale," 248–58, quote on 256–57.

17. Ibid., 255–56.

18. Haunted History Tour with tour guide Paul Chasse, March 22, 2008.

19. Nash, *Look for the Woman*, 247; Floyd, *More Great Southern Mysteries*, 171–74; Bradley, *The Book of Secrets*, 149.

20. Valentino, *Nightmares and Fairytales: 1140 Rue Royale*.

21. *Ghost Source*, www.ghostsource.com/800spotlight.html; *New Orleans Paranormal and Occult Research Society*, www.neworleansghosts.com/haunted_new_orleans.htm; *Haunted New Orleans*, www.prairieghosts.com/lalaurie.html, accessed April 5, 2008.

22. *Haunted America Tours*, www.hauntedamericatours.com/hauntedhouses/lalauriemansion/lalaurie, accessed April 5, 2008.

23. "Marie Delphine Lalaurie," www.everything2.com/index.pl?node_id=1189970, accessed April 5, 2008.

24. See www.youtube.com/watch?v=EW3immRJ9SA&feature=related, www.youtube.com/watch?v=bzgX4wiffG0&feature=related, and www.youtube.com/watch?v=17uSDIoVNEk&feature=related. A video of a tour conducted by Haunted History tour guide Matthew Yaddoshi is at www.youtube.com/watch?v=JtIrKYGh26A, accessed October 27, 2008.

25. Hambly, *Fever Season*, 48–49, 51, 122–23, 206–10, 365, 381. *Fever Season* is the second volume in a series of mysteries set in 1830s New Orleans. The main character, Benjamin January, is a free man of color who is both a musician and a surgeon; he encounters Madame Lalaurie when giving music lessons to her daughters and when working at Charity Hospital during the 1832 yellow fever epidemic.

Chapter 1. The Macartys

1. Published sources, none of which provide any documentation, disagree about the arrival date and parentage of Jean Jacques (also called Jean Baptiste) and Barthélémy Daniel de Macarty. Leng, in *Staten Island and Its People, a History*, 71, states that Daniel Maccarthy-Mactaig "went to France about 1690 and served under His Majesty, Louis XIV of France. . . . Théodore MaCarty, his son . . . married Catherine Flechier in 1704. . . . [Théodore's sons] Jean Jacques [and] Barthelemy Daniel . . . both officers in the French Army, the former a captain and the latter a lieutenant, came to New Orleans . . . in 1732." Arthur (*Old Families of Louisiana*, 330–33) and King (*Creole Families of New Orleans*, 368) both say that Jean Jacques and his brother Barthélémy Daniel were the sons of Bartholomew Maccarthy-Mactaig, the elder a captain and the younger a lieutenant. Leng and Arthur give 1732 as their arrival date, and King gives 1730. Three archival records document the Macartys in French Louisiana. A "Sieur de Macarty, Lieutenant, agreement of April 30, 1720" was listed among the passengers, under Monsieur Delormes, director general of Louisiana, who embarked for Louisiana on the ship *Alexandre* from Lorient, France, on June 26, 1720 (Conrad, *First Families of Louisiana*, 85). The July 9, 1735, marriage contract between Jean Jacques de Macarty and Françoise Trépagnier identifies him as a native of Languedoc, son of Théodore de MacCarty and Catherine Flechy (Forsyth and Pleasonton, *Louisiana Marriage Contracts*, 28). Barthélémy Daniel de Macarty is identified in the will of his son Jean Baptiste as a "captain in the service of his most Christian majesty, native of Languedoc" (Will of Jean Baptiste de Macarty, November 21, 1808, Acts of Narcisse Broutin, vol. 18, pp. 491–92, NARC).

2. Johnson, "Colonial New Orleans"; Ingersoll, *Mammon and Manon in Early New Orleans*, 3–65. The numbers ascribed to the various segments of the 1731 population are from Ingersoll, "Free Blacks in a Slave Society," 155, 173 n. 7.

3. Wallace, *History of Illinois and Louisiana*, 312–13; Wallace, "Fort de Chartres-Its Origin, Growth and Decline," www.riverweb.cet.uiuc.edu/Archives/transactions/1903/Fort_20de_20Chartres.html, accessed February 10, 2008; Stanley, *New France*, 42; Barron, *The Vaudreuil Papers*; Bossu, *New Travels in North America*, 122. The Royal and Military Order of St. Louis was established by Louis XIV for officers who had served meritoriously in the king's navy for at least ten years.

4. Alejandro O'Reilly assumed power as captain-general and governor of Louisiana on August 18, 1769, and the executions of the five rebel leaders were carried out on October 25, 1769. For more on the conspiracy to overthrow the Spanish government, see French, *Historical Memoirs of Louisiana*, 178–233; and Din and Harkins, *New Orleans Cabildo*, 46–49.

5. "Census of Families living below the city taken by Sieur Bauré, Captain of the Militia, September, 1763," 45, and "List of farms on both sides of the river below the city, January, 1770," 239, in Voorhies, *Some Late Eighteenth-Century Louisianians*. Land measurements of the time were given in arpents. One linear arpent equals approximately 192 feet, and a "superficial" or square arpent is about 0.84 acres; therefore de Macarty's 205-arpent plantation was about 172 acres.

6. Succession of Don Bartólomé de Macarti, Judicial Records of the Spanish Cabildo, February 14, 1781, box 38, no. 640, LHC; translation by Nilda Aponte.

7. Marriage contract for Luis Bartolomé Macarty and Maria Juana Lerable, widow of Charles le Comte, July 3, 1776, Acts of Juan Garic, vol. 7, p. 196, NARC. Marriage of Charles le Comte and Marianne [Marie Jeanne] Lerable, Parish Church of St. Louis (became St. Louis Cathedral in 1793), July 12, 1763; for unexplained reasons, it is found in Baptismal Book 5, part 2 (June 1765–June 1767), p. 170b, act 15, AANO. Marie Jeanne Lerable was the daughter of Laurent Lerable *dit* St. Laurent, native of Rohan, France, and Marie Jeanne Derbonne, native of Louisiana. The children of Marie Jeanne Lerable's first marriage were Alexandre, Marie Adelaide, and Andre Charles Lecomte.

8. Baptism of Maria Delfina de Macarty, December 26, 1793, SLC/WP, unnumbered volume for 1786–1796, part 3, p. 291, AANO. The baptism of Louis Barthélémy *fils* is missing from the sacramental register.

9. The plantation brought to the marriage by Marie Jeanne Lerable was eighteen linear arpents fronting the river by forty arpents in depth. Sale of plantation of twelve arpents fronting the river by forty arpents depth, with buildings, livestock, and twenty-four slaves, by Juan Bautista Buenvenu to Luis Macarty and wife Maria Juana Lerable for $35,000, Acts of Raphael Perdomo, November 4, 1785, vol. 6, p. 635; sale of plantation of four arpents fronting the river by forty arpents depth by Pedro de la Roche to Luis Macarty for $7,000, Acts of Francisco Broutin, January 17, 1794, vol. 30, p. 3 verso; sale of plantation of six arpents fronting the river by forty arpents depth, with buildings, by Joseph Bonneville to Luis Macarty for $7,468, Acts of Pierre Pedesclaux, February 12, 1794, vol. 20, p. 139, all from NARC. Translations by Nilda Aponte.

10. "Plan of the City and Suburbs of New Orleans from an actual survey made in 1815 by Jacques Tanesse," New Orleans 1817, and "Plan of the City and Environs of New Orleans," Barthélémy Lafon, 1816, both reproduced in Lemmon et al., *Charting Louisiana*, plates 173 and 175.

11. Toledano, Evans, and Christovich, *New Orleans Architecture: The Creole Faubourgs*, 40–41.

12. Letter journal of Joseph Xavier Delfau de Pontalba to his wife, 1796. The original French document, which belonged to the Louisiana Historical Society, has now disappeared. An English translation was made in the late 1930s by the WPA Louisiana Writers' Project, and remains at the Louisiana State Museum's Historical Center. Thanks to Kathryn Page, archivist of the LHC, for allowing me to photocopy the typescript. Many extracts from the original letter journal were published in King's *Creole Families of New Orleans*, and Vella quotes from the typed translation in the third chapter of *Intimate Enemies*, 70–98.

13. Jeanne Louise le Breton des Chapelles was the daughter of Jean Baptiste Césaire le Breton and Jeanne Françoise de Macarty, Delphine's aunt. Jeanne Louise was married to Joseph Xavier de Pontalba on October 5, 1789, SLC/WP, vol. 2, part 2, p. 66, AANO.

14. Pontalba to his wife, June 17, 1796, typescript pp. 133–34, July 4, 1796, typescript p. 157, and July 20, 1796, typescript pp. 189–90, all in LHC.

15. Porteous, "Torture in Spanish Criminal Proceedings"; Wardill, "Scene of the le Breton Murder." The le Breton plantation was taken over by Delphine's uncle Jean Baptiste de Macarty and was inherited by his children Jean Baptiste Barthélémy, Edouard, and Céleste, the wife of Paul Lanusse. It was destroyed by floodwaters when the Mississippi River broke through the levee on May 6, 1816.

16. Pontalba to his wife, May 3, 1796, typescript p. 76, LHC.

17. James, *The Black Jacobins*; Fick, *The Making of Haiti*; Sublette, *The World That Made New Orleans*, 148–60, 191–201.

18. Pontalba to his wife, March 5, 1796, typescript p. 16, LHC. For more on the attempted Pointe Coupeé slave revolt of 1791, see Hall, *Africans in Colonial Louisiana*, 319–32.

19. Acts and Deliberations of the Cabildo, vol. 4, April 25, 1795–May 9, 1795, pp. 2, 8, 23, typed translation by the WPA Louisiana Writers' Project, NOPL. For more on the Pointe Coupée slave revolt of 1795, see Debien and Le Gardeur, "Saint-Domingue Refugees in Louisiana," 176–88; Hall, *Africans in Colonial Louisiana*, 344–74; and Din and Harkins, *New Orleans Cabildo*, 176–77.

20. The Spanish *Codigo Negro* was based on *La Recopilación de Castilla* (The Law of Castile), *La Recopilación de leyes de las reynos de las Indias* (The Law of the Spanish West Indian Colonies), and *Las Siete Partidas* (The Law of Seven Parts). Acts and Deliberations of the Cabildo, vol. 1, June 21, 1771, p. 65, October 8 and 15, November 12, 1773, pp. 133, 163, 165, February 6, 1778, p. 279, April 9, 1779, p. 313; vol. 2, April 26 and 30, May 28, June 4, 1784, pp. 214, 215, 221, 224, and February 26, 1790, book 3, vol. 2, p. 96; all are typed translations, NOPL.

21. Pontalba to his wife: Augustin, May 4, 1796, typescript p. 78; Jeannete, May 9, 1796, typescript p. 85; Lucille, July 10, 1796, typescript p. 167; all in LHC.

22. Cable, *Creoles of Louisiana*, 284–308; Clapp, *Autobiographical Sketches*, 115–37; Din and Harkins, *New Orleans Cabildo*, 224–30; Vella, *Intimate Enemies*, 85; Trask, *Yellow Fever in New Orleans*, 1–30.

23. Pontalba to his wife, September 20, 27, October 9, 28, 30, 1796, typescript pp. 228–29, 239, 255–56, 264, 270, and 284–86, LHC.

24. Robin, *Voyages to Louisiana*, 56, 250.

25. This theory first appeared in Bremer, *Homes of the New World*, 244, and was further developed by Benfey, *Degas in New Orleans*, 42, and Morlas, "La Madame et la Mademoiselle," 123–24.

26. Donation of Eulalia, daughter of Maria Juana, by Philippe de Marigny de Mandeville to his mother, Francisca Delille de Mandeville, Acts of Andres Almonester y Roxas, November 7, 1777, vol. 2, p. 545, NARC. A later document identifies Eulalie's mother as Marie Jeanne Duteuil (see note 43, chapter 7). The quote "that magnificent and courtly citizen" is from King, *Creole Families of New Orleans*, 21.

27. Emancipation of Eulalie by Antoni Marignie de Mandeville (Antoine Philippe Marigny de Mandeville), Acts of Andres Almonester y Roxas, November 9, 1779, vol. 2, p. 572 verso, NARC.

28. Information about the relationship between Eulalie Mandeville and Eugène Macarty comes from the Second District Court records for Nicolas Théodore Macarty et al. v. Eulalie Mandeville f.w.c., docket no. 195, filed with Supreme Court of Louisiana docket no. 626, SCHA. Testimony about Eulalie's childhood was given by her half brother Bernard de Marigny (p. 135); by Jacques Enoul Livaudais, husband of her half sister Céleste de Marigny (p. 164); and by Charles Olivier, cousin of Bernard and Céleste (p. 86).

29. In Macarty v. Mandeville, Bernard de Marigny explained in detail the bequests made to Eulalie by their father and other family members (ibid., 135–44).

30. Baptism of Artemise Emelita, August 13, 1794, SLC/S-FPC, vol. 1, p. 7, act 32; Eugène Macarty signed the baptismal register, and a marginal note states that Don Eugenio Macarty "recognizes his natural daughter and declares [her] as his own." Baptism of Théofilo Macarty et Mandeville, November 17, 1795, SLC/S-FPC, vol. 5, part 2, p. 244, act 969; a marginal note added on July 28, 1800, states that "Théofilo is the natural son of Don Eugenio Macarty" and was signed by Fr. Antonio [de Sedella] and Eug^e Macarty. Baptism of Ysidro Bartolomé, St. Bernard Church, February 11, 1797, SLC/S-FPC, vol. 1, p. 10, act 43; Eugène Macarty acknowledged his natural son and signed the register. Baptism of Eulalia, July 15, 1799, SLC/S-FPC, vol. 6, part 2, p. 148, act 469; Eulalia was recorded as a "free quadroon, natural daughter of Eugenio Macarti and Eulalia Mandeville," and Eugène Macarty signed the register. Baptism of Bernardo Théofilo, April 26, 1806, SLC/S-FPC, vol. 9, part 1, p. 56, act 265; the godparents were Bernard and Céleste de Marigny, and Fr. Sedella and Eugène Macarty signed the register. Baptism of Pierre [later known as Villarceaux], April 6, 1811, SLC/S-FPC, vol. 12, part 1, p. 25 verso, act 126; Fr. Sedella and Eugène Macarty signed the register. Baptism of Esteban Eugenio, April 6, 1815, SLC/S-FPC, vol. 14, part 2, p. 100; Fr. Sedella signed the register, but Eugène Macarty did not. All baptisms from AANO.

31. Sale of lot with buildings and improvements by the syndics of the creditors of Samuel D. Earle and Joseph Torres to Eugène Macarty for $2,400, Acts of Stephen de Quiñones, May 17, 1808, vol. 10, p. 582; sale by Eugène Macarty to Eulalie Mandeville for $3,000, Acts of Quiñones, June 29, 1810, vol. 11, p. 388, both NARC. The chain of title for this property is found in the Vieux Carré Survey, square 82, lot 23047-01, Williams Research Center, THNOC, with additional information from the Historic American Buildings Survey.

32. Testimony regarding Eulalie and Eugène's business ventures comes from Louisiana Supreme Court, Macarty v. Mandeville, 135–44. See also Gould, "In Full Enjoyment of Their Liberty," 148, 150, 171, 179.

33. Baptism of Théodore, natural son of Eugène Macarty and Totote Detreez, May 17, 1817, SLC/S-FPC, vol. 15, part 2, p. 130 verso; this child was baptized at age seven, meaning he was born around 1810. His funeral was held on August 2, 1817, SLC/S-FPC, vol. 6, part 2, p. 122, act 939. Marie was born June 1, 1815, and Françoise was born April 8, 1817; both were designated as natural daughters of Eugène Macarty and Marie Jeanne Destreez, and were baptized on May 8, 1819, SLC/S-FPC, vol. 16, part 1, p. 110, acts 342 and 343. Baptism of Eugène and Rose, twins, natural children of Mr Eugène Macarty and Marie Detré, May 22, 1823, SLC/S-FPC, vol. 18, part 1, p. 33 verso, acts 111 and 112; Eugène and Rose were stated to be two and a half years old. All baptisms from AANO. Birth records for Eugène and Eugenia [Rose] McCarty, children of Eugène Macarty and Totote Destrees, born August 2, 1820, Orleans Parish Births, vol. 2, p. 46, LSA.

34. Helöise Croy is identified as the mother of Eugène Victor Macarty, later a well-known musician, on the record of his marriage to Louise Galland (St. Mary's Church, October 28, 1846, Marriages of Persons of Color 1805–1880, act 165, AANO), and his marriage to Lucie Elizabeth Lee (Immaculate Conception Church, May 2, 1866, vol. 16, p. 20, act 16, AANO). The June 25, 1881, death record for Victor Eugène Macarty gives his age as sixty-four, indicating that he was born in 1817. His funeral announcement calls

him "E. V. Macarty-Croy," *Bee*, French edition, June 26, 1881, p. 1, col. 4. Thanks to Sonja Macarthy for providing this information.

35. Baptism of Dorsino Bartholome Macarty, natural son of Henriqueta Prieto and Bartolomé Macarty, May 2, 1800, SLC/S-FPC, vol. 6, part 3, p. 273, act 884, AANO. There is no baptismal record or birth date for their daughters Céleste and Lucine, but judging from their death certificates they were born around 1797 and 1805, respectively. Baptism of Drosin Prieto [Drauzin Barthélémy Macarty], natural son of Henrietta Prieto and an unknown father, June 6, 1806, SLC/S-FPC, vol. 9, part 1, p. 73, act 343, AANO. There are no records for the fifth daughter, Adele.

36. Baptism of Armand Henry de Macarty, July 15, 1814, SLC/WP, vol. 7, p. 131, act 758, AANO (note that this baptism was recorded in the register for white persons); birth record for Armand Henry de Macarty, born December 15, 1813, New Orleans Recorder of Births and Deaths, Orleans Parish Births, vol. 10, p. 93, LSA. Birth record for Laurent Gustave de Macarty, born April 1, 1815, Orleans Parish Births, vol. 19, p. 93, LSA. The birth records, which do not specify race, were not filed until 1848, and stated that the children were the "issue of the legitimate marriage of Jean Baptiste Barthélémy Macarty and Magdeleine Carpentier." These birth records specified that the maternal grandparents were "Mr Charles Carpentier and Mrs Eulalie Lefevre f.w.c., both of St. Domingo." Jean Boze identified Luce Lefevre's "protector" as Monsieur L'angagnera, who was "employed in the administration in Saint-Domingue" (Boze to Ste-Gême, March 25–May 4, folder 238, pp. 5–6, Ste-Gême Papers). Acknowledgment by Barthélémy Macarty of his natural sons Armand, age 6, and Gustave, age 5, "born of himself and Madelaine Carpentier *dite* CéCé, free woman of color," Acts of Philippe Pedesclaux, April 18, 1820, vol. 14, p. 39, act 794, NARC.

37. Augustin François de Macarty's daughter with Sanitté Rivére was Philonise, for whom there is no baptismal record. His daughters with Victoria Wiltz were Josephine and Bridgette (baptism of Maria [Josephine] Macarty, free quadroon, daughter of [name omitted], *alferez* of the fixed regiment of this city, and Victoria [surname omitted], born January 1, 1792, February 13, 1792, SLC/S-FPC, vol. 4, part 3, p. 287, act 421, AANO). Baptism of Patricio Macarty, natural son of Céleste Perrault, born February 15, 1799, baptized May 26, 1799, SLC/S-FPC, vol. 6, part 2, p. 127, AANO.

38. Baptism of Delphina Emesia Macarty, December 26, 1816, SLC/S-FPC, vol. 15, p. 90 verso, act 542, AANO.

39. Gayarré, "Barthélémy de Macarty's Revenge," 278–79. Paxton's *Directory and Register* for 1822 shows the Chevalier de Macarty and his son Louis Barthélémy living on Levee Street below Olivier's Rum Distillery. After the Chevalier died in 1824, the 1830 census shows Louis Barthélémy Macarty living alone, the only white person in a household of thirty slaves (U.S. Census for Orleans Parish, Louisiana, 1830, schedule of the number of inhabitants between the F^{bg} Danois [Faubourg D'Aunoy] and the Fisherman's Canal, sheet 55, line 18, NARA microfilm publication M19, roll 45, accessed through www.ancestry.com).

Chapter 2. López y Ángulo

1. King, *Creole Families of New Orleans*, 359–60.
2. Arthur, *Old Families of Louisiana*, 116; Arthur, *Old New Orleans*, 148.

3. Kendall, "Old New Orleans Houses," 698. Kendall's "curious story" might have come from Arthur Preston Whitaker's brief summary of the political career and subsequent downfall of Ramon López y Ángulo in his 1934 publication, *The Mississippi Question*. Thanks to Dr. Gilbert Din for directing me to this source, which led me to the López material in the Archivo General de Indias.

4. The Archivo General de Indias (AGI) is housed at the Casa Lonja de Mercaderes (Merchants' Exchange) in Seville, Spain. The documents are arranged in *legajos* (bundles) of related materials. Photostats of some legajos of the Papeles Procedentes de la Isla de Cuba (PPC) and the Audiencia de Santo Domingo (ASD) are located in the Manuscript Division of the Library of Congress, and a more complete series from the AGI is available on microfilm at THNOC. Legajo 2607 of AGI/ASD contains the papers of the intendants of Louisiana; approximately 400 pages are devoted to López y Ángulo. The photostats at the Library of Congress, made in the 1930s, are not numbered. When the documents were microfilmed in 1968, each page was stamped with a number, which is cited in these notes.

5. A. P. Whitaker, *The Mississippi Question*, 161.

6. Mariano Luis Urquijo to Ramon López y Ángulo, López to Urquijo, López to Miguel Cayetano Soler, Urquijo to Soler, and Francisco de Mella to Soler, May–June 1799, AGI/ASD, legajo 2607, pp. 178–220, microfilm, THNOC, translation by Nilda Aponte.

7. López to Soler, October 23, 1799, AGI/ASD, legajo 2607, pp. 239–40, microfilm, THNOC, translation by Nilda Aponte.

8. López to the king of Spain, appended to a letter of Bishop Luis Peñalver y Cardenas to José Antonio Caballero, Ministro de Gracia y Justicia, July 31, 1801, AGI/ASD, legajo 2607, p. 331, microfilm, THNOC, translation by Nilda Aponte.

9. The age at which women could marry was stated in the 1808 *Digest of the Civil Laws*, Book I, "Of Persons," Title IV, "Of Husband and Wife," article 6, p. 24. Ministers and magistrates who performed a marriage ceremony for "any male under the age of fourteen and any female under the age of twelve" were to be "removed from office." The position of the Catholic Church on this issue is stated in Ayrinhac, *Marriage Legislation on the New Code of Canon Law*, Chapter IV, "Diriment Impediments," article 135, p. 137.

10. Thanks to Dr. Gilbert Din for helping me to understand Spanish policy on the marriage of government officials to local women (personal communication, February 16, 2007).

11. Din, *Spaniards, Planters, and Slaves*, 48–49, 65, 71, 268 n. 3; Holmes, "Do It! Don't Do It!" 28–30.

12. López to Soler, April 25, 1800, AGI/ASD, legajo 2607, pp. 316–17, microfilm, THNOC, translation by Nilda Aponte.

13. Bishop Luis Peñalver y Cardenas to José Antonio Caballero, July 31, 1801, AGI/ASD, legajo 2607, p. 332, microfilm, THNOC, translation by Nilda Aponte.

14. The circumstances surrounding Ramon López y Ángulo's hasty marriage to Delphine Macarty are drawn from the letter of Bishop Luis Peñalver y Cardenas to Caballero, July 31, 1801, to which are attached copies of earlier statements by Peñalver, López, and others, AGI/ASD, legajo 2607, pp. 328–33, microfilm, THNOC, translation by Nilda Aponte.

15. Marriage of Don Ramon López y Ángulo, Intendant of this province, widower of Francisca Borja Enderis, son of Don José Antonio de López y Ángulo and Doña Ana

Fernandes, with Doña Maria Delphina Macarty, witnesses Luis Macarty and Maria Juana Lerable, the bride's parents, and Rev. Isidoro Quintero, diocesan secretary, June 11, 1800, SLC/WP, vol. 2, part 2, p. 129, act 505, AANO.

16. A copy of Peñalver y Cardenas's report of April 18, 1800, is attached to his July 31, 1801, letter to José Antonio Caballero, AGI/ASD, legajo 2607, p. 330, microfilm, THNOC, translation by Nilda Aponte.

17. Governor Manuel Gayoso de Lemos to Peñalver y Cardenas, May 9, 1799, AGI/ PPC, legajo 102, 505, microfilm, THNOC, translation by Nilda Aponte. Gayoso's role as a "marriage counselor" is mentioned in Holmes, *Gayoso*, 226 n. 75.

18. *Libro Primero de Confirmaciones de esta Parroquia de San Luis de la Nueva Orleans, 1789–1841*, 147–48. Delphine's sponsor at confirmation was Petrona de Reggio, wife of the Spaniard Pedro Marin de Argote. Ana Maria Thomasa Laureana de Reuda was the daughter of Miguel de Rueda, registrar of the Royal Hospital (Nolan, *Sacramental Records*, 5:125).

19. Marriage of D^n Pablo Lanusse y Laurent and D^a Maria Céleste de Macarty y Fazende, February 6, 1802, SLC/WP, vol. 2, part 2, p. 140, act 569, AANO.

20. Acts and Deliberations of the Cabildo, book 4, vol. 3, February 19, 1796, p. 92, typed translation, NOPL; Din, *Spaniards, Planters, and Slaves*, 185, 203.

21. Acts and Deliberations of the Cabildo, book 4, vol. 3, August 8 and 16, 1800, pp. 202–16, and book 4, vol. 4, October 24, 1800, the Marquis de Casa Calvo to Don Nicolas Maria Vidal, pp. 13–29, typed translation, NOPL.

22. Din, *Spaniards, Planters, and Slaves*, 205, 206, 209, 312–13 nn. 47 and 48. The original of López y Ángulo's proclamation of November 29, 1800, quoted by Din on page 209, is found in AGI/PPC, legajo 68. See also Din and Harkins, *New Orleans Cabildo*, 178–80.

23. Notice to Captain-General Salvador de Muro y Salazar, Marqués de Someruelos, January 7, 1801, AGI/ASD, legajo 2607, n.p., microfilm, THNOC. This appears to be a copy of the original document, whose whereabouts are unknown.

24. A. P. Whitaker, *The Mississippi Question*, 31, 158–59.

25. López to Morales, October 3, 1801, Papers of Panton, Leslie, and Company, abstracts/translations at www.microformguides.gale.com/Data/Download/3040000A.pdf, accessed January 28, 2007. The original letter, written in Spanish, is from AGI/ASD, legajo 2607, microfilm reel 13, John C. Pace Library, University of West Florida, Pensacola.

26. López to Charles DeHault DeLassus, January 10, 18, 27, March 22, 27, 1800, January 24, 26, February 12, March 2, 10, and May 16, 1801, Box 5, Official Dispatches of the Spanish Governors Subseries, MHM. Thanks to Christopher Gordon for providing me with copies and translations of these documents.

27. Captain-General Salvador de Muro y Salazar, Marqués de Someruelos, to Ministerio de Hacienda de Indias, September 22, 1801, AGI/PPC, Reales Ordenes, legajo 1737, photostat, LC, Facsimiles from Spanish Archives, Box 3035, packet E, part 9, translation by Nilda Aponte.

28. Juan Ventura Morales to Soler, March 12, 1802, AGI/ASD, legajo 2607, p. 400; López to Soler, April 12, 1802, AGI/ASD, legajo 2607, p. 402; and Muro y Salazar to Soler, July 29, 1802, AGI/ASD, legajo 2607, p. 406, microfilm, THNOC; and AGI/PPC, legajo 1737, photostat, LC, translations by Nilda Aponte.

29. López to the "Prince of Peace" (Manuel Godoy) January 17, 1803, AGI/ASD, legajo 2607, pp. 444–50, microfilm, THNOC, translation by Nilda Aponte.

30. "Biografias y Vidas," entry for Mariano Luis de Urquijo, www.biografiasyvidas. com/biografia/u/urquijo_mariano.htm, accessed February 9, 2009; Lea, *History of the Inquisition in Spain*, 396.

31. López to Soler, June 4, 1803, AGI/ASD, legajo 2607, pp. 530–33, microfilm, THNOC, translation by Nilda Aponte.

32. Juan Ventura Morales closed the port of New Orleans to all foreign commerce and rescinded the American right of deposit on October 16, 1802. William E. Huling, Vice Consul for the United States at New Orleans, to W. C. C. Claiborne, Territorial Governor of Mississippi, October 18, 1802; Claiborne to Huling, October 28, 1802; Claiborne to Don Manuel de Salcedo, Spanish Governor of Louisiana, October 28, 1802; Claiborne to Secretary of State James Madison, October 29, 1802; Claiborne to Madison, November 6, 1802; Salcedo to Claiborne, November 15, 1802; Claiborne to Madison, January 3, 1803; Claiborne to Huling, January 12, 1803; Madison to Claiborne, January 17, 1803. All in Rowland, *Official Letter Books*, 1:207, 208, 209, 210, 221, 233, 253, 255.

33. Dispatch of January 11, 1805, AGI/ASD, legajo 2607, unnumbered page [549?], microfilm, THNOC, translation by Nilda Aponte. The exact death date for López y Ángulo is not stated. The 1941 *Times-Picayune* article "Epitaph-Plate of 'Haunted' House Owner Found Here" gives a death date of March 26, 1804, but López had not yet left Spain at that time. A. P. Whitaker's *The Mississippi Question* states that "after the transfer of Louisiana to the United States [López y Ángulo] was finally pardoned and appointed consul at New Orleans; but as he was proceeding to his post . . . the ship ran aground and he died of heart failure from the shock" (161).

34. Despatch of January 11, 1805.

35. Thanks to Elizabeth Shown Mills for explaining the French custom of naming a daughter for the husband's deceased wife (personal communication January 27, 2010).

36. The notion that "Borquita" was born on the ship returning from Spain appears in a January 10, 1910, letter from Edouard DeLassus of St. Martinsville, Louisiana, to Walter B. Douglas of St. Louis, Missouri. The writer, descended from Delphine Macarty's daughter Jeanne Blanque DeLassus, stated in a discussion of family genealogy that "Miss MacCarty at the age of thirteen was married to a grandee of Spain by the name of Lopez de Angulo and by this marriage had one daughter, who was born at sea" (DeLassus–St. Vrain Collection). See also Arthur, *Old Families of Louisiana*, 116.

37. Louis Chevalier Macarty appointed as tutor to the orphaned minor Françoise Borja de López y Ángulo, Court of Probates, May 12, 1808; Widow Blanque v. Paul Poultz, Syndic of the Creditors of Jean Blanque, Parish Court, November 15, 1815, docket no. 1145; Borja López y Ángulo v. Cyprien Gros, under-tutor for the Blanque minors, Parish Court, November 15, 1815, docket no. 1146, all microfilm, NOPL.

38. Claiborne to Huling, January 13, 1803, and Claiborne to Madison, January 28, 1803, in Rowland, *Official Letter Books*, 1:257, 267.

39. Proclamation of William C. C. Claiborne issued on surrender of Louisiana; Claiborne's address to the "large assemblage of citizens" in the "Grand Salee" of the Cabildo, ibid., 1:307–10. Claiborne to Madison, February 14, 1803; Madison to Claiborne March

27, 1803; Claiborne to Madison, November 18, 1803; and Claiborne to Colonial Prefect Pierre Clément de Laussat, November 18, 1803, ibid., 1:282, 283, 284, 290.

40. Claiborne to Madison, July 14, 1804; Claiborne to His Excellency the Marquis de Casa Calvo, July 25, 1804; Claiborne to Casa Calvo, September 1, 1804; Casa Calvo to Claiborne, September 5, 1804; Claiborne to Madison, October 5, 1804; Claiborne to Casa Calvo, October 9, 1804; Casa Calvo to Claiborne, October 10, 1804; and Claiborne to Madison, October 20, 1804, ibid., 2:248–49, 265–67, 315, 319, 347, 369–71. The quote is from Claiborne to Madison, August 10, 1805, ibid., 3:158.

41. Claiborne to Madison, April 7, 8, and 9, 1804; Claiborne to Casa Calvo, July 25, 1804; and Claiborne to Madison, July 25, 1804, ibid., 2:83–85, 88–89, 265–67; Claiborne to Casa Calvo, July 28, August 3, 1805; Claiborne to Madison, August 7, 10, 1805; Claiborne to Casa Calvo, August 14, 1805; Casa Calvo to Claiborne, August 17, 1805; and Claiborne to Casa Calvo, August 17, 1805, ibid., 3:139–40, 146, 154, 158, 167, 172–76; letter of safe conduct for Casa Calvo, in E. Carter, *Territorial Papers—Orleans*, 665.

42. Claiborne to Madison, January 20, 1809, in Rowland, *Official Letter Books*, 4:305. Gayarré gives a good summary of Claiborne's troubles with the Spanish in his *History of Louisiana: The American Domination*, 69–105.

43. Claiborne to Madison, January 24, 1804, and February 6, 1804, in Rowland, *Official Letter Books*, 1:345–46, 363–65. Laussat left on April 21, 1804, to become colonial prefect of Martinique.

44. Tregle, "Creoles and Americans," 134.

45. Claiborne to Jefferson, January 16, 1804, in E. Carter, *Territorial Papers—Orleans*, 161. Claiborne expressed similar opinions to Madison, January 10, 1804, in Rowland, *Official Letter Books*, 1:329–30.

Chapter 3. Blanque

1. Marriage of Juan Blanque, widower of Juana Pouyet, son of Paul Blanque and Marie Fargues, and Maria Delphina de Macarty, widow of Ramon López y Ángulo, witnesses Pedro Marin de Argote, Esteban Boré, Santiago Livaudais, Eugenio de Macarty, and Luis Macarty, the bride's father, March 19, 1807, SLC/WP, vol. 3, part 1, p. 12 verso, act 37, AANO.

2. Sally K. Reeves has noted that in notarial acts between 1803 and 1816 both brothers signed their names *Laffite*, not *Lafitte* as most writers have rendered it (Reeves, "Cruising Contractual Waters," 7–15).

3. Laussat appointed Blanque as the commercial agent for the French government in New Orleans. Claiborne wrote that Blanque had declined the assignment, which was then given to the planter Evan Jones (Claiborne to Madison, March 11, 1804, in Robertson, *Louisiana under the Rule of Spain, France, and the United States*, 293–95). Claiborne to Madison, August 1, 1804, in Rowland, *Official Letter Books*, 2:285.

4. Funeral of Dª Maria Juana Lerable, February 26, 1807, SLC/WP, unnumbered volume for 1803–1807, part 2, p. 155, act 410, AANO.

5. Succession of Marie Jeanne Lerable, wife of Chevalier Louis Barthélémy Macarty, Court of Probates, 1807, [no docket no.], microfilm, NOPL; Succession of Marie Jeanne Lerable, Acts of Narcisse Broutin, May 9, 1808, vol. 18, p. 166, and March 29, 1811, vol.

24, p. 74, NARC. The statement that there was no marriage contract is found in Widow Blanque v. Syndics of the creditors of Jean Blanque, Parish Court, November 15, 1815, docket no. 1145, microfilm NOPL. Calculation of the value of Delphine's inheritance from her mother, based on the commodity price index, from Officer and Williamson, www.measuringworth.com/ppowerus/.

6. Dora Richards Miller's letters to George Washington Cable are dated March 25, April 3, 9, 20, and May 6, 1889, and the undated research notes were sent along with these letters. Cable Papers.

7. J. P. Coleman, "The Famous Haunted House in Royal Street," *Daily States*, November 2, 1924. This version of the story is repeated in Kendall, "Old New Orleans Houses," 697–98.

8. WPA Louisiana Writers' Project, *Louisiana: A Guide to the State*, 481. The tale of the severed ear is included in a paragraph about the Macarty house on the Chalmette Battlefield, which was General Jackson's headquarters during the Battle of New Orleans; this house actually belonged to Delphine's cousin Augustin Macarty, not to her parents. The severed-ear story is also found in Early, *New Orleans Holiday*, 86.

9. Brown, "Proof That Madame Lalaurie . . . Rests Here," *States*, January 27, 1941. A version of this story turns up in Ebeyer's strange little self-published book, *Paramours of the Creoles*, 74–75. The theory resurfaced in 1975, by which time the scene of Madame de Macarty's murder by slaves had shifted to the Macarty/Lanusse plantation in Carrollton ("Ask A. Labas—History of the Warrington House," *States-Item*, Lagniappe section, May 6, 1975, B-7, cols. 1–2).

10. The 1812 plot occurred among slaves on the Bellechasse, Castantato, Bienville, and Macarty/Lanusse plantations ("The Louisiana Purchase: A Heritage Explored—An Online Educational Resource from LSU Libraries Special Collections"). The trial transcripts available online are docket no. 227 Orphee, slave of Pere Thomas; no. 228 Isaac, slave of Dominique Fletas; no. 229 Honoré, slave of Mr. Lemenge; no. 231 Joseph, slave of Col. Bellchase; nos. 232 and 233 Charles and Lindor, slaves of A. Bienveneau; no. 240 Colin, slave of Mr. Velamil; no. 241 Antoine, slave of Mr. Boniquet; no. 242 Charles, slave of Mr. Marigny. www.lib.lsu.edu/special/purchase/history.html#revolts1, accessed February 8, 2011.

11. Inventory of goods, succession of Marie Jeanne Lerable, Acts of Narcisse Broutin, May 9, 1808, vol. 18, 166, NARC. This document lists the land, slaves, and other goods that went to Delphine and her brother and half sister. On March 20, 1809, Delphine officially transferred the same fifty-two slaves to her husband Jean Blanque, Acts of P. F. S. Godefroy, vol. 1, p. 97, NARC.

12. Donation by the Chevalier Louis Barthélémy de Macarty to Jean Blanque and Dame Marie Delphine Macarty his wife, Acts of Narcisse Broutin, June 20, 1808, vol. 18, p. 228, NARC. Calculation of the value of Delphine's inheritance from her father from Officer and Williamson, www.measuringworth.com/ppowerus/.

13. Sale of property by Chevalier de Macarty to Louis Barthélémy Macarty and Jean Blanque for $165,650, Acts of Narcisse Broutin, July 2, 8, 1808, vol. 18, pp. 247, 260, NARC.

14. Vieux Carré Survey, Square 63, lot 11272, present-day 409 Royal Street, THNOC; Sheriff's auction, property of Godefroi du Jarreau to Jean Blanque, Acts of Narcisse Broutin, July 16, 1808, vol. 18, p. 273, NARC.

15. After the settlement of Jean Blanque's estate, Delphine and her brother Louis

Barthélémy Macarty each owned half interest in the Royal Street townhouse; the description was published in the auction notice for L. B. Macarty's real estate after his death, *Bee*, May 14, 1847, p. 2, col. 7.

16. "Plan of the City and Suburbs of New Orleans . . . by Jacques Tanesse," THNOC accession no. 1971.4.

17. Arthur, *Old New Orleans*, 43–45.

18. Baptism of Maria Louisa Paulina, born April 6, 1809, baptized June 29, 1809, godparents Luis de Macarty, infant's maternal grandfather, and Maria Francisca Borja de Candelaria Lopez y Angulo, infant's sister, vol. 6, part 1, p. 6 verso, act 18. Baptism of Luisa Maria Laure, born January 13, 1813, baptized October 12, 1813, godparents Luis Bartolomé de Macarty and Maria Luisa Paulina Blanque, infant's sister, vol. 7, p. 98, act 555. Baptism of Juana Luisa Maria, born April 16, 1814, baptized July 1, 1815, godparents Bartolomé de Macarty and Luisa Maria Laura Blanque, vol. 8, p. 2. Baptism of Juan Pedro Paulino, born April 22, 1815, baptized July 1, 1815, godparents Pedro Blanque, resident of France, absent, proxy Luis Bartolomé de Macarty, and Maria Luisa Paulina Blanque, vol. 8, p. 2. All are from SLC/WP, AANO.

19. Claiborne to Jefferson, March 4, 1810, in E. Carter, *Territorial Papers—Orleans*, 869–71.

20. Faye, "Louis de Clouet's Memorial to the Spanish Government." The original of Clouet's report is found in AGI, Indiferente General, legajo 146-3-8.

21. Walsh to Claiborne, July 11, 1805, Rowland, *Official Letter Books*, 3:121–22; Claiborne to Dearborn, October 8, 1806, ibid., 4:25–26.

22. Peters, ed., *Public Statutes at Large*, Acts of the 8th Congress, 1st session, chapter 38, section 10, 2:283–86: "An act to prohibit the importation of slaves into the Louisiana Territory," March 26, 1804.

23. Dr. John Watkins (Claiborne's agent) to Claiborne, February 2, 1804, Rowland, *Official Letter Books*, 2:12; Hatch Dent to James H. McCulloch, July 14, 1804, E. Carter, *Territorial Papers—Orleans*, 265–66.

24. Claiborne's anti-slavery sentiments, fear of rebellion, and concerns about importing foreign slaves into the Territory of Orleans are expressed in Claiborne to Madison, March 10, June 22, July 1, 12, and 15, 1804, Rowland, *Official Letter Books*, 2:25, 217, 233, 237, 235. See also Lachance, "The Politics of Fear."

25. Claiborne to Madison, March 10, June 22, July 1 and 5, 1804, Rowland, *Official Letter Books*, 2:25, 217, 233, 237.

26. The description of the Laffites is from Davis, *The Pirates Laffite*, xi. The brothers' origin in Bordeaux, their emigration from Saint-Domingue to New Orleans, and the establishment of their Barataria headquarters are discussed in detail on pages 1–153.

27. For South Carolina's newly reopened African slave trade, see Sublette, *The World That Made New Orleans*, 225–26; Leglaunec, "Slave Migrations," 205–6; Rasmussen, *American Uprising*, 21–24.

28. Sale of female slave Surprise, age 16, *brut*, arrived on the *Aura* from Charleston, Captain Laporte, by Blanque to Henriette Villascusa for $400, Acts of Pierre Pedesclaux, August 2, 1806, vol. 53, folder 5, p. 578. Sale of two unnamed male slaves, ages 12 and 20, Congo, arrived on the *Aura* from Charleston, Captain Laporte, by Blanque to Bernard

Cheriol for $960, Acts of P. Pedesclaux, August 6, 1806, vol. 53, folder 6, p. 596. Sale of four unnamed male slaves, *brut*, arrived on the *Lanna* from Charleston, Captain Laporte, by Blanque to Jacques Villeré for $6,200, Acts of Narcisse Broutin, September 29, 1806, vol. 14, p. 28. Sale of two unnamed male slaves, both fourteen, *brut*, arrived on the *Lanna* from Charleston, Captain Laporte, by Blanque to Gabriel Villeré for $1,000, Acts of N. Broutin, September 29, 1806, vol. 14, p. 28 verso. Sale of male slaves of the Mandan [Mende] nation, four years in the colony [*sic*] Cando age seventeen, and Gacemoire, age 15, by Blanque to Pierre Dulcide Barran for $1,500, Acts of N. Broutin, October 17, 1806, vol. 14, p. 54 verso. Sale of two unnamed male and two unnamed female slaves, adults, *brut*, arrived on the *Lanna* from Charleston, Captain Laporte, by Blanque to Jacques Villeré, for $2,000, Acts of N. Broutin, October 29, 1806, vol. 14, p. 101. Sale of four unnamed male slaves, adults, *brut*, arrived on the *Franklin* from Charleston, Captain Lauve, by Blanque to Joseph Lefebvre for $2,200, Acts of P. Pedesclaux, March 17, 1807, vol. 54, p. 115 verso. Sale of fourteen unnamed male and female slaves, adults, *brut*, arrived on the *Franklin* from Charleston, Captain Lauve, by Blanque to Charles Jumonville Villiers for $7,700, Acts of N. Broutin, June 10, 1807, vol. 16, pp. 90, 93. Sale of ten unnamed male slaves, adults, *brut*, arrived on the *Lanna* from Charleston, Captain Laporte, by Blanque to Charles Jumonville Villiers, for $5,000, Acts of N. Broutin, June 10, 1807, vol. 16, p. 94. Sale of six unnamed male and female slaves, adults, *brut*, arrived on the *Franklin* from Charleston, Captain Lauve, by Blanque to Joseph Montegut for $3,600, Acts of N. Broutin, June 30, 1807, vol. 16, p. 160. All citations are from Hall's *Louisiana Slave Database* and were accessed at NARC.

29. Hall, *Louisiana Slave Database*, using "Charleston" as a search term; Leglaunec, "Slave Migrations," 205–7.

30. Peters, ed., *Public Statutes at Large*, Acts of the 9th Congress, 2nd session, chapter 22, sections 1–10, 2:426–30: "An act to prohibit the importation of slaves into any port or place within the jurisdiction of the United States," March 2, 1807.

31. Hall's *Louisiana Slave Database* shows that Blanque made a total of 136 transactions—73 purchases and 63 sales—often buying or selling slaves in groups.

32. For a detailed explanation of why the Saint-Dominguen émigrés were forced out of Cuba, see Sublette, *The World That Made New Orleans*, 249–50.

33. Peters, ed., *Statutes at Large*, 11th Congress of the United States, 1st session, chapter 8, 2:549–50: "An act for the remission of certain penalties and forfeitures," June 28, 1809. On August 9, 1809, Claiborne forwarded a copy of the act to New Orleans mayor James Mather; in Rowland, *Official Letter Books*, 4:401.

34. A breakdown of these figures shows that there were 1,373 white men, 703 white women, and 655 white children; 428 free men of color, 1,377 free women of color, and 1,297 free colored children; and 962 enslaved men, 1,330 enslaved women, and 934 enslaved children. Debien and Le Gardeur, "Saint-Domingue Refugees in Louisiana," 239; Lachance, "The 1809 Immigration of Saint-Domingue Refugees to New Orleans"; Lachance, "The 1809 Immigration of Saint-Domingue Refugees," Table I, 247, 251, 262–63; Lachance, "The Foreign French," 103–11.

35. A sixteen-year-old Creole mulatto named Charles is included in the "List of Slaves Owned by the late Jacques Deslondes and M. Picou, October 1795," transcription and

translation in Thrasher, *On to New Orleans*, 281. Manuel Andry identified Charles Deslondes as the "principal leader of these bandits" (Andry to Claiborne, January 11, 1811,
printed in the *Le Moniteur* January 15, 1811, transcription and translation in Thrasher, *On
to New Orleans*, 156).

36. The ethnicity and place of origin for some of the slaves is found in the "Declara-
tions for Compensation for Slaves Killed in the 1811 Uprising," St. Charles Parish Original
Acts, February 20, 1811, Book 1810–1811, act 17, transcription and translation in Thrasher,
On to New Orleans, 212–21. The plantation inventories published by Thrasher show a
high proportion of Africans among those enslaved on the German Coast plantations.

37. The execution of Charles is described in a letter of Samuel Hambleton to David
Porter, January 25, 1811, quoted in Paquette, "A Horde of Brigands?" 78.

38. Hall's *Louisiana Slave Database* lists 113 men who were killed during the uprising,
executed after judgment, in prison, or missing.

39. "Verdicts of the St. Charles Parish Tribunal for the Slaves Charged with Rebellion," St. Charles Parish Original Acts, January 13, 1811, Book 1810–1811, act 2, pp. 17–20,
transcription and translation in Thrasher, *On to New Orleans*, 210–11. "Court documents
Relating to the 1811 Slave Revolt from New Orleans City Court," City Court, January 16,
1811, docket nos. 184–95, NOPL, transcription and translation in Thrasher, *On to New
Orleans*, 226–46.

40. In *American Uprising*, Rasmussen discusses the supposition that the revolt was
instigated by "foreign" slaves (175).

41. Governor Claiborne's rather terse reports of the 1811 uprising are found in Clai-
borne to various recipients, January 9–17, 1811, Rowland, *Official Letter Books*, 5:93–103.
The idea that Charles Deslondes and other members of his rebel band were from Saint-
Domingue was promulgated until recently by most historians. See, for example, Kendall,
"Shadow over the City," 143–46; Dormon, "The Persistent Specter"; Thompson, "National
Newspaper and Legislative Reactions"; Davis, *The Pirates Laffite*, 72–74. For the histori-
cally correct version of the 1811 uprising, see Hall, "Franco-African Peoples of Haiti and
Louisiana"; Paquette, "A Horde of Brigands?"; and Rasmussen, *American Uprising*.

42. Davis, *The Pirates Laffite*, 211–21.

43. Ibid., 158–62.

44. Edward Nicholls, proclamation, August 29, 1814, quoted in ibid., 168.

45. J. Laffite to Blanque, September 4, 1814, English translation in the appendix to
Latour, *Historical Memoir*, xii–xiv. For more on Latour's collection of these documents,
see Davis, *The Pirates Laffite*, 227–28. For Pierre Laffite's escape from jail, see ibid., 175–
76. All of the Laffite materials are now preserved in the Parsons Collection, Center for
American History, University of Texas at Austin. Davis notes that these original documents "were part of cases no. 0573 and/or no. 0574, United States District Court. By the
early twentieth century, they had been stolen from the District Court archives in New
Orleans, along with most of the other documents now in the Parsons Collection" (*The
Pirates Laffite*, 552 n. 60, 555 n. 78).

46. Lachance, "1809 Immigration of Saint-Domingue Refugees"; Davis, *The Pirates
Laffite*, 165–75, quoting from J. Laffite to Blanque, September 7, 1814, J. Laffite to Claiborne, n.d. [September 10, 1814], P. Laffite to Blanque, September 10, 1814, and Deposition

of John Blanque, April 22, 1815, United States v. Certain Goods taken at Barataria, docket no. 0746.

47. Davis, *The Pirates Laffite*, 183–210. Interestingly, there is no mention in Claiborne's *Official Letter Books* of Blanque's delivery of the Laffites' letters or of the Baratarians' involvement in the Battle of New Orleans.

48. Davis, *The Pirates Laffite*, 211–21.

49. Funeral of Dⁿ Juan Blanque, husband of Dᵃ Maria Delfina de Macarty, October 8, 1815, SLC/WP, unnumbered vol. 1815–1820, part 1, p. 6, act 42, AANO.

50. Inventory of the succession of Jean Blanque, Acts of Pierre Pedesclaux, November 10, 1815, vol. 71, p. 1025, NARC; Widow Blanque v. Paul Poultz, Syndic of the Creditors of Jean Blanque, Parish Court, November 15, 1815, docket no. 1145, and Borja Lopez y Angulo v. Cyprien Gros, under-tutor for the Blanque minors, November 15, 1815, docket no. 1146, microfilm, NOPL. Delphine's renunciation of the community of goods between herself and her husband is reiterated in Acts of Pierre Pedesclaux, January 17, 1816, vol. 72, p. 15, and in P. Pedesclaux, July 9, 1816, vol. 73, p. 410, NARC.

51. *Digest of the Civil Laws* (1808), Book III, "Of the Different Modes of Acquiring the Property of Things," Title V, "Of Marriage Contract," Section IV, "Of the Partnership or Community of Acquests or Gains," article 72, p. 338.

52. Creditors of the Succession of Jean Blanque, Acts of Philippe Pedesclaux, February 22, 1816, vol. 72, p. 751, NARC; L. Macarty, P. J. Poutz, and L. Blanq, Syndics of the creditors of the estate of the late Jean Blanque (hereafter the Syndics) v. Delphine Macarty, Widow Blanque, tutrix of her children, Parish Court, March 28, 1816, docket no. 990, microfilm, NOPL.

53. All sales by Delphine Macarty, Widow Blanque, and the Syndics: sale of Joseph to Joseph Ducros for $1,000, Acts of Pierre Pedesclaux, May 13, 1816, vol. 72, p. 338. Sale of unidentified negress, Jacques, Catherine and children Azenor, Felix, Manuel, and Rosa to Andre Rixner for $4,710, Acts of Michel de Armas, May 14, 1816, vol. 10, act 241. Sale of Annette, Isaac, and Zilia to Baptiste St. Amant for $3,410, Acts of M. de Armas, May 22, 1816, vol. 10, act 397. Sale of Philippe, LaGuerre, Beard, Fevrier, Jacques London, Henry, Augustin, Marguerite, and an unidentified infant to Onesifort St. Amant and François Mayronne for $12,495, Acts of M. de Armas, May 22, 1816, vol. 10, act 398. Sale of Adonis, Lubin, Bazile, and Charlotte and her daughters Célestine and Louise to the Chevalier Macarty for $5,060, Acts of M. de Armas, May 22, 1816, vol. 10, act 399 (note that Célestine and Louise were later included in Delphine's 1828 marriage inventory). Sale of Jacques Anglais and Senegal to Albin Michel for $1,500, Acts of M. de Armas, May 22, 1816, vol. 10, act 400. Sale of Honore to Vincent Joseph Trabuc for $1,200, Acts of M. de Armas, May 22, 1816, vol. 10, act 401. Sale of Henry Bambara and Françoise and son Joseph for $1,960 to David S. John, Acts of Pierre Pedesclaux, May 24, 1816, vol. 72, act 292. Sale of Jean Pierre to François Loiseau for $600, Acts of P. Pedesclaux, May 25, 1816, vol. 72, act 295. Sale of Gaibel, Lindor, Silvie, Medor, Jean Pierre, and Marie for $4,870 to Pierre Lefebre, Acts of P. Pedesclaux, May 28, 1816, vol. 72, act 300. Sale of Luke and Achem for $1,920 to François Dupais, Acts of P. Pedesclaux, May 28, 1816, vol. 72, act 302. Sale of Simonne to Jean Rondeau for $960, Acts of P. Pedesclaux, June 3, 1816, vol. 72, act 320. Sale of Figaro and Fabianne to Ursin and Louis Bouligny for $1,560, Acts of

M. de Armas, May 31, 1816, vol. 11, act 424. sale of Marseille to Valery Dantilly for $1,300, Acts of P. Pedesclaux, June 3, 1816, vol. 72, p. 321. Sale of Etienne and François to Edmond Meance for $510, Acts of P. Pedesclaux, June 4, 1816, vol. 72, act 327. Sale of Anna and Euphrosine to Benoit Milbrouck for $1,425, Acts of P. Pedesclaux, June 6, 1816, vol. 72, p. 331. Sale of Joseph to Joseph Ducros for $1,000, Acts of P. Pedesclaux, June 8, 1816, vol. 72, p. 339. Sale of Jean Baptiste to Bernard de Marigny for $1,790, Acts of P. Pedesclaux, June 16, 1816, vol. 72, p. 332. Sale of Rose to François Rapp for $750, Acts of P. Pedesclaux, June 25, 1816, vol. 72, p. 391. Sale of Nagot to Augustin Massicot for $2,105, Acts of M. de Armas, May 28, 1816, vol. 11, act 413. Sale of Jack to Albin Michel for $690, Acts of M. de Armas, August 16, 1816, vol. 11, act 603. Sale of Isaac to John Stephen David for $130, Acts of M. de Armas, August 16, 1816, vol. 11, act 604. All citations are from Hall's *Louisiana Slave Database* and were accessed at NARC.

54. All sales by Delphine Macarty, Widow Blanque, and the Syndics: sale of land to Louis Chevalier Macarty and Louis Barthélémy Macarty for $9,471, Acts of Michel de Armas, May 22, 1816, vol. 10, act 396; sale of lot with house and dependencies on Bienville Street to Louis Barthélémy Macarty for $2,500, Acts of M. de Armas, November 26, 1817, vol. 13A, act 583, NARC.

55. Sale of the Pointe de la Hache plantation by Delphine Macarty, Widow Blanque, and the Syndics to Albin Michel for $16,000, Acts of Michel de Armas, May 31, 1816, vol. 11, act 425, NARC.

56. All sales by Delphine Macarty, Widow Blanque, and the Syndics: sale of eight lots in Bourg Pontchartrain to Philippe Pedesclaux for $245, Acts of Michel de Armas, June 9, 1817, vol. 13, act 346; sale of two lots in Bourg Pontchartrain to Louis Nicolas Fortin for $1,810, Acts of Philippe Pedesclaux, October 15, 1816, vol. 72, p. 604; sale of a lot in Bourg Pontchartrain to Delmasse Guénon for $100, Acts of Ph. Pedesclaux, October 29, 1816, vol. 72, p. 604, NARC.

57. Auction sale of Royal Street property from the succession of Jean Blanque to Jean Françoise Girod and Widow Chole for $17,800, Acts of Pierre Pedesclaux, June 13, 1816, vol. 72, p. 352, NARC.

58. Exact figures for the proceeds from the sale of Blanque's assets would be $1,503,625 in today's currency, and his total indebtedness would be $2,435,735, Officer and Williamson, www.measuringworth.com/ppowerus/.

59. Sale of property by the Syndics to the Widow Blanque for $17,000, Acts of Pierre Pedesclaux, June 25, 1816, vol. 72, p. 391, NARC.

60. Syndics v. Delphine Macarty, Widow Blanque, tutrix of her children, Parish Court, March 28, 1816, docket no. 990, microfilm, NOPL; succession of Jean Blanque, inventory, Acts of Pierre Pedesclaux, July 9, 1816, vol. 73, p. 410, NARC.

61. Donation of Pauline by Louis Chevalier Macarty to Marie Delphine Macarty his daughter, Acts of Michel de Armas, August 1, 1817, vol. 13, act 439, NARC.

62. Orleans Parish Count, Petitions for the Emancipation of Slaves 1813–1843, no. 89E, microfilm, NOPL. The slave Jean Louis, valued at $800, is listed in Jean Blanque's estate inventory, with a note that he is to be freed by Madame Blanque. Jean Blanque acquired Jean Louis from Pierre Rene de St. Germain for $400 on June 9, 1814; Acts of Marc Lafitte, vol. 4, p. 189, NARC.

63. Funeral for Eliza, negress, age 15, daughter of Hélène, slave of Dame Blanque, February [illegible], 1816, vol. 6, part 1, p. 101, act 445. Funeral for Jean Pierre Paulin, [no age], slave of M^de Vve Blanque, June 27, 1819, vol. 7, part 1, act 173. Funeral for Genevieve, quadroon born in Illinois, age 40, slave of M^de Blanc, September 9, 1819, vol. 7, part 1, act 472. Funeral for Zoé, of the Congo nation, age 20, slave of Madame Blanque née Macarty, November 17, 1820, vol. 7, part 1, act 366. Funeral for Enriette, age 3, daughter of Célestine, negress slave of Blanque Macarty, June 25, 1821, vol. 7, part 1, act 1081. Funeral for Clemént, age 23 months, slave of Madame Blanque née Macarty, August 31, 1822, vol. 7, part 2, p. 105, act 1607. Funeral for Marie Françoise, [no age], negress slave of Widow Jean Blanque, December 26, 1823, vol. 7, part 2, p. 147, act 2363. Funeral for Jean, age 5, son of Rosette, slave of Widow Jean Blanque, December 29, 1823, vol. 7, part 2, p. 148, act 2366. All in SLC/S-FPC. AANO.

64. Funeral of Caballero D^n Luis de Macarty, age 68, widower of Juana Lerable, October 22, 1824, SLC/WP, unnumbered vol. 1824–1828, part 1, p. 2, AANO.

65. Will of Louis Chevalier Macarty, filed January 8, 1825, Will Book 4, pp. 54–55, microfilm, NOPL. The two slaves bequeathed to his natural daughter Emesie were named Rosa and Théophile. Macarty's will was enacted before the notary Marc Lafitte, but it could not be located among Lafitte's acts at the NARC.

66. Petition by Eugène Macarty and Louis Barthélémy Macarty, testamentary executors of Louis Chevalier Macarty, to Judge James Pitot of the Probate Court, filed January 28, 1825, microfilm, NOPL; partition of property by the heirs of Louis Chevalier Macarty, Acts of Marc Lafitte, October 22, 1825, vol. 28, p. 354, NARC.

Chapter 4. Lalaurie

1. Marriage record for Jean-Marie Lalaurie and Françoise Depenne, 10 Pluviôse, année V [January 29, 1797], Villeneuve-sur-Lot, microfilm 5Mi26/R52, ADL. Birth registration for Leonard Louis Nicolas Lalaurie, 16 Frimaire, année XX [born December 6, 1802], Arrondissement de Villeneuve-sur-Lot, Départmente de Lot-et-Garonne, France, LDS Family History Library, microfilm no. 735555, which cites p. 18, Naissances 1802–1807, Registres de l'état civil 1793–1892, series 4E [Féodalité, communes, bourgeoisie, familles 1790–1940], vol. 322, p. 11, ADL.

2. Letters to Louis Lalaurie, étudiant en médecine, rue de Sorbonne no. 4, Paris, and rue l'Angouléme no. 23, Toulouse, from his father, brother, and others, Villeneuve-sur-Lot, 1823–1824; letters to Louis Lalaurie, Chez Monsieur Laroque, Rue Bouquiére, Bordeaux, and Chez Monsieur Cazentre, médecine, Pauillac, from his father, brother, and others, Villeneuve, 1824, DeLassus–St. Vrain Collection. Thanks to Christopher Gordon, archivist at MHM, for providing photocopies of these materials.

3. Brasseaux, The "Foreign French," 312. Passenger Lists of Vessels Arriving at New Orleans 1820–1902, NARA microfilm publication M259, roll 4 (February 9, 1824–May 30, 1825), Ship Fanny, December 8, 1824. The passenger list incorrectly gives Lalaurie's age as twenty. Also traveling on the Fanny were the merchant Emile Doumeing; J. Rondil and P. Durand, both weavers; and C. Cousse [Cossé], a tailor. The other passenger, Charles Barthélémy Lanusse, married Eleanor Mirtile de Macarty, daughter of Edmond de

Macarty and Justina Maria Eleonor Destrehan, on January 21, 1826, at St. Louis Cathedral (Nolan, *Sacramental Records*, 17:111, 255).

4. Notes taken during the trip of the *Fanny* from Bordeaux to New Orleans by Louis Lalaurie, DeLassus–St. Vrain Collection, translation by Larry Franke, MHM staff.

5. Ship *Fanny*, Bordeaux, cargo and recipients, *Courier*, February 17, 1825, p. 3, col. 2.

6. "To the Editor," *Courier*, March 19, 1825, French edition p. 2, col. 3, English edition p. 3, col. 3. The apothecary Antoine Dalché shared space with the physician Dr. Felix Formento, and later with Dr. Louis Lalaurie, at his shop on the corner of Dumaine and Bourbon. Lalaurie's announcement is referenced in Duffy, *Rudolph Matas History of Medicine*, 1:293. Duffy does not appear to have realized that this Dr. Lalaurie was the husband of the infamous Madame Delphine Lalaurie. For more on the Comité Médical de la Nouvelle-Orléans and the licensing of physicians and apothecaries, see Duffy, *Rudolph Matas History of Medicine*, 1:309–10 and 326–44.

7. For number of druggists and physicians, see Paxton's *Directory and Register* for 1824 (there was no 1825 directory). The Orthopaedic Institution of doctors Choppin and Schuppert was located at 215 Carondelet Street (Duffy, *Rudolph Matas History of Medicine*, 2:234).

8. The birthplace of Pierre Dulcide Barran in Villeneuve is known from the record of his marriage to Jeanne Dessales, St. Mary's Church/WP, December 17, 1808, vol. 1, p. 29 verso, act 70, AANO, and from his death record, November 26, 1840, Orleans Parish Deaths, vol. 8, p. 652, LSA. Barran was not listed in the city directory, and we therefore do not know where Dr. Lalaurie lived in 1825.

9. Advertisements for theaters, ballrooms, and Carnival events are from the *Courier* and the *Bee*, 1825–27. For more on the early theaters, see Belsom, *Celebrating 200 Years of Opera in New Orleans*, 1–3.

10. The chapter on "Secret and Benevolent Associations" in (no author) *Biographical and Historical Memoirs of Louisiana*, 170–78, lists the officers (including Jean Blanque and Augustin Macarty) of the Grand Lodge of Louisiana from 1812 to 1891, but it does not name ordinary members such as Louis Lalaurie would have been. See also Greene, *Masonry in Louisiana*, 39–42, 60–64, 83–86.

11. Théodore Delboch, Villeneuve, to Louis Lalaurie, New Orleans, March 9, 1827, DeLassus–St. Vrain Collection, translation by Gail Moreau.

12. Paxton's *Directory and Register* for 1823 listed Madame Widow Blanque, 249 Levee below D'Enghien (now Franklin), and the Chevalier de Macarty and Louis B. Macarty, planters, on Levee below Olivier's rum distillery.

13. The negative descriptions of Louis Lalaurie are from Saxon, *Fabulous New Orleans*, 205; Asbury, *The French Quarter*, 248; Nash, *Look for the Woman*, 247–48; and Benfey, *Degas in New Orleans*, 35.

14. J. M. Lalaurie, Villeneuve, to his son Louis Lalaurie, New Orleans, October 15, 1825, September 8, 1826, DeLassus–St. Vrain Collection, translation by Gail Moreau.

15. L. [Laurent] Lalaurie, Villeneuve, to his brother Louis Lalaurie, New Orleans, December 24, 1826 (incorrectly labeled 1829), DeLassus–St. Vrain Collection, translation by Gail Moreau. This brother—who simply signed his name "L."—is listed in his mother's succession as "Laurent Eugène Lalaurie, doctor" (Succession of Françoise Depenne,

wife of J. M. Lalaurie, June 11, 1827, series 3Q, Domaines, enrégistrements, hypothèques, 1790–1940), vol. 35, p. 943, ADL).

16. Richards, "Madame Lalurie Legend Just Fiction," photocopied newspaper clipping incorrectly labeled *New Orleans Morning Tribune*, August 10, 1936, DeBuys Family Papers; Richards quoted Corrine DeBuys and DeBuys family friend William Warrington throughout the article. Brown, "Proof That Madame Lalaurie . . . Rests Here," *States*, January 27, 1941; Brown claims to have heard this story from Miriam DeBuys. The "crippled daughter" was first mentioned by Saxon in *Fabulous New Orleans* (205), but Saxon did not imply that she was receiving treatment from Dr. Lalaurie.

17. The theory and practice of this branch of medicine is discussed in detail, with illustrations, in Bigg, *Orthopraxy*, 63–130.

18. J. M. Lalaurie, Villeneuve, to his son Louis Lalaurie, New Orleans, July 25, 1825, and L. [Laurent] Lalaurie, Villeneuve, to his brother Louis Lalaurie, New Orleans, December 24, 1826, DeLassus–St. Vrain Collection, translation by Gail Moreau.

19. J. M. Lalaurie, Villeneuve, to his son Louis Lalaurie, New Orleans, January 5, 1827, DeLassus–St. Vrain Collection, translation by Larry Franke, MHM staff. Death record for Françoise Depenne, wife of J. M. Lalaurie, December 25, 1826, microfilm 5Mi26/R67, ADL.

20. J. M. Lalaurie, Villeneuve, to his son Louis Lalaurie, New Orleans, March 7, 1827, DeLassus–St. Vrain Collection, translation by Gail Moreau.

21. L. [Laurent] Lalaurie, Villeneuve, to his brother Louis Lalaurie, New Orleans, February 12, 1827, DeLassus–St. Vrain Collection, translation by Gail Moreau.

22. J. M. Lalaurie, Villeneuve, to his son Louis Lalaurie, New Orleans, March 7, 1827, DeLassus–St. Vrain Collection, translation by Gail Moreau.

23. Ibid.

24. Assignment of revenues by Louis Lalaurie to his father, J. M. Lalaurie, August 9, 1827, DeLassus–St. Vrain Collection, translation by Gail Moreau.

25. Procuration by Louis Lalaurie to Jean Guerin, Acts of Felix de Armas, October 20, 1827, vol. 12, act 1104, NARC.

26. Sale of John, age 15, by Louis Miller of Natchez to Delphine Macarty, Widow of Jean Blanque, for $600, Acts of Felix de Armas, January 11, 1828, vol. 13, act 29, NARC. The list of slaves is from Marriage Contract between Delphine Macarty and Louis Lalaurie, Acts of F. de Armas, January 12, 1828, vol. 13, pp. 4–5, act 43, NARC.

27. Marriage Contract between Delphine Macarty and Louis Lalaurie, Acts of F. de Armas, January 12, 1828, vol. 13, pp. 4–5, act 43, NARC. Calculation of the value of Delphine's fortune in today's currency from Officer and Williamson, www.measuringworth.com/ppowerus/.

28. Marriage of Leonard Louis Nicolas Lalaurie and Marie Delphine Macarty, witnesses Charles Jumonville de Villiers and Manuel Andry, January 12, 1828, SLC/WP, vol. 4, part 2, p. 111, act 505, AANO. Baptism of Jean Louis Lalaurie, legitimate son of Leonard Louis Nicolas Lalaurie and Marie Delphine Macarty, godparents Jean Guerin and Marie Louise Eleanor Charnet Coquillon, January 13, 1828, SLC/WP, vol. 12, p. 106, act 272, AANO; Guerin was the man whom Lalaurie had put in charge of his financial affairs when he left town in October 1827.

29. Arthur, *Old New Orleans*, 148; "Epitaph-Plate of 'Haunted' House Owner Found Here," *Times-Picayune*, January 28, 1941.

30. Marriage of Francisco Placido Forstall and Maria Francisca Borja López y Angulo, May 31, 1821, SLC/WP, vol. 3, part 3, p. 257, act 1066. Baptism of Juana Maria Céleste Forstall, born April 4, 1823, July 5, 1823, SLC/WP, vol. 10, part 1, p. 36, act 207. Baptism of Maria Luisa Emma, born October 11, 1824, December 24, 1824, SLC/WP, vol. 10, part 2, p. 149, act 695. Baptism of Juan Julio Forstall, born September 6, 1826, March 6, 1827, SLC/WP, vol. 11, p. 313, act 871, all in AANO.

31. Sale of Adonis, chief miller, by Henri de Ste-Gême to Jean Blanque for $1,200, Acts of Michel de Armas, May 25, 1812, vol. 7, page 142, act 354. Sale of Pierre Louis and Gregoire by Ste-Gême to Chevalier Louis Barthélémy de Macarty for $1,400, Acts of M. de Armas, May 30, 1812, vol. 152, act 370. Both in NARC.

32. Nathalie Dessens, "De Jean Boze á Henri de Ste-Gême," 3. Marriage of Baron Henrique de Ste-Gême, native of Bazens, Department of Lot-et-Garonne, France, and Margarita Delmaz, native and resident of this parish, widow of Laufroy Dreux, April 29, 1816, SLC/WP, vol. 3, part 3, p. 172, act 574, AANO.

33. Information on Henri de Ste-Gême and Jean Boze comes from the finding aid to the Ste-Gême Family Papers 1799–1904, Mss 100, THNOC, and from Nathalie Dessens, "De Jean Boze á Henri de Ste-Gême." Thanks to Dr. Judith Schafer for first alerting me to the Lalaurie references in the Ste-Gême Papers, and to Dr. Nathalie Dessens for providing additional information.

34. Boze to Ste-Gême, December 1, 1828, folder 134, pp. 8–9, and Boze to Ste-Gême, July 20, 1829, folder 143, p. 10, Ste-Gême Papers, translation by Gail Moreau.

35. U.S. Census for Orleans Parish 1830, Lalaurie (no first name), Schedule of the number of inhabitants between the F^{bg} Danois [Faubourg D'Aunoy] and the Fisherman's Canal, sheet 52, line 25, NARA microfilm publication M19, roll 45, accessed through www.ancestry.com. In 1830 the census listed only the name of the head of household; others were represented by check marks in various categories for gender, age, and race. The entry for the Lalaurie family shows one white male under age five [Jean Louis]; one white male age ten to fourteen [Paulin]; one white male age twenty to twenty-nine [Louis]; one white female age ten to fourteen [Jeanne]; two white females ages fifteen to nineteen [Laure and Pauline], and one white female age thirty to thirty-nine [Delphine, who was actually forty-three]. The slaves were two males and four females under age ten, four males and three females ages ten to twenty-four, eight males and two females ages twenty-four to thirty-five; and one male age thirty-six to fifty-four.

36. Sale of lot in the Faubourg Annunciation by Delphine Macarty, wife of Lalaurie, to Samuel Dorance Dixon for $600, Acts of Octave de Armas, May 26, 1831, vol. 10, p. 393, act 238, and mortgage by Delphine Macarty, wife of Lalaurie, from the Insurance Company of Louisiana, Acts of Felix de Armas, July 2, 1831, vol. 33, act 535, both in NARC.

37. Public auction of building lots belonging to Delphine Macarty, wife of Lalaurie, in the Faubourg Delphine; two lots to Jacques Lefort for $6,000 and one lot to François Rabouam for $5,000, Acts of Felix de Armas, May 19, 1831, vol. 32, acts 388 and 389, NARC.

38. Sale of property by Delphine Macarty, wife of Lalaurie, along with Jacques Lefort

and François Rabouin, to Lucien Guillaume Miligsberg representing the Levee Steam Cotton Press Company for $30,100, Acts of Felix de Armas, July 26, 1831, vol. 33, act 585, NARC. Toledano, Evans, and Christovich, *New Orleans Architecture: The Creole Faubourgs*, 19.

39. J. P. Coleman, "The Famous Haunted House in Royal Street," *Daily States*, November 2, 1924, p. 10, cols. 1–6.

40. The chain of title for the property at present-day 1140 Royal, Square 50 (bounded by Royal, Governor Nicholls, Bourbon, and Chartres), lot 22782-30, comes from the Vieux Carré Survey, THNOC: brevet of Louis XV in favor of the Ursuline Nuns, September 18, 1726; letters patent, U.S. Government to the Ursulines Nuns, February 17, 1824; Ursuline Nuns to Germain Ducatel, March 16, 1825, Acts of Philipe Pedesclaux, vol. 30, p. 120; Ducatel to Edmond Soniat Dufossat, March 6, 1828, Acts of H. K. Gordon, vol. 7, p. 101, NARC.

41. Sale of lots designated nos. 1 and 2 and partially built dwelling by Edmond Soniat Dufossat to Delphine Macarty, wife of Lalaurie, Acts of Octave de Armas, August 30, 1831, vol. 11, p. 381, act 433, NARC. Lot no. 1 was described as being "46 feet 6 inches facing on Royal Street and 90 feet in depth facing on Hospital Street." The back lot, no. 2, was "28 feet facing on Hospital Street by 74 feet in depth."

42. Boze to Ste-Gême, March 10, 1830, folder 160, pp. 13–14; August 20–November 20, 1831, folder 189, p. 8; October 15, 1831, folder 190, p. 2; February 20, 1832, folder 197, p. 1 and 3; March 10, 1832, folder 200, p. 2, Ste-Gême Papers.

43. Heard, *French Quarter Manual*: "Creole Town House," 38–43; "Balconies and Galleries," 82–87; "Ironwork," 93–99; "Carriageways," 100–101; "Courtyards," 104–9; "Service Buildings and Wings," 110–15. Vogt, *Historic Buildings of the French Quarter*: "The Courtyard," 54–58; "Townhouses," 60–61; "Outbuildings," 62. Russell, "Cast Iron and New Orleans," 10–11. The floor plan of the Lalaurie house is similar to that of the American-influenced Hermann-Grima house, 820 St. Louis Street (Vogt, *Historic Buildings*, 126).

44. Percy's *Directory of the City and Suburbs* for 1832 lists L. Lalaurie, M.D., at the corner of Royal and Hospital.

45. Marriage of Auguste DeLassus and Marie Louise Jeanne Blanque, January 6, 1833, SLC/WP, vol. 5, part 2, act 274, AANO. Among the friends and relatives who signed the marriage register was Louis Lalaurie, who was only a few years older than his stepdaughter.

46. Paulin Blanque's presence at Yale University is documented in Silliman, *Statistics of the Class of 1837*, 34, where it is stated that "Paulin Blanque, New Orleans, La., left the class freshman year [1834]."

47. Percy's *Directory of the City and Suburbs* for 1832 and Michel's *Annual and Commercial Register* for 1834 show that Placide Forstall, of the firm of Gordon, Forstall, and Co., lived at the corner of Bourbon and St. Ann. Eugène Macarty and his partner Eulalie Mandeville were at 381 Dauphine corner Barracks; Eugène's second partner, Totote Destrés, was listed as Miss T. Detrey, dry goods, corner Conde (Chartres) and Ursulines; his third partner, Helöise Croy, was at 50 Victoire (Decatur). Jean Baptiste Macarty's first partner, Henriette Prieto, lived at 170 Burgundy, and his second partner, Magdeleine "CéCé" Carpentier, lived at the corner of Rampart and Customhouse (Iberville). Sophie

Mousante, the woman with whom Delphine's father had cohabited, lived at 18 Esplanade, and her daughter Emesie Macarty lived with a white merchant named Benjamin Hart at the corner of Rampart and Ursulines. Céleste Perrault lived with Augustin Macarty at 275 Camp in the American sector above the Vieux Carré.

48. Donation of Firmin, age 15, from the succession of the late Louis Chevalier Macarty, by Delphine Macarty, wife of Lalaurie, and Louis Barthélémy Macarty to Delphine Emesie Macarty, Acts of Octave de Armas, February 11, 1834, vol. 21, act 113, NARC. Firmin was not one of the slaves (Rosa and Théophile) bequeathed to Emesie by her father in his will.

49. Gould, "In Full Enjoyment of Their Liberty," 149–54.

50. *Civil Code* (1825), Book I, "Of Persons," Title V, "Separation from Bed and Board," articles 136–39, pp. 40–42.

51. Delphine Macarty, wife of Louis Lalaurie v. Louis Lalaurie, her husband, First Judicial District Court, November 16, 1832, docket no. 10,237, NOPL.

52. *Civil Code* (1825), Book I, "Of Persons," Title IV, "Of Husband and Wife," article 124, p. 36, and article 125, p. 38.

53. Authorization by Louis Lalaurie to Delphine Macarty his wife, Acts of Felix de Armas, April 11, 1833, vol. 38, act 183, NARC. This document lists all of the real estate and slaves, including some that had already been sold, that Delphine brought to the marriage in 1828. Lalaurie's residence in Plaquemines Parish is borne out by a notice he placed in the *Courier* of May 23, 1832 (p. 3, col. 6), asking for the return of a "note of hand for $500, drawn by L. Lalaurie to the order of Andre Cossé of Plaquemines." The finder was asked to return it to Judge Leonard of Plaquemines Parish, or to P. Forestier, druggist, at the corner of Royal and St. Peter in New Orleans.

Chapter 5. "Passive Beings"

1. The *Code Noir* for French Louisiana derives from the code formulated in 1685 for France's colonies in the Antilles; see Palmer, "Origins and Authors of the *Code Noir*." A translation of Louisiana's *Code Noir* is published in Fortier, *Louisiana . . . in Cyclopedic Form*, 97–99.

2. Schafer, *Slavery, the Civil Law, and the Supreme Court of Louisiana*, 6.

3. *Acts Passed at the First Session of the First Legislature of the Territory of Orleans* (1807), Black Code, Crimes and Offences, Sec. 16 and 17, pp. 206–8.

4. *Digest of the Civil Laws* (1808), Chapter III, "Of Slaves," article 16, p. 40, and article 27, p. 42.

5. For an overview of the development of the 1825 Louisiana *Civil Code*, see Stone, "The Law with a Difference."

6. *Civil Code* (1825), Book I, "Of Persons," Title VI, "Of Master and Servant," Chapter 3, art. 173, p. 52; art. 177, p. 54; art. 192, p. 58. For more on slave law in Louisiana, see Schafer, *Slavery, the Civil Law, and the Supreme Court of Louisiana*, especially the first chapter.

7. Pontalba to his wife, May 4, 1796, typescript p. 78; July 10, 1796, typescript p. 167; and November 3, 1796, typescript p. 292, LHC.

8. Robin, *Voyages to Louisiana*, 238–41.

9. Stoddard, *Sketches . . . of Louisiana*, 324. Stoddard's chapter on the "State of Slavery" expresses his views in strong terms (331–43).

10. Latrobe, *Impressions Respecting New Orleans*, 53–54. Bernard de Marigny was Eulalie Mandeville's white half brother; his first wife was Mary Ann Jones.

11. Ibid., 54; Boze to Ste-Gême, March 25–May 4, 1834, folder 238, p. 5, Ste-Gême Papers, translation by Gail Moreau.

12. Bremer, *Homes of the New World*, 244.

13. *Bee*, English edition, June 20, 1829, p. 3, col. 2; Boze to Ste-Gême, July 20, 1829, folder 143, p. 9, Ste-Gême Papers.

14. "The Torture Reviled," *Bee*, June 20, 1854. This and other articles were hand-copied on index cards by the "Negro Unit" of the Louisiana Writers' Project, and are now housed in the Marcus Christian Collection, WPA file, "crimes against slaves," Louisiana and Special Collections, Earl K. Long Library, University of New Orleans.

15. "Cruelty to Slaves," *Daily Delta*, April 1, 1855, index cards, Christian Collection.

16. "Cruelty to a Slave," *Daily Delta*, May 14, 1856, index cards, Christian Collection.

17. "Infamous Woman," *Bee*, October 21, 1854; "Cruelty to Slaves," *Daily Delta*, October 21, 1854; "The Case of Fanny Smith," *Bee*, October 25, 1854; "Fanny Smith," *Bee*, October 31, 1854; "Charge of Cruelty to a Slave," *Bee*, December 2, 1854; all from index cards, Christian Collection.

18. "Cruel Treatment by Mistress," *Daily Delta*, September 28, 1858; "Ill-Treatment," *Daily Delta*, March 15, 1855; both from index cards, Christian Collection.

19. Schafer, *Slavery, the Civil Law, and the Supreme Court of Louisiana*: *Womack v. Nicholson*, Caddo Parish (1842), 42–43; *Kennedy v. Mason*, Ouachita Parish (1855), 47–48; *Humphries v. Utz*, Madison Parish (1856), 49–52.

20. Ibid., *State v. Morris* (1849), 31–32.

21. Sale of Nelson, age 21, Jack, age 22, Rochin, age 19, Samson, age 14, Cyrus, age 12, Matilda, age 20, and Maria, age 18, by Stephen Peillon to Delphine Macarty, wife of Lalaurie, for $3,869, Acts of Felix de Armas, November 4, 1828, vol. 18, act 1061, NARC.

22. Sale of Lucinda, age 19, by Thornton Alexander of Stafford County, Virginia, to Delphine Macarty, wife of Lalaurie, for $400, Acts of Felix de Armas, April 17, 1830, vol. 27, act 400; sale of Lucinda by Lalaurie to Louis Tabary for $600, F. de Armas, January 24, 1833, vol. 38, act 40, NARC.

23. Sale of Abram, age 21, James, age 22, Amos, age 21, and Frederick, age 22, by James Barnes Diggs of Norfolk to Delphine Macarty, wife of Lalaurie, for $2,140, Acts of Felix de Armas, February 9, 1831, vol. 31, act 79; sale of Sally, age 22, by Jean Baptiste Philippé to Lalaurie for $600, F. de Armas, April 12, 1831, vol. 32, act 254; sale of Patsy, age 19, by William W. Eldridge of Bourbon County, Kentucky, to Lalaurie for $500, F. de Armas, April 21, 1831, vol. 32, act 287; and sale of Mary, age 31, by Francis Herries to Lalaurie for $600, F. de Armas, June 2, 1831, vol. 33, act 444, all in NARC.

24. Sale of Diana, age 21, by Joseph Hardy, f.m.c., to Delphine Macarty, wife of Lalaurie, for $400, Acts of Felix de Armas, August 21, 1832, vol. 37, act 458; sale of Mary Anne alias Anne Saunders, age 18, by Louis François Feinturier to Lalaurie for $550, F. de Armas, December 20, 1832, vol. 37, act 597, both in NARC.

25. Sale of Eulalia alias Lively, age 22, by Sarah Lee, free negress, to Delphine Macarty, wife of Lalaurie, for $600, Acts of Felix de Armas, April 22, 1833, vol. 39, act 220, NARC. Sale of Priscilla, age 17, by Thomas German of Jefferson Parish to Lalaurie for $500, Acts of William Christy, November 19, 1833, vol. 16, p. 45, NARC; in this act, written in English, Priscilla is designated as a "slave for life," guaranteed against all vices and maladies except the habit of running away.

26. Sale of Louise, Célestine, Suzette, Edouard, Ben, and Juliette by Delphine Macarty, wife of Lalaurie, to Louis Brugnière of St. Bernard Parish for $4,900, Acts of Felix de Armas, November 22, 1828, vol. 18, act 1114; sale of Célestine, Edouard, Ben, and Juliette by Louis Brugnière to Andre Dussumier for $2,600, F. de Armas, February 13, 1829, vol. 20, act 218; sale of Célestine, Edouard, Ben, and Juliette by Dussumier to Delphine Macarty, wife of Lalaurie, for $2,600, F. de Armas, May 12, 1830, vol. 28, act 480, all in NARC. Brugnière corresponded with Delphine and her family and was a special friend of Louis Barthélémy Macarty's; Dussumier's kinswoman Amanda Andry would later marry Delphine's son Paulin Blanque.

27. Emancipation of Hélène, age 40, Acts of Felix de Armas, March 6, 1828, vol. 14, act 270; sale of Hélène by Adelaide Lecomte Piernas to Jean Blanque, Acts of Narcisse Broutin, December 19, 1810, vol. 23, p. 645, both in NARC.

28. Emancipation of Devince, Parish Count, October 26, 1832, extracts from the records of the deliberation of the police jury of the Parish of Orleans, Sitting of 15th February, 1834, Petitions for the Emancipation of Slaves 1813–1843, no. 42B, microfilm, NOPL. The emancipation was not finalized until February 15, 1834.

29. Boze to Ste-Gême, July 20, 1829, folder 143, p. 10, Ste-Gême Papers, translation by Gail Moreau.

30. Bremer, *Homes of the New World*, 244.

31. Boze to Ste-Gême, May 1–31, 1832, folder 204, pp. 3–4, Ste-Gême Papers, translation by Gail Moreau.

32. Saillard, *Les Aventures du Consul de France*, August 20, 1834, 101–3.

33. Amédée Ducatel, as a clerk in the office of Felix de Armas, signed as a witness to many of the property transactions enacted before de Armas, including Louis Lalaurie's April 11, 1833, permission for his wife to "administer their goods and affairs without his consent and authorization."

34. The notary Amédée Ducatel was interviewed by J. W. Guthrie sometime in 1889, undated general notes, Cable Papers. Dora Richards Miller wrote to George Washington Cable that she had searched the pages of the *Courier* and the *Louisiana Advertiser* for any account of Madame Lalaurie's court appearance but "could not even find her name," and that J. W. Guthrie had searched the Louisiana Supreme Court index and found nothing (Miller to Cable, April 20, 1889, Cable Papers).

35. Martineau, *Retrospect of Western Travel*, 264–65. Cable elaborated on Martineau's telling of the story in "The Haunted House in Royal Street," 204–5.

36. Julia Duralde, born in 1775, married John Bruce Clay in 1807. Her late husband was the brother of Kentucky senator Henry Clay, and her sister had been married to Governor Claiborne. She is listed as Madame Clay in Michel's 1834 *Annual and Commercial Register* and as Mrs. Julia Clay in Gibson's 1838 *Guide and Directory*. The chain of

title for the house is found in the Vieux Carré Survey, square 50, lot 22782, present-day 628 Governor Nicholls, THNOC.

37. Delavigne, "Haunted House of the Rue Royale," 250.

38. See, for example, "New Orleans Paranormal Research Society Ghostly Gallery—The Haunted Mansion," www.neworleansghosts.com/haunted_new_orleans.htm, accessed November 30, 2005.

39. Boze to Ste-Gême, March 25–May 4, 1834, folder 238, pp. 5–6, Ste-Gême Papers, translation by Gail Moreau.

40. Funeral for Florence, negress, age 10, daughter of Bonne, slave of Mr Lalaurie, February 16, 1831, SLC/S-FPC, vol. 9, part 1, p. 106, act 698. Funeral for Leontine, negritte age 22 months, child of Bonne, both slaves of Paulin Blanque, August 26, 1831, SLC/S-FPC, vol. 9, part 1, p. 163, act 906. Funeral for Bonne, negress, age 30, slave of Mr Macarty, February 7, 1833, SLC/S-FPC, vol. 10, part 1, p. 34, act 217. Funeral for Juliette, negress, age 13, slave of Mr Lalaurie, February 26, 1833, SLC/S-SPC, vol. 10, part 2, p. 43, act 276. Funeral for Jules, négrillon, age 6, slave of Lalaurie Macarty, May 29, 1833, SLC/S-FPC, vol. 10, part 2, p. 102, act 650. All in AANO.

41. Sale of Bonne, age 18, by Sanitté Bataille, f.w.c., to Paul Lacroix for $450, Acts of Pierre Pedesclaux, April 15, 1814, vol. 68, p. 148; sale of Bonne, age 25, by Lacroix to the Chevalier de Macarty for $425, Acts of Marc Lafitte, May 20, 1816, vol. 8, p. 236, both in NARC. There is no record of Delphine Macarty, Widow Blanque, receiving Bonne, Juliette, Florence, and Jules from her father's succession.

42. Funeral for Célestine, negress, [no age given, calculated from estimated birth date], slave of Madame Lalaurie née Macarty, June 20, 1831, vol. 9, part 1, p. 138, act 716. Funeral for Edouard, negro, age 18, slave of Madame Lalaurie née Macarty, June 30, 1831, vol. 9, part 1, p. 149, act 739. Funeral for Rose, negress, age 19, slave of Mr L. Lalaurie, September 24, 1832, vol. 9, part 2, p. 305, act 1931; note that Rose is not the same as the much older woman named Rosette inherited by Delphine from the estate of Jean Blanque. Funeral for Nicolas, mulatto, age 26, slave of Mr L. Lalaurie, September 30, 1832, vol. 9, part 2, p. 306, act 1942. Funeral for Marianne, negress, age 22, slave of Mr Lalaurie, February 17, 1833, vol. 10, part 2, p. 39, act 246. Funeral for Maria, negress, age 20, slave of L. Lalaurie, November 22, 1833, vol.10, part 2, p. 233, act 1502. Funeral for Sally, negress, [no age given, calculated from estimated birth date], slave of Mr Lalaurie, November 26, 1833, vol.10, part 2, p. 232, act 1513, all from SLC/S-FPC, AANO. The interments of Maria and Sally, slaves of L. Lalaurie, are also recorded in the Burial Book for St. Louis Cemetery no. 1 (June 27, 1833-January 29, 1834), November 22 and 26, 1833, p. 160 and 163, AANO).

43. Thanks to Elizabeth Shown Mills for explaining the correlation between Catholic baptism and a Catholic funeral and interment in a Catholic cemetery (personal communication, February 28, 2010).

44. Martineau, *Retrospect of Western Travel*, 264–65.

45. In *Slavery, the Civil Law, and the Supreme Court of Louisiana*, Schafer gives three examples of cases in which a slave owner was accused by another citizen: *Markham v. Close* (1831), Opelousas, 54; *Barrow v. McDonald* (1857), Terrebonne Parish, 55; *Ney v. Richard* (1860), St. Landry Parish, 55–56.

46. Information on the creation of the Criminal Court of the First District for Orleans

Parish in 1821 is found in vol. 1 of Louis Moreau Lislet's *Digeste General des Acts de la Legislature de la Louisiane*, "Cour Criminelle de la Nouvelle-Orleans," 409–16.

47. Criminal Court of the First District, State v. Bernard Chipiau, Minute Book 1, June 16, 1831; State v. Pierre Soulé, f.m.c., Minute Book 2, June 14, 1832; State v. Patrick Sheeran, Minute Book 2, December 29, 1834; State v. Louis Donnet, Minute Book 2, May 14, 1832; all in NOPL.

48. The receipt from John Grymes is included in the lawsuit Delphine Macarty, wife of Lalaurie, v. John R. Grymes, Parish Court, June 28, 1830, docket no. 5673, microfilm, NOPL. Grymes had borrowed $350 from Madame Lalaurie without formalizing the loan before a notary; she paid him $300 for his legal fee and asked him to pay her the $50 difference, a request he did not honor. Proving to be a formidable adversary, Delphine took the case all the way to the Louisiana Supreme Court, April 20, 1831, docket no. 2021, mss 106, Box 92, SCHA. Calculation of the value of $300 in today's currency from Officer and Williamson, www.measuringworth.com/ppowerus/.

49. Sparks, *Memories of Fifty Years*, 432–40; D. K. Whitaker, "Some Stories of Bench and Bar," 72; "A Beauty of Former Days" [obituary for Susana Bosque Grymes], *New York Times*, August 11, 1881, p. 2, col. 6; Gayarré, "New Orleans Bench and Bar," 650–53.

50. Davis, *The Pirates Laffite*, 85, 102–4, 127, 159–60, 204, 207–8, 225, 293; Alexander, *Notorious Woman: The Celebrated Case of Myra Clark Gaines*, 60–61, 168, 204, 215; Baily, *The Lost German Slave Girl*, 124–83; C. Wilson, *Two Lives of Sally Miller*, 9, 41, 74; Schafer, *Brothels, Depravity, and Abandoned Women*, 108–25.

Chapter 6. The Fire

1. George Washington Cable's research assistant Dora Richards Miller made handwritten transcriptions/translations of the articles in English and French from the *Courier*, the *Bee*, and the *Advertiser*. These have been preserved in the Cable Papers. There is no hard copy or microfilm of the *Courier* for April 10–15, 1834. The *Bee* (French and English editions) and the *Advertiser* are available on microfilm, but Miller's transcriptions/translations from the *Courier* are the only existing source. Miller wrote to Cable that "curiously, the French pages of the *Bee* were much . . . more intense in every way. I translated as exactly as possible."

2. Jean Boze mentioned that Judge Canonge "resides facing the house of Mme. Lalaurie on Royal Street," Boze to Ste-Gême, March 25–May 4, 1834, folder 238, p. 6, Ste-Gême Papers. Michel's *Annual and Commercial Register* for 1834 lists J. F. Canonge, attorney and counsellor at law, 341 Royal.

3. *Courier*, English edition, April 10, 1834, handwritten transcription by D. R. Miller, Cable Papers; reprinted in the *Advertiser* on April 11, p. 2, col. 1.

4. *Bee*, French edition, April 11, 1834, handwritten translation by D. R. Miller, Cable Papers.

5. *Courier*, English edition, April 10, 1834, handwritten transcription by D. R. Miller, Cable Papers; *Bee*, English edition, April 11, 1834, p. 1, col. 1.

6. *Bee*, French edition, April 11, 1834, handwritten translation by D. R. Miller, Cable Papers.

7. *Courier*, English edition, April 10, 1834, handwritten transcription by D. R. Miller, Cable Papers.

8. *Bee*, French edition, April 11, 1834, handwritten translation by D. R. Miller, Cable Papers. New Orleanians would have been well acquainted with the infamous character of Lucrezia Borgia. Lucrezia was depicted as both a sadistic poisoner and a loving mother in Victor Hugo's melodrama *Lucrèce Borgia*. Hugo completed the play in July 1832, and it was first performed in Paris on February 2, 1833. Gaetano Donizetti's opera *Lucrezia Borgia*, inspired by Hugo's play, opened in Milan on December 26, 1833, a few months before the fire at the Lalaurie mansion (*Washington National Opera Magazine*, Fall 2008, 34).

9. *Advertiser*, April 11, 1834.

10. "Authentic Particulars" (deposition of Judge Jacques François Canonge before Judge Gallien Préval of the Parish Court), *Bee*, English and French editions, April 12, 1834, p. 1, col. 1. The original deposition has not survived. According to Irene Wainwright, archivist for the Louisiana Division of the New Orleans Public Library, the Canonge deposition would not have been connected to a specific case before the court; it could only be in the minute books if it were transcribed into the record at all. There is a gap in the minute books of the Parish Court from 1831 to 1842.

11. Starr, *Bamboula: The Life and Times of Louis Moreau Gottschalk*, 32–33.

12. "Application of the Lynch Law," *Courier*, English edition, April 11, 1834, handwritten transcription by D. R. Miller, Cable Papers. A similar account appeared in the *Bee*, English edition, April 11, 1834. Miller noted that "no account of the escape is given in either paper."

13. *Advertiser*, April 11, 1834.

14. *Bee*, English edition, April 12, 1834, p. 1, col. 1.

15. *Courier*, English edition, April 12, 1834, and *Bee*, French edition, April 12, 1834, handwritten transcription/translation by D. R. Miller, Cable Papers.

16. Boze to Ste-Gême, March 25–May 4, 1834, folder 238, pp. 5–6, and July 18–August 10, folder 243, p. 6, Ste-Gême Papers, translation by Gail Moreau.

17. Boze to Ste-Gême, March 25–May 4, 1834, folder 238, p. 6, Ste-Gême Papers; Latrobe, *Impressions Respecting New Orleans*, 53.

18. *Advertiser*, April 14, 1834, p. 2, col. 1; Martineau, *Retrospect of Western Travel*, 264–65.

19. *Bee*, English edition, April 15, 1834, p. 2, col. 1; D. R. Miller to Cable, undated general notes, Cable Papers.

20. "Shocking Brutality," *Daily National Intelligencer*, April 29, 1834, p. 3, col. 4; "A Horrible Affair," *Niles' Weekly Register*, May 3, 1834, p. 152, col. 2, and p. 153, col. 1.

21. "Horrid Fruits of Slavery," *The Emancipator*, May 6, 1834, quoted in Harwood, "Abolitionist Image," 284.

22. *Le Temps*, daily column, "Extérieur: Revue des journaux étrangers"; and *Le National*, daily column, "Coréspondence," April 15–August 31, 1834. Both newspapers carried news from foreign journals, but the few items from the United States were concerned with politics and finance, never with such sensational topics as the Lalaurie incident.

23. Saillard, *Les Aventures du Consul de France*, 101–3. Michel's *Annual and Commercial Register* for 1834 shows the French Consul's office at 100 Royal Street, near Conti.

24. Interview with Amédée Ducatel by J.W. Guthrie, about 1889, attached to typed chain of title for the Lalaurie house, Cable Papers; Cable, "Haunted House in Royal Street," 208, 218. For more on Ducatel, see Arthur, *Old Families of Louisiana*, 127–32.

25. Heidari, *To Find My Own Peace: Grace King in Her Journals*, 10, 210 n. 9. The Grace King Papers are housed at the Hill Memorial Library, Louisiana State University, Baton Rouge. Gayarré (1805–95) was a friend of Grace King's family and became her mentor. Arthur, *Old Families of Louisiana*, 131.

26. Martineau, *Retrospect of Western Travel*, 265–66.

27. Ibid.

28. Charles F. Zimpel, "Topographical Map of New Orleans and its Vicinity, Embracing a Distance of twelve miles . . . ," 1834, accession no. 1955.19, THNOC.

29. Martineau, *Retrospect of Western Travel*, 266. Cable elaborated further on Martineau's version of Madame Lalaurie's escape in "The Haunted House in Royal Street," 212–15.

30. The story by L. Souvestre appeared in *Le Courrier des États-Unis* on December 8, 1838, and the 1968 translation by Harriet Molenaer was published as "Madame Lalaurie: A Contemporary French Account," 378–90. The editor, Katherine Bridges, commented that L. Souvestre might have been Madame Lesbazeilles-Souvestre, "who is remembered chiefly for her French translation of Charlotte Bronte's *Jane Eyre*, and who was a contributor to *Le Courrier des États-Unis.*"

31. Bremer, *Homes of the New World*, 243–45.

32. Cable, "Haunted House in Royal Street," 192–219.

33. Charity Hospital Admission Book 5, November 1833–July 1834, microfilm, NOPL; funerals for April 1834 through 1842, SLC/S-FPC, when the church ceased to keep a register of interment services.

34. Arthur, *Old New Orleans*, 149; Saxon, "Haunted House of Old New Orleans," 13–15, 20; Asbury, *The French Quarter*, 247, 250.

35. Loggins, *Where the Word Ends: The Life of Louis Moreau Gottschalk*, 28; Nash, *Look for the Woman*, 248; Benfey, *Degas in New Orleans*, 42–43.

36. Sale of Bastien, negro, age 24, by the creditors of Joseph Montegut *père* to Jean Blanque for $1,670, Acts of Marc Lafitte, June 28, 1815, vol. 7, p. 183, NARC. There is no record of Montegut's purchasing Bastien.

37. Frost, "Was Madame Lalaurie . . . Victim of Foul Plot?" *Times-Picayune*, February 4, 1934.

38. *Bee*, April 11, 1834, French edition, handwritten translation by D. R. Miller, Cable Papers; Saillard, *Les Aventures du Consul de France*, 102.

39. Marriage contract for Maria Macarty and Francisco Montreuil, April 4, 1786, Acts of Fernand Rodriguez, vol. 8, p. 398, NARC; marriage of Maria Macarty and Francisco Montreuil, June 21, 1783, SLC/WP, vol. 1, part 2, p. 165, AANO. Baptism of Bartólome Roberto Montreuil, born February 9, 1785, baptized April 5, 1785, SLC/WP, unnumbered volume for 1777–1786, part 2, p. 379, act 1168, AANO. Baptism of Theodulo Joseph Montreuil, born September 17, 1786, baptized October 7, 1786, SLC/WP, unnumbered volume for 1786–1791, part 1, p. 15, act 54, AANO; death record for Théodule Joseph Montreuil, Orleans Parish Deaths, March 10, 1832, vol. 1, p. 367, LSA. Barthélémy

Montreuil is listed in Michel's *Annual and Commercial Register* for 1834 as a collector of taxes on taverns, City Hall, with no residential address given.

40. Will of Francisco Roberto Gauthier Montreuil, Acts of Pierre Pedesclaux, October 1, 1797, vol. 30, p. 540 verso, NARC, translation by Nilda Aponte. There is no funeral record for François Montreuil.

41. Manette Macarty Montreuil died on February 2, 1837 (Orleans Parish Deaths, vol. 7, p. 98, LSA). The 1808–1837 records concerning her business dealings in settling the estate of her husband are too numerous to list. They can be found in the acts of notaries Michel de Armas and Octave de Armas, NARC.

42. Death record for Barthélémy Montreuil, Orleans Parish Deaths, June 12, 1834, vol. 5, p. 172, LSA.

43. Saillard, *Les Aventures du Consul de France*, 102; Martineau, *Retrospect of Western Travel*, 264; Cable, "Haunted House in Royal Street," 207; Benfey, *Degas in New Orleans*, 45.

44. "Famous Haunted Crime Scenes," www.trutv.com/library/crime/notorious_murders/classics/haunted_crimescenes/6.html; "New Orleans Paranormal Research Society Ghostly Gallery—The Haunted Mansion," www.neworleansghosts.com/haunted_new_orleans.htm; see also "New Orleans and Its Ghosts," www.essortment.com/all/neworleansghos_rmpo.htm; "Lalaurie Mansion of New Orleans," www.bellaonline.com/articles/art60461.asp. All accessed February 3, 2009.

45. Valentino, *Nightmares and Fairytales: 1140 Rue Royale*, unpaginated.

46. Information on these practices comes from Savitt, "Use of Blacks for Medical Experimentation"; Deyle, *Carry Me Back*; and Washington, *Medical Apartheid*. Thanks to Jonathan Pritchett of Tulane University for directing me to these sources.

Chapter 7. Exile

1. Boze to Ste-Gême, March 25–May 4, 1834, folder 238, p. 5, Ste-Gême Papers; Martineau, *Retrospect of Western Travel*, 266.

2. Marriage of Juan Nelder, son of Artord Nelder and Elisa Pearsy, native of Plymouth, England, and Maria Luisa Adelaida Piernas, daughter of José Piernas and Maria Adelaida Lecomte [Delphine's half sister], December 24, 1815, SLC/WP, vol. 3, part 2, p. 165, act 540, AANO; Among the witnesses was Marie Delphine Macarty, Widow Blanque. "The New Hotel at Claiborne-Covington," *St. Tammany Farmer*, February 19, 1890, p. 2, col. 4; the article states that it was Nelder "whose chivalry prompted him to offer his mill house as a refuge." Thanks to Steve Ellis for directing my attention to this information.

3. Power of attorney by Delphine Macarty, wife of Lalaurie, to Placide Forstall, and power of attorney by Louis Lalaurie to Auguste DeLassus, Acts of Louis Feraud, April 30, 1834, vol. 11, act 73, NARC.

4. Cable, "Haunted House in Royal Street," 217; Castellanos, *New Orleans as It Was*, 60; Asbury, *The French Quarter*, 251; Frost, "Was Madame Lalaurie . . . Victim of Foul Plot?" *Times-Picayune*, February 4, 1934; Brown, "Proof that Madame Lalaurie . . . Rests Here," *Daily States*, January 27, 1941; Early, *New Orleans Holiday*, 87.

5. Navard ("Andre Cajun"), *Stories of New Orleans*, 57–60. The Tulane connection

was repeated by Marjorie Roehl in "Paul Tulane Remained a Mystery to the End," *Times-Picayune*, January 29, 1989, p. K-15, cols. 1–3.

6. Journal of William Cullen Bryant, Paris, July 23, 1834, Bryant Homestead Collection of the Trustees of Reservations, Cummington, Massachusetts, in Bryant and Voss, eds., *Letters of William Cullen Bryant*, 412. A less accurate version of this journal entry is found in Godwin, *A Biography of William Cullen Bryant*, 307–8.

7. J. M. Lalaurie, Villeneuve, to his son Louis Lalaurie, New Orleans, March 7, 1827, DeLassus–St. Vrain Collection, translation by Gail Moreau.

8. Auguste DeLassus, Paris, to his father, Charles DeHault DeLassus, New Orleans, August 14, 1836, DeLassus–St. Vrain Collection, translation by Larry Franke, MHM staff.

9. Succession of Françoise Depenne, wife of J. M. Lalaurie, Acts of Maurice Bosq, November 17, 1834, series 3E, vol. 977, p. 10, ADL. The ambiguity surrounding Laurent Eugène Lalaurie's death is found in a list of health professionals in Villeneuve, April 21, 1829, where it is noted: "He is not any more in the country. He is believed dead" (series 5M4, 1829–1847, ADL). In the succession record of J. M. Lalaurie, Laurent Eugène is said to be "deceased for several years although one cannot produce the legal and material proof of his death" (Acts of Maurice Bosq, April 25, 1843, series 3Q, vol. 35, p. 485, ADL).

10. Auguste DeLassus, Paris, to his father, Charles DeHault DeLassus, New Orleans, August 14, 1836, DeLassus–St. Vrain Collection, translation by Larry Franke, MHM staff. The French online dictionary *Un Mot par Jour* (www.jclat.typepad.com/think), defines *Jean-Foutre* as "un homme incapable, sur qui on ne peut pas compter." French researcher Jérôme Malhache gives the more colloquial definition of "ass-hole," commenting that the term was "frequently used in the nineteenth century and was considered strong enough to be not fully written out by DeLassus in a polite, respectful letter to his father" (personal communication, June 24, 2008).

11. Sale of Sam, age 28, his wife, Letty, age 22, and their children Angela and Alfred by Auguste DeLassus, attorney in fact for Louis Lalaurie, to Benjamin Franklin French for $3,060, Acts of Octave de Armas, September 23, 1834, vol. 23, act 447. Sale of Manuel, age 16, by DeLassus to François Auguste f.m.c. for $570, O. de Armas, September 23, 1834, vol. 23, act 449. Both in NARC.

12. Sale of Eulalia, age 23, by Placide Forstall, attorney in fact for Delphine Macarty, wife of Lalaurie, to Antonio Miranda for $1,100, Acts of Octave de Armas, September 19, 1834, vol. 23, act 428. Sale of Priscilla, age 19, by Forstall to Eugene Dillatte for $420, O. de Armas, September 19, 1834, vol. 23, act 430. Sale of Abraham, age 21, by Forstall to David Adams for $1,100, O. de Armas, September 23, 1834, vol. 23, act 449. Sale of Nelson, age 26, by Forstall to Jean Jacques Jandot for $1,000, O. de Armas, October 30, 1834, vol. 23, act 505. Sale of James, age 23, by Forstall to Louis Dansac for $750, O. de Armas, October 30, 1834, vol. 23, act 506. Sale of Célestin, age 24, by Forstall to François Daubert for $650, O. de Armas, October 30, 1834, vol. 23, act 507. Sale of Théodore, age unknown, to Marie Françoise Labostrie, O. de Armas, October 30, 1834, vol. 23, act 508. Sale of Ben, age 21, for $500, and Frederick, age 27, for $1,000, by Forstall to Felix Forstall, Acts of Felix de Armas, June 11, 1836, vol. 1, act 182. All in NARC.

13. Sale of Bastien, age 42, for $1,000, and Diana, age 23, for $400, by Placide Forstall, attorney in fact for Delphine Macarty, wife of Lalaurie, to Louis Moreau, Acts of Octave

de Armas, September 19, 1834, vol. 23, act 429; cancellation of sale of Bastien and Diana, O. de Armas, March 30, 1836, vol. 29, p. 178; sale of Bastien, age 44, and Diana, age 25, for $2,500 total by Forstall to Robert and Buxton Layton and Nathaniel Hyde, Acts of Felix de Armas, June 11, 1836, vol. 1, act 181; all in NARC.

14. Emancipation of Bastien, Acts of H. B. Cenas, May 25, 1849, vol. 42, p. 761, NARC. The petition to the Council of the First Municipality is attached to this notarial act.

15. This figure was arrived at by subtracting the number of slaves who were sold, freed, or died from those inventoried in the 1816 settlement of the Blanque estate and the 1828 marriage contract, plus the twenty slaves Delphine bought between 1828 and 1833.

16. Sale of property by Placide Forstall, attorney in fact for Delphine Macarty, wife of Lalaurie, to Pierre Edouard Trastour for $14,000, Acts of Amédée Ducatel, March 24, 1837, vol. 4, act 132, p. 245; sale of property by Trastour to Charles Caffin for $14,000, Acts of Felix Grima, February 24, 1837, vol. 17, no. 578; both in NARC.

17. Martineau, *Retrospect of Western Travel*, 266; Bremer, *Homes of the New World*, 245; Points, "The Haunted House . . . Events in the Life of Madame Lalaurie," *Daily Picayune*, March 13, 1892.

18. Castellanos, *New Orleans as It Was*, 60; Heidari, *To Find My Own Peace: Grace King in Her Journals*, 10.

19. Jeanne Marie Céleste Forstall was born on April 4, 1823, and was baptized at St. Louis Cathedral on July 5, 1823 (SLC/WP, vol. 10, part 1, p. 36, act 207, AANO). The godparents were the infant's uncle Edmond Jean Forstall and her grandmother Marie Delphine Macarty. Lalaurie née Macarty, Paris, to Céleste Forstall, New Orleans, October 29, 1835, and January 12, 1836, translation by Gail Moreau. Mary Gehman provided copies of the letters from a 1999 University of New Orleans student video project obtained from the DeBuys Family Papers. A copy of another letter to Céleste from her grandmother, also included in the DeBuys Papers, is too faint to read. It was not written from Paris; the top line might be "Villeneuve, December 16, 1834."

20. Auguste DeLassus, Paris, to his father, Charles DeHault DeLassus, New Orleans, July 1, 1836, and Jeanne Blanque DeLassus to Charles DeHault DeLassus, July 26, 1836, DeLassus–St. Vrain Collection, translation by Larry Franke, MHM staff.

21. Paulin Blanque, Paris, to Auguste DeLassus, New Orleans, June 15, 1838, DeLassus–St. Vrain Collection, translation by Gail Moreau.

22. Will of Jean Marie Lalaurie, Acts of Maurice Bosq, January 16, 1840, and succession of Jean Marie Lalaurie, Acts of Joseph Rataboul, November 7, 1842, no. 767, series 3E, vol. 977, p. 30, ADL; inventory of the estate of Jean Marie Lalaurie, Acts of Maurice Bosq, April 25, 1843, Déclarations des Mutations par Décès, no. 275, series 3Q, vol. 35, p. 485, ADL.

23. Louis Lalaurie, Havana, to Auguste Delassus, New Orleans, October 9, 1842, DeLassus–St. Vrain Collection, translation by Larry Franke, MHM staff.

24. Cuban Genealogy Club of Miami, Espada Cemetery, www.cubangenclub.org/members/espada/espada_|_1.htm, accessed January 21, 2007; "Nombre—Dr. Leonard Lalaurie; Fecha de Defuncion—September 3, 1863; Patio—Quinto; Direccion—centro; Nicho—62; Pagina—156." Thanks to Christopher Gordon of the Missouri History Museum for directing me to this source.

25. Substitution of procuration by Placide Forstall to Auguste DeLassus, Acts of Octave de Armas, September 17, 1840, vol. 30, act 400, and procuration by Louis Barthélémy Macarty to Auguste DeLassus, Acts of O. de Armas, August 6, 1840, vol. 30, act 141, NARC.

26. Information on the Panic of 1837 from Starr, *Bamboula*, 32, and C. Wilson, *Two Lives of Sally Miller*, 57.

27. Louis Barthélémy Macarty v. DeLassus and Pellerin, Fourth District Court, docket no. 22,964, microfilm, NOPL. In addition to addressing the issue of DeLassus's appropriation of L. B. Macarty's funds, the court ordered that he produce an account of his administration of Madame Lalaurie's financial affairs from September 25, 1840, to August 31, 1842.

28. Louis Brugnière, with note appended by Jean Louis Lalaurie, Paris, to Louis Barthélémy Macarty, New Orleans, August 18, 1840, DeLassus–St. Vrain Collection, translation by Gail Moreau. Delphine sold to Brugnière the group of slaves who were subsequently returned to her.

29. Lalaurie née Macarty, Paris, to Auguste DeLassus, New Orleans, May 31, 1842, DeLassus–St. Vrain Collection, translation by Larry Franke, MHM staff.

30. Jean Louis Lalaurie, Paris, to Auguste DeLassus, New Orleans, August 15, 1842, DeLassus–St. Vrain Collection, translation by Larry Franke, MHM staff.

31. Paulin Blanque, Paris, to Auguste DeLassus, New Orleans, August 15, 1842, DeLassus–St. Vrain Collection, translation by Larry Franke, MHM staff.

32. Pauline Blanque, Paris, to Auguste DeLassus, New Orleans, December 1, 1842, DeLassus–St. Vrain Collection, translation by Gail Moreau.

33. For a discussion of concubinage, natural and illegitimate children, and inheritance, see Domínguez, *White by Definition*, 56–89.

34. The laws governing the complex topic of successions and donations are found in the *Civil Code* (1825), Book III, "Of the Different Modes of Acquiring the Property of Things," Title I "Of Successions," inheritance by legitimate children or grandchildren, article 898; inheritance by ascendants (parents), article 899; inheritance by brothers and sisters, article 900 and 908; inheritance by collaterals (other relatives), article 910, pp. 284, 288, 292, and 299.

35. Laws governing donations to concubines, *Civil Code* (1825), Book III, Title II, "Of Donations," article 1468, p. 474.

36. Definition of natural children, *Civil Code* (1825), Book I, "Of Persons," Title VII "Of Father and Child," articles 220 and 221, p. 66.

37. Inheritance by natural children, *Civil Code* (1825), Book III, Title I, articles 912 and 913, p. 292, and Title II, article 1473, p. 476.

38. Domínguez, *White by Definition*, 26, 83, referring to article 1481 of the revised Civil Code of 1870.

39. Death record for Eugène Macarty, Orleans Parish Deaths, October 25, 1845, vol. 9, p. 847, LSA. Eugène was interred in St. Louis Cemetery no. 2 in a tomb purchased for the purpose by Eulalie Mandeville. When Eulalie died on October 21, 1848, she was interred in the same tomb (Burial record for Eugène Macarty, St. Louis Cemetery no. 2, part 2, 1843–1847, p. 188, and burial record for Eulalie Mandeville, September 1847–November 1869, p. 451, AANO).

40. Marriage of Eugène Macarty and Eulalie Mandeville, St. Augustine's Church, October 22, 1845, AANO. St. Augustine's was founded in 1841 by a congregation mostly composed of free people of color.

41. *Civil Code* (1825), Book I, "Of Persons," Title IV, "Of Husband and Wife," article 95, p. 30.

42. Diana Williams addresses "private religious marriages" or "marriages of conscience," such as that between Eugène Macarty and Eulalie Mandeville, in her 2007 Harvard University dissertation "They Call It Marriage." Thanks also to Elizabeth Shown Mills for further insights on deathbed marriages.

43. The ceremony was performed by Father C. E. Lomnig. The record was inserted into vol. 1-B, Marriages of White Persons (1842–1853), between p. 78 (December 22, 1849) and p. 79 (December 29, 1849). There is no mention of the race of either party. Eugène is identified as the son of Barthélémy Macarty and Marie Belisle Pellerin, and Eulalie as the daughter of Philippe Pierre Mandeville, with the mother's name omitted. At the bottom of the page is an asterisk followed by "Marie Jeanne Duteuil"; recall that Eulalie was the daughter of a Mandeville family slave named Marie Jeanne (Maria Juana). The witnesses were Charles Emannuel Lamini, Michel Valecourt Durel, and Drauzin Barthelemy Macarty (son of Jean Baptiste Barthélémy Macarty with the free woman of color Henriette Prieto). Thanks to Sonja MacCarthy, a descendant of Eugène Macarty and Helöise Croy, for sharing this information, and to Jack Belsom of the AANO for locating it.

44. Testament of Eugène Macarty, Acts of Victor Foulon, October 7, 1845, vol. 17, p. 230, act 298, NARC; Will Book 8, pp. 166–67, microfilm, NOPL. Quittance and discharge by Eugène Macarty Jr. on behalf of the other heirs, Acts of Victor Foulon, September 12, 1846, vol. 19, p. 422, act 210, NARC. Macarty named as his natural children and heirs Théophile, Pierre Villarceaux, and Eugène Macarty Jr., all of New Orleans, and Isidore Barthélémy Macarty and the children of the late Emelitte Macarty, all of Santiago de Cuba.

45. Distribution of the estate of Eugène Macarty among his heirs, December 7, 1846, Acts of Victor Foulon, vol. 19, p. 519, act 260; testimony of witnesses and judgment of E. A. Canon, Second District Court, in Louisiana Supreme Court docket no. 626, SCHA. *Macarty et al. v. Mandeville*, *Annual Reports of Cases Argued and Determined in the Supreme Court of Louisiana*, 3:239. The value of Eulalie Mandeville's bank account is calculated from Officer and Williamson, www.measuringworth.com/ppowerus/.

46. Gayarré, "Barthélémy de Macarty's Revenge," 279–82. The ending of Gayarré's story is pure fantasy. Gayarré has Louis Barthélémy Macarty depart suddenly for France after receiving a letter from the eighteen-year-old daughter of a woman, now dead, whom Macarty had once loved and lost. Macarty's rival, "Monsieur Vermandois," had embezzled money from a Louisiana bank, fled to France with Macarty's sweetheart, and established himself as a merchant. Deeply in debt, Vermandois intended to force his daughter into marriage with an elderly millionaire when her true affections were centered on a young military officer of no fortune. Macarty proposed to Vermandois that unless he allowed the girl to marry the man of her choice, his crimes would be revealed, his creditors would descend upon him, and he would be ruined. The marriage took place, and Macarty's "revenge was complete."

47. Baptism of Adelaide Gormans, daughter of Thomas Gormans and Marie Théotiste Hubert Sauvagin, born August 23, 1817, baptized October 24, 1823, SLC/WP, vol. 10, part 1, act 287, p. 71, AANO. The baptismal record does not indicate whether Adelaide was a legitimate or a natural child, but when her mother, Marie Théotiste, died in 1827, she was specified as "single" (*de estado soltera*), not as a wife or widow (Funeral for Marie Théotiste Hubert Sauvagin, October 11, 1827, SLC/WP, unnumbered vol. for 1824–1828, p. 223).

48. Information about the relationship between Eugènie Adelaide "Pancine" Gomez and Louis Barthélémy Macarty comes from the record of the Supreme Court of Louisiana, Succession of Louis Barthélémy Macarty on the Opposition of Mrs. Delphine Macarty, docket no. 1710, SCHA. Ambroise Assumption Pardo was a New Orleans merchant who handled Macarty's business affairs and became, along with Victor Roumage, the executor of his estate. In the record of the Fifth District Court, docket no. 1710 (a copy of which is filed with the supreme court record), Roumage stated that "the mother of the minor child [Louise Macarty] was a relation of Pardo's wife." The printed "Brief for the Opponent and Appellant," prepared by Janin and Taylor, attorneys for the opponent, also stated that "Pancine Gomez" was related to Pardo's wife (pp. 10 and 15). Pardo was married to Eugènie Adelaide Gaye (January 28, 1832, SLC/WP, vol. 5. part 1. act 158), the daughter of Thomas B. Gaye and Marie Euphrosine Hubert. The relationship between Pancine Gomez and Madame Pardo must have been through the Hubert line, but no direct connection has come to light.

49. Thomas Gorman, inspector of the revenue, 103 Bayou Road below St. Claude, was listed in Paxton's *Directory and Register* for 1822; in 1823 he was listed at 533 Dauphine, on the corner of Hospital.

50. Donation of a house on Elysian Fields, a lot on Frenchmen Street, and an enslaved woman and her young son by Louis Barthélémy Macarty to Eugénie Adelaide Gomez, Acts of Amédée Ducatel, September 26, 1836, vol. 2, act 320, p. 315, and donation of a slave by Macarty to Gomez, Ducatel, March 26, 1838, vol. 7, act 112, p. 215, NARC.

51. Birth record for Marie Jeanne Louise Philomène Macarty, natural daughter of Louis Barthélémy Macarty and Eugénie Adelaide Gormens alias Gomez, white, September 30, 1839, Orleans Parish Births, vol. 9, p. 748, LSA.

52. Donation of two houses on Madison Street in the Vieux Carré, two lots on Frenchmen Street in the Faubourg Marigny, two lots downriver on Bartholomew Street near the Macarty Plantation, and five slaves by Louis Barthélémy Macarty to his natural daughter Philomène Gomez, represented by her mother, Acts of Octave de Armas, July 31, 1840, vol. 30, act 134, and donation of household furnishings by Louis Barthélémy Macarty to Eugénie Adelaide Gomez, O. de Armas, August 1, 1840, vol. 30, act 135, NARC.

53. Information about the relationship between Eugénie Adelaide Gomez and Louis Barthélémy Macarty comes from the record of the Louisiana Supreme Court, Succession of Louis Barthélémy Macarty on the Opposition of Mrs. Delphine Macarty, docket no. 1710, SCHA. The printed *Opposition of Delphine Macarty, wife of Louis Lalaurie, to the provisional account of the Executors* (p. 10) states that "they [L.B. Macarty and Pancine Gomez] went together to France; and from two notarial acts prepared in Paris, it appears that there . . . they lived in the same house, rue Duphot No. 28."

54. Paulin Blanque, Paris, to Auguste DeLassus, New Orleans, December 5, 1840, DeLassus–St. Vrain Collection, translation by Gail Moreau.

55. Louis Barthélémy Macarty's trip to Italy is discussed in Paulin Blanque, Paris, to Auguste DeLassus, New Orleans, August 15, 1842, DeLassus–St. Vrain Collection, translation by Larry Franke, MHM staff. Donation of house on Royal Street by Louis Barthélémy Macarty to his natural daughter Marie Jeanne Louise Philomène Macarty, Acts of Antoine-Jules Fourchy, March 19, 1841, Etude LVIII, no. 766, Minutier Central des Notaires Parisiens, Archives Nationales, Paris. The donation was confirmed before Octave de Armas, July 6, 1841, vol. 32, act 162, NARC. Louis Barthélémy Macarty had paid $19,600 for this building to the creditors of Antoine Louis Boimare at a public auction on January 7, 1835, Acts of Théodore Seghers, vol. 11, act 21, NARC. Confirmation of donations to Eugénie Adelaide Gomez and Louise Macarty made before Octave de Armas on July 31 and August 1, 1840, Acts of Antoine-Jules Fourchy, March 19, 1841, Etude LVIII, no. 766, Minutier Central des Notaires Parisiens, Archives Nationales, Paris.

56. The September 28, 1841, civil birth record for Pancine's son Louis Barthélémy Paulin identifies him as the "son of Charles Casadavant and Adelaide Gormans," Prefecture du Department de la Seine, 2nd (now 5th) arrondissement de Paris, Archives de Paris, actes de naissance, microfilm 5Mi1/514. On April 21, 1846, Pancine gave birth to another child, called Charles Marie Casadavant, for whom there is no civil birth record. Finally, on November 16, 1846, Pancine married Charles Casadavant at the city hall of the 5th arrondissement, and two days later they appeared at their neighborhood church, Saint Laurent, to have their marriage blessed and to legitimize their son Charles Marie, born April 21, 1846. Marriage record for Charles Casadavant, rentier, residing at no. 24 rue Saint Laurent, born in Martinique November 23, 1818, son of Théophile Casadavant and Marguerite Adelaïde Germa, both deceased, and of Adelaide Gormans, rentière, also residing at no. 24 rue Saint Laurent, daughter of Thomas Gormans and Marie Théodide Hubert Sauvagin, both deceased, Prefecture du Department de la Seine, 5th arrondissement de Paris, Archives de Paris, actes de mariage, microfilm 5Mi1/2168. Marriage record for Charles Casadavant and Adelaide Gormans, Church of Saint Laurent, D6J/673, Archives de Paris.

57. Death record for Louis Barthélémy Macarty, December 4, 1846, Orleans Parish Deaths, vol. 11, p. 238, LSA.

58. Will of Louis Barthélémy Macarty, Acts of Octave de Armas, September 19, 1846, vol. 39, act 140, NARC. Macarty made additional clarifications to his will before de Armas on November 10, 1846, act 172, and November 22, 1846, act 173, NARC. The slaves to be emancipated were Louis, age 20; Jackson, age 28; Henri, age 55; Cyprian, age 52; Sansnom, age 48; Phébe, age 50; Louise daughter of Betsy, age 18; Betsy, age 38; Rachael, age 56; Eliza age 35; and Aimée age 38. None of these can be identified as former slaves of Madame Lalaurie; *Sansnom* should not be confused with her much younger American slave *Samson*.

59. Inventory of the estate of Louis Barthélémy Macarty, Acts of Octave de Armas, December 9–21, 1846, vol. 39, act 192. Supplementary inventory of the estate of Louis Barthélémy Macarty, O. de Armas, January 24, 1849, vol. 44, act 15, NARC. Value in today's currency, Officer and Williamson, www.measuringworth.com/ppowerus/.

60. Procuration by Delphine Macarty, wife of Lalaurie, to Théodore Bailly Blanchard and Paulin Blanque to "collect the legacy due to her from the succession of M. Macarty her brother," Acts of Benjamin Labarbe, January 27 and 30, 1847, Etude LVI, no. 26, Minutier Central des Notaires Parisiens, Archives Nationales, Paris.

61. Process-verbal, inventory of goods apportioned to Mlle Jeanne Louise Philomène Macarty, Acts of Octave de Armas, April 7, 1847, vol. 40, act 73, NARC. The slaves were Zelie and her daughter Mathilde, Louison, Couassy, and Lucie; the real estate consisted of a lot and house on Frenchmen Street between Grandhommes (Dauphine) and Craps (Burgundy), three lots at the corner of Barthélémy and Casacalvo (Royal), two houses on Madison Street between Levee (Decatur) and Conde (Chartres), and a house on Royal between Toulouse and St. Peter. Value of Louise Macarty's inheritance in today's currency from Officer and Williamson, www.measuringworth.com/ppowerus/.

62. "Judicial Sales—Estate of the late Louis Barthélémy Macarty," May 14, 1847, *Bee*, May 14, 1847, p. 2, cols. 6 and 7. The site of the Macarty property can be seen in Norman's 1845 "Plan of New Orleans & Environs," where it appears on Levee Street between Independence and Bartholomew extending back to St. Claude Avenue. In the later nineteenth century Levee was renamed North Peters, but North Peters disappeared in the twentieth century when this area along the riverfront was taken for railroad tracks and wharves. Thanks to map expert Norm Hellmers for clarifying this issue.

63. Succession of Louis Barthélémy Macarty, Fifth District Court, docket no. 319, microfilm, NOPL. "Succession of L. B. Macarty, on the opposition of Mrs. Lalaurie," printed brief submitted by A. Pitot, L. Eyma, and R. Preaux, attorneys for the Executors and Appellees; "Opposition of Delphine Macarty, wife of Lalaurie, to the provisional account of the Executors," printed brief submitted by Janin and Taylor, attorneys for Delphine Macarty, wife of Lalaurie; "Brief for the minor Louise Macarty," printed brief submitted by G. Legardeur, attorney for the minor; handwritten summary filed May 13, 1850; the sum of $159,347 "coming to Mrs. Lalaurie" is listed on p. 18 of the "provisional account rendered by Victor Roumage and A. A. Pardo, testamentary executors of L. B. Macarty," on April 8, 1850, Succession of Louis Barthélémy Macarty on the Opposition of Mrs. Delphine Macarty, Louisiana Supreme Court docket no. 1710, SCHA.

64. The old 1st arrondissement became the new 8th arrondissement in 1860, when the original twelve arrondissements of Paris were increased to twenty by absorbing what had been small, independent towns outside the city limits.

65. Delphine's addresses at no. 72 rue de la Madeleine, no. 6 rue Greffulhe, and no. 8 rue d'Isly were found by Jérôme Malhache while searching the files of Delphine's notary, Benjamin Labarbe. Malhache also located notarial acts concerning Céleste Macarty, widow of Paul Lanusse, and her son Jean Baptiste Lanusse and daughter-in-law Marie Thérèse Bailly Blanchard, residing at no. 53 rue de la Madeleine.

66. Emancipation of Oreste, Journal of Minutes and Proceedings of the Council of the First Municipality, vol. 6 (1849–1850), April 16, 1849, Emancipations, p. 51, microfilm, NOPL. On May 31, 1850, Paulin Blanque authorized the family attorney Théodore Bailly Blanchard to free Oreste and two other slaves from the succession of Delphine Macarty, wife of Lalaurie.

67. Frost, "Was Madame Lalaurie ... Victim of Foul Plot?" *Times-Picayune*, February 4, 1934.

68. Cable, "Haunted House in Royal Street," 217; Miller to Cable, undated general notes, Cable Papers.

69. Brown, "Proof that Madame Lalaurie ... Rests Here," *Daily States*, January 27, 1941; "Epitaph-Plate of 'Haunted' House Owner Found Here," *Times-Picayune*, January 28, 1941, p. 5, cols. 2–3.

70. Death record for Marie Delphine "Maccarthy," wife of Lalaurie, Republic of France, filed December 8, 1849, attached to her succession papers, microfilm, NOPL.

71. Funeral record for Marie Delphine "Machaty," Church of Saint Louis d'Antin, *Sépultures* 1834–1869, LDS Family History Library, microfilm no. 312900. Thanks to Gail Moreau for providing this document.

72. Interment and exhumation of Marie Delphine "Maccarthy," no. 3517, Register of Burials, Office of the Caretaker, Cimetière de Montmartre, Paris. The location of the Notta tomb was given as 20th division, 6th line, no. 21.

73. On February 4, 1941, Bob Brown wrote to Miriam DeBuys, thanking her for providing the photograph of the tomb. The letter and photograph are now in the collection of Macarty descendant John Ellis.

74. Ownership and burial record, tomb of *Famille Paulin Blanque*, book 1, title B-199, lot 3, alley 2, right, facing Basin Street, New Orleans Archdiocesan Cemeteries Office. Thanks to Alana Mendoza for providing this document. The earliest burial was for Dame H. J. Stouse, age 21, interred June 15, 1884. This would have been Marie Josephine Amable Ducros, born February 27, 1863, to Laure Forstall and Felix Ducros (Orleans Parish Births, vol. 33, p. 3, LSA). Marie Josephine married Henry Jules Stouse on September 20, 1883 (Orleans Parish Marriages, vol. 10, p. 155, LSA), and died on June 14, 1884 (Orleans Parish Deaths, vol. 85, p. 290, LSA). The ownership record appears to have been created in 1924, at which time the title holder was a "Miss Tanney." This might have been Ruby Taney, born May 1, 1898, to Robert J. Taney and Jeanne Lafferranderie (Orleans Parish Births, vol. 113, p. 976, LSA). Taney had previously been married to Delphine's granddaughter Julia Forstall, who died on May 25, 1882 (Orleans Parish Deaths, vol. 80, p. 925, LSA). Paulin Blanque was interred in the tomb of the Forstall Family (Burial Book, St. Louis Cemetery no. 1, 1865–1869, September 23, 1868, p. 331).

Chapter 8. Denouement

1. Succession of Delphine Macarty, wife of Lalaurie, opened January 14, 1850, docket no. 3224, Fifth District Court, microfilm, NOPL.

2. The notary who oversaw the appraisal of Madame Lalaurie's estate was Théodore Guyol. Note that the inventory gives the total value as $256,321, but adding all of the items together produced the sum of $245,420, a difference of $10,901. Calculations of the estate's worth in today's currency and the amount received by each of the heirs from Officer and Williamson, www.measuringworth.com/ppowerus/.

3. Inventory for Marie Delphine Macarty, wife of Lalaurie, Déclarations des Muta-

tions par Décès, June 20, 1850, no. 398, series DQ7, vol. 35, p. 23, Archives de Paris. Thanks to Gisele Bourdier for discovering and copying this document.

4. Procuration par M^elles^ Blanque et Mme DeLassus a Me Blanchard, Acts of Ferdinand Leon Ducloux, December 10, 1849, Etude LVI, no. 802, Minutier Central des Notaires Parisiens, Archives Nationales, Paris. The procuration is also filed in Acts of Théodore Guyol, February 20, 1850, act 118, NARC.

5. Procuration by Pauline and Laure Blanque, Jeanne Blanque DeLassus, and Jean Louis Lalaurie in favor of Théodore Bailly Blanchard, authorizing him to emancipate the slaves Patsy and Elodie, Acts of Benjamin Labarbe, May 31, 1850, Etude LVI, no. 804, Minutier Central des Notaires Parisiens, Archives Nationales, Paris. Procuration by Paulin Blanque in favor of Théodore Bailly Blanchard, Acts of Théodore Guyol, June 21, 1850, vol. 17, act 33, NARC.

6. Funeral for Elizabeth, age eight days, natural daughter of "Paccy" [Patsy?] slave of Placide Forstall, died June 17, 1838, at the home of her master, SLC/S-FPC, vol. 11, part 1, act 295, p. 147, AANO.

7. The petition for the emancipation of Patsy and Elodie should have been made before the Judiciary Committee of the Council of the First Municipality, as was the petition in behalf of Oreste. A search of the Journal and Minutes of the Council between May 1850 and April 1852, when the record ends, shows no such petition (Emancipation Dockets, Journal and Minutes of the Council of the First Municipality, vol. 6 [1849–1850] and vol. 7 [1850–1852], microfilm, NOPL). I searched the Conveyance Office Index to Vendors from 1850 until 1855; slave manumissions should turn up in the Index to Vendors, because such acts were considered a transfer of property from the owner to the enslaved person. I also searched the indexes for notaries Adolphe Mazureau, Théodore Guyol, Achille Chiapella, and Philippe Lacoste, before whom the heirs of Madame Lalaurie enacted their property transactions.

8. Death record for Louise Marie Pauline Blanque, age 40, "died at ten o'clock in the morning in the House of Rouquette," Maire de Biarritz, Service de l'Etat Civil. The death was reported by Pierre Lariviere and Martin Doyhainle, "neighbors of the deceased."

9. Procuration in favor of Théodore Bailly Blanchard, authorizing him to oversee the succession of Pauline Blanque, Acts of Benjamin Labarbe, September 23, 1850, Minutier Central des Notaires Parisiens, Etude LVI, no. 806, Archives Nationales. Paris. Louis Barthélémy Macarty donated $5,000 to his niece Pauline Blanque in an act before the New Orleans notary Amédée Ducatel on April 7, 1838.

10. Announcement for auction of the estate of Mrs. Lalaurie by the auctioneers N. Vignie and P. E. Tricou, Bee, March 5, 1853, p. 2, col. 9; partition of property from the succession of Delphine Macarty, wife of Lalaurie, and Pauline Blanque by the heirs, Acts of Adolphe Mazureau, March 19, 1853, vol. 46, part 1, pp. 37–101, NARC.

11. Sale of lots in the Faubourg Pontchartrain by the heirs to Louis Conti for $600 and to Louis Lambert for $500, Acts of Achille Chiapella, February 10, 1852, vol. 26, acts 90 and 91. Sale of lots on Conti Street by the heirs to Garnier Fréres and to Eugène Rochereau for $25,000, Acts of Adolphe Mazureau, March 19, 1853, vol. 46, part 1, pp. 37 and 45. Sale of lots in Jefferson Parish by the heirs to Athalie Drouillard for $300, to David Barbour for $300, to Victor Fortier for $330, to Thomas Winston for $250, Mazureau,

April 27, 1853, vol. 46, part 2, pp. 91–124. Sale of lots in the 2nd District by the heirs to Francisco Mercadal for $40,950, Mazureau, July 14, 1854, vol. 49, act 59. Sale of lot in Faubourg St. Mary to Nicolas Fitzsimmons for $2,000, Acts of Philipe Lacoste, March 19, 1853, vol. 21, p. 75, all in NARC. Sale of lots in the 2nd District by Jean Louis Lalaurie to Henry Denis for $20,000, Lacoste, January 27, 1855, Conveyance Office Book 65, p. 602.

12. Jeanne Blanque et al. v. Succession of L. B. Macarty, Fifth District Court, docket no. 319, January 24, 1851, attached to Succession of Louis Barthélémy Macarty on the Opposition of Mrs. Delphine Macarty, Louisiana Supreme Court docket no. 1710, SCHA.

13. Sale of the property of the late Louis Barthélémy Macarty by the sheriff of Orleans Parish to John McDonogh for $41,250, Acts of Octave de Armas, May 28, 1847, vol. 40, act 122, NARC.

14. Will of John McDonogh, December 29, 1838; 1851 published edition available through "Making of America," www.quod.lib.umich.edu/cgi/t/text/pageviewer, accessed October 27, 2008.

15. Devore and Logsdon, *Crescent City Schools*, 33.

16. Sale of Macarty property from the estate of John McDonogh, Acts of Eusebe Bouny, May 10, 1859, vol. 5, acts 171–78, NARC. Some of the lots are illustrated in Plan Book 67, folio 31, "McDonogh's Property, 30 lots of Ground, Third District, Macarty's Place," between Pauline, Jeanne, and Barthelemy Streets, Dauphine and Burgundy Streets, and St. Claude, Marais, Villere, and Robertson Streets, NARC. Marais, Villere, and Robertson are beyond St. Claude, specified in the advertisement in the *Bee* on May 14, 1847, as being the back boundary of L. B. Macarty's land.

17. "The Dismemberment of the Macarty Plantation," *Daily Crescent*, August 11, 1859, p. 1, col. 4.

18. The "McCarthy" School for "colored boys and girls" first appeared in Gardner's *New Orleans Directory* in 1867 and continued to be listed in Soards' *New Orleans Directory* at 621 Pauline Street until 1926. The school also appears in Robinson's Atlas, 1883, sheet 20, square 134; Sanborn Fire Insurance Map, 1893, vol. 4, sheet 146 and 148; Sanborn Fire Insurance Map, 1896, vol. 4, sheet 348; and Sanborn Fire Insurance Map, 1909, vol. 1, sheet 34. The Sanborn Fire Insurance Map for 1937, sheet 909, shows houses facing the 3800 block of Royal and Chartres, with a large open space in the center where the school formerly stood; sheet 962 shows the new location of the Macarty School in the square bounded by North Claiborne, Caffin, North Derbigny, and Lamanche.

19. R. Coleman, *Blue Monday*, 18, 20.

20. Sale of lot by Frederic Buisson, testamentary executor of Adolphe Pichot, to Placide Forstall for $760, Acts of Andre Doriocourt, September 18, 1844, vol. 1, act 84; sale of lot by City of New Orleans from the estate of John McDonogh to Placide Forstall for $3,700, Acts of Eusebe Bouny, March 3, 1859, vol. 5, act 96; sale of lot with buildings and improvements by the succession of Delphine [Borja] Lopez, Widow of Placide Forstall, to Delphine Forstall for $12,600, Acts of Omer Villere, April 9, 1884, April 9, 1884, vol. 4, act 500; all in NARC. The description of the property is from printed notices attached to the 1884 act.

21. Headmistress Annette Pratz, RSCJ (Religieux du Sacré Coeur de Jésu), to Archbishop Antoine Blanc, August 14, November 15, and November 21, 1850, Archdiocese of

New Orleans Collection, V-5-n, Archives of the University of Notre Dame. According to the *Metropolitan Catholic Almanac and Laity's Directory* for 1851, the institution at St. Michael's had "31 religious, 120 boarders, and 10 orphans; Madame Pratz, Superior" (178). Thanks to William Kevin Cawley, Archivist and Curator of Manuscripts, University of Notre Dame, for providing copies of the letters and information on St. Michael's School, and to Jay Schexnaydre for additional information about the school.

22. The surviving children of Borja López y Ángulo and Placide Forstall were Jeanne Marie Céleste, b. 1823, married Henry A. Rathbone, a banker; Marie Louise Emma, b. 1824, married Emile DeBuys, a broker; Pauline, b. 1834, married Eugène Peychaud, a banker; Jeanne Marie Charlotte Philomène (Laure), b. 1836, married Felix Ducros, a broker; Jean Jules Anatole, b. 1838, married Rosa Gelpi; Joseph Charles Octave, b. 1840, married his cousin Louise Forstall; Marie Octavie (Adelaide), b. 1845, married Jules Lemore, a broker; Marie Jeanne Octavie Julia, b. 1846, married Robert Tanney, a clerk; and Delphine, b. 1848, never married. Information on the Forstall children comes from the sacramental registers of St. Louis Cathedral and from civil marriage and birth records.

23. Death record for Placide Forstall, March 18, 1876, Orleans Parish Deaths, vol. 65, p. 720, LSA; death record for Widow Placide Forstall, January 19, 1884, Orleans Parish Deaths, vol. 84, p. 359, LSA.

24. Interview with John Ellis, November 5, 2007, and March 16, 2008, and with Henry George "Mac" McCall, March 16, 2008. Both are descended from the Forstall-Rathbone-DeBuys line.

25. Marriage contract of Amanda Andry, daughter of Hortaire Michel Andry and Marie Louise Zoé Desforges, and Paulin Blanque, Acts of Adolphe Mazureau, December 8, 1852, vol. 44, p. 457, NARC; marriage of Amanda Andry and Paulin Blanque, December 8, 1852, SLC/WP, vol. 10, part 3, p. 534, act 43, AANO.

26. Sale of two-story brick house by the heirs of Delphine Macarty, wife of Lalaurie, to Amanda Andry, wife of Blanque, for $5,200, March 19, 1853, Acts of Adolphe Mazureau, vol. 46, p. 53, NARC.

27. Birth record for Charles Macarty Blanque, born September 11, 1853, Orleans Parish Births, vol. 14, p. 215, and for François Placide George Blanque, born May 8, 1856, Orleans Parish Births, vol. 19, p. 532, LSA.

28. Felicité Amanda Andry, wife Blanque, v. her husband, Second District Court, December 13, 1858, docket no. 14,597, microfilm, NOPL. The witnesses were Amanda Shepard, owner of the slave Charlotte whom Amanda punished; Bridget Abadie, a servant in the Blanque household; and Ann Wilson, also a servant.

29. U.S. Census for Orleans Parish 1860, Ward 5, p. 364, line 11, Paulin Blanque, age 51, no occupation, living in the household of J. L. Fabre [Ursulines Street near Rampart], along with Horton [Hortere] DeBuys, NARA microfilm publication M653, roll 418, accessed through www.ancestry.com. Death record for Paulin Blanque, September 23, 1868, Orleans Parish Deaths, vol. 43, p. 277, LSA; burial record for Paulin Blanque, interred in the Forstall family tomb, St. Louis Cemetery no. 1, Burial Book 1865–1869, p. 331, AANO.

30. Mortgage of property by Amanda Andry, separated wife of Paulin Blanque, to Henry Laquie for $1,800, Acts of Amédée Ducatel, February 20, 1866, vol. 87, p. 28;

mortgage of property by Amanda Andry, separated wife of Paulin Blanque, to Alcide Delpeuch for $3,000, Ducatel, June 27, 1867, vol. 90, p. 44, both NARC. Henry Laquie v. Amanda Andry, separated wife of Paulin Blanque, Third District Court, June 12, 1867, docket no. 23,778; A. Eimer Bader and Co. and Samuel Smith and Co. [agents for Alcide Delpeuch] v. Amanda Andry, separated wife of Paulin Blanque, Fifth District Court, March 22, 1869, second series, docket no. 396, microfilm, NOPL. Sheriff's sale to Frederick Zambelli by virtue of a writ of seizure and sale directed by the Fifth District Court, May 10, 1870, Conveyance Office Book 96, p. 684.

31. Soards' *New Orleans Directory* gave the following addresses for Amanda Blanque: 1875, 151 Gasquet; 1882, 295 North Roman; 1886, 151 St. Anthony; 1887, 367 Frenchmen; 1889, 168 Marigny; 1892, 86 Desire; 1896, 3223 Dauphine; 1897, 714 Piety; 1898, 740 St. Ferdinand. U.S. Census for Orleans Parish 1910, Precinct 8 (part), Ward 7 (part), Enumeration District 116, "Armanda" Blanque, age 70, feebleminded, Asylum of the Little Sisters of the Poor, sheet 8B, line 84, NARA microfilm publication T624, roll 521, accessed through www.ancestry.com. Death record for Charles Gabriel Blanque, age 36, died at Charity Hospital from morphine poisoning, May 29, 1900, Orleans Parish Deaths, vol. 122, p. 563; death record for Amanda Andry Blanque, died at the Asylum of the Little Sisters of the Poor, North Johnson corner of Laharpe, May 10, 1913, Orleans Parish Deaths, vol. 157, p. 777, both at LSA.

32. Procuration by Jean Louis Lalaurie to Théodore Bailly Blanchard, Acts of Théodore Guyol, March 30, 1850, vol. 15, act 229, NARC.

33. In February 1852, Jean Louis Lalaurie "of Paris" was represented by Théodore Bailly Blanchard in a sale of property by the heirs of Delphine Macarty, wife of Lalaurie (Acts of Achille Chiapella, February 10, 1852, vol. 26, acts 90 and 91, NARC). In October 1852, Blanchard appeared before the notary Théodore Guyol with instructions to destroy a will that Jean Louis had made in Paris (Acts of T. Guyol, October 1, 1852, vol. 24, act 583, NARC). Another act before Guyol, in January 1854, refers to T. B. Blanchard as the "agent of Jean Louis Lalaurie, residing in Paris, France" (payment of debt by Blanchard, agent for Jean Louis Lalaurie, to Mathieu Jules Bejac, Guyol, January 19, 1854, vol. 28, act 32, NARC).

34. U.S. Census for New Orleans 1880, Enumeration District 27, Jean L. Lalaurie, age 46, broker, boarder in the household of Anton Yoeger, baker, Exchange Alley, sheet 4, line 43, NARA microfilm publication T9, roll 460, accessed through www.ancestry.com.

35. In 1866 Jean Louis Lalaurie borrowed $2,000 from Neuville Bienvenu, and in 1871 he borrowed an additional $2,000 from William Geddes and $16,000 from Benjamin Harrison. Bienvenu v. Lalaurie, filed April 15, 1874, Sixth District Court, docket no. 6075, cites not only Lalaurie's obligation to Neuville Bienvenu (acts of A. E. Bienvenu, March 12, 1866, NARC) but also the mortgages in favor of William M. Geddes (acts of Charles Stringer, August 8, 1871, NARC) and Benjamin S. Harrison (acts of James Fahey, December 22, 1871, NARC). As security he used "three lots, with fine and substantially built four-story brick store buildings with granite pillars" on each, in the squares bounded by Decatur, Iberville, Bienville, and Clinton Streets. In 1872 Jean Louis became involved in a shady financial scheme with Victor Girodias, a state tax collector, to use tax revenues to buy stock in the Crescent City Landing and Slaughter House Company (J. Louis Lalaurie

v. C. S. Sauvinet, Sheriff, et al., filed May 5, 1873, Louisiana Supreme Court docket no. 626, SCHA; advertisement for the sheriff's auction April 11, 1872, *New Orleans Republican*, attached to Louise Alida Hacker, wife of Victor Gerodias, v. Jean Louis Lalaurie, Fifth District Court, docket no. 4084, microfilm, NOPL; sheriff's auction January 26, 1874, Conveyance Office Book 103, p. 216; sheriff's auction June 5, 1875, Conveyance Office Book 107, p. 5).

36. "Duels on the Tapis," *New Orleans Times*, April 23, 1870, p. 1, cols. 2–3; "Another Duel," *Bee*, April 24, 1870, p. 1, col. 3. Thanks to Jack Belsom for identifying the opera that was playing on the night of the "insult."

37. Tallant, *Romantic New Orleanians*, 211.

38. Death record for J. Louis Lalaurie, December 13, 1883, Orleans Parish Deaths, vol. 84, p. 92, LSA.

39. This case is listed in the index for the First District Court as docket no. 348, but it was not included in the microfilming project and the hard copy is now lost.

40. The January 15, 1888, death date for Auguste DeLassus in St. François, Missouri, is given in the "Biographical Sketch" of the DeLassus–St. Vrain Family, www.mohistory. org/files/archives_guides/DelassusCollection.pdf, accessed June 12, 2008.

41. Death record for Laure Blanque, age 68, May 1, 1881, actes de décès, series V4E, p. 484, Archives de Paris. Death record for Jeanne Louise Marie Blanque, widow of the Marquis [*sic*] Pierre Gilbert Auguste DeHault DeLassus, age 85, March 30, 1900, actes de décès, microfilm 5Mi3/2078, Archives de Paris.

42. Marriage of Marie Jeanne Louise Philomène Macarty and Henri Ferdinand Berthod, December 29, 1860, in "Paris, France & Vicinity Marriages 1710–1907," database, www.ancestry.com, citing Maurice Coutot, comp., *Etat Civil Reconstitué 1798–1860: Mariages, Naissances, Décès* (Paris: AFIDO S.A., 2006).

43. Mortgage by Mrs. Henri F. Berthod to Pierre Leblanc, Acts of Eusebe Bouny, January 20, 1874, vol. 16, act 9, NARC; Pierre Leblanc v. Louise Macarty, wife of Henri F. Berthod, Sixth District Court, October 6, 1875, docket no. 7941 NOPL; sale of property seized from Louise Macarty Berthod by Eugène Waggaman, sheriff of Orleans Parish, to Smithson H. Davis for $5,100, Conveyance Office Book 106, pp. 19–20.

44. Death record for Eulalie Mandeville, age 74, October 20, 1848, Orleans Parish Deaths, vol. 10, p. 576. Death record for Totote Destrés, age 60, September 4, 1847, Orleans Parish Deaths, vol. 10, p. 489. Death record for Magdeleine Carpentier, age 38, April 11, 1834, Orleans Parish Deaths, vol. 4, p. 121. Death record for Henriette Macarty born Prieto, age 58, May 9, 1860, Orleans Parish Deaths, vol. 20, p. 640, all at LSA. There is no Orleans Parish death record for Helöise Croy, but Gardner's *New Orleans Directory* for 1861 shows her operating a rooming house at 167 Tremé, and the 1870 census shows her living in the home of her son. There are also no Orleans Parish death records for Sophie Mousante or Céleste Perrault.

45. Boze to Ste-Gême, March 25–May 4, folder 238, pp. 5–6, Ste-Gême Papers.

46. Baptism of Benjamin Hart, born June 16, 1833, SLC/S-FPC, vol. 25, part 1, p. 29, act 87, AANO; the godparents were the child's paternal grandfather, Jacob Hart, and his maternal grandmother, Sophie Mousante. Young Benjamin died on March 18, 1836, in a house on Rampart between Hospital and Barracks (death record for Benjamin Hart,

colored, natural son of Benjamin Hart and Marie Delphine Emesie Macarty, March 18, 1836, Orleans Parish Deaths, vol. 6, p. 20, LSA). A daughter named Marie Delphine Emesie Hart was born on December 19, 1837 (birth record for Marie Delphine Emesie Hart, colored, natural daughter of Benjamin Hart and Delphine Emesie Macarty, Orleans Parish Births, vol. 6, p. 191, LSA).

47. U.S. Census for Philadelphia 1850, New Market Ward, Benjamin Hart, age 45, native of New York, no occupation; Delphina Hart, age 30, native of Louisiana; Charles, age 14; Mary D. [Marie Delphine Emesie], age 12; Joseph, age 3; Alfred, age 6 months; all at sheet 376, line 40, continued sheet 377, line 1, NARA microfilm publication M432, roll 817. U.S. Census for Philadelphia 1860, 10th Ward, Benjamin Hart, age 56, gentleman, native of New York; Delphine Hart, age 40, native of Louisiana; Laura Hart, age 7, sheet 199, line 24, NARA microfilm publication M653, roll 1160. U.S. Census for Philadelphia 1870, 3rd District, 10th Ward, Delphine Hart, age 50, music teacher, real estate valued at $7,000; Louisa [Laura] Hart, age 17; all at sheet 8, line 11, NARA microfilm publication M593, roll 1395. U.S. Census for Philadelphia 1880, "Delphrine" Hart, age 64, living in the household of her son Charles Hart, age 40, lawyer, ED 452, sheet 19, line 1, NARA microfilm publication T9, roll 1181. All census records accessed through www.ancestry.com. Between 1848 and 1851 Benjamin Hart, agent, was listed in McElroy's *Philadelphia Directory*.

48. Sophie Mousante/Macarty appeared for the last time in Michel & Co.'s *New Orleans Annual and Commercial Register* for 1846, living at 207 Ursulines Street.

49. Jean Boze wrote to Henri de Ste-Gême that CéCé's "two natural children by Macarty were very well educated in colleges in the North, a legacy that is still of great value" (March 25–May 4, folder 238, pp. 5–6, Ste-Gême Papers). Marriage notice for "Armand de Macarty of Cuba and Matilda W. Post of this city, on Tuesday, July 31st, 1849, at the Church of the Divine Unity, by the Rev. Mr. Bellows," newspaper clipping pasted into vol. II, New York Society Library, NYC Marriage Notices 1843–1856 (www.nysoclib.org/king/king2.html, accessed through www.ancestry.com). Matilda was the widow of Abraham Kintzing Post. Interestingly, although Armand was born in 1813, his New Orleans birth record was filed in 1848, just before his marriage; no race was specified, and he was stated to be the "issue of the legitimate marriage of Jean Baptiste Barthélémy Macarty and Magdeleine Carpentier" (Orleans Parish Births, vol. 10, p. 93, LSA).

50. U.S. Census for New York City 1860, Ward 21, District 2, sheet 1199, line 1, Armand de Macarty, native of Louisiana, merchant; his wife, Matilda de Macarty; daughters Henrietta and Irene Macarty, natives of Cuba; and Jeanetta Macarty, native of New York, plus three servants born in Ireland, NARA microfilm publication M653, roll 819, accessed through www.ancestry.com. Trow's *New York City Directory* for 1860–1861 lists Armand de Macarty, merchant, Macarty and Cairnes, 42 Pine Street, residence 15 E. 32nd Street. Death record for Armand de Macarthy, U.S. Census Mortality Schedules, New York, 1850–1880, line 25, Albany, New York, New York State Library microfilm, accessed through www.ancestry.com.

51. Post, *The Post Family*, 208. Irene de Macarty Clark, widow of the Honorable Lester W. Clark, supplied the section on the Macarty-Post family in Leng, *Staten Island and Its People*, 71.

52. Marriage of Drauzin Barthélémy Macarty and Louise Anne Courcelle, June 20, 1837, SLC/S-FPC, vol. 3, part 1, p. 80, act 103, AANO. Pitts and Clark's *Guide and Directory* for 1842, Drauzin B. Macarty, fancy dry goods, business at 238 Bourbon, residence Marais between Dumaine and St. Philip. U.S. Census for Orleans Parish 1870, Ward 5, "Dovisen" [Drauzin] Macarty, age 62, broker, real estate valued at $7,770 and personal estate of $300, and wife Louise, age 54, sheet 136, line 27, NARA microfilm publication M593, roll 521, accessed through www.ancestry.com. For more on Drauzin Macarty's wealth and leadership position in the free-colored community, see Toledano and Christovich, eds., *New Orleans Architecture: Faubourg Tremé and the Bayou Road*, 103–4. Burial record for D. B. Macarty, November 20, 1870, St. Louis Cemetery no. 2, Burial Book 1868–1871, p. 181, AANO. Sale of property from the estate of Drauzin Barthélémy Macarty, Acts of Eusabe Bouny, February 16, 1874, vol. 16, act 26, NARC.

53. Pitts and Clark's *Guide and Directory* for 1842, Eugène Macarty Jr., exchange broker. There are many entries in the Conveyance Office Index to Purchasers and Vendors for Pierre Villarceaux and Théodule Macarty.

54. Patricio Macarty's occupation is known from the later lawsuit by his father's white family, who claimed that they had been defrauded of the estate of Augustin Macarty (Marie L. Badillo and Sylvester Chauvin v. Francisco Tio, January 20, 1851, Louisiana Supreme Court docket no. 1745, SCHA).

55. U.S. Census for Orleans Parish 1850, 1st ward, Eug. V. Macarty, age 22, musician; his mother, Helöise Croy, age 56, native of S^{to} Domingo, sheet 12, line 28, NARA microfilm publication M432 roll 235; U.S. Census for Orleans Parish 1870, Ward 6, "Eugine" Macarthy, age 45, clerk at city hall; his wife, Rosalie [Hugon], their children Rose, Emile, and Henri, and his mother "Elouise" [Croy] Macarthy, native of S^{to} Domingo, 6th Ward, sheet 102, line 21, NARA microfilm publication M593, roll 522; U.S. Census for West Baton Rouge, 1880, V. E. McCarthy, age 54, schoolteacher, living in the household of Alex Banes, 4th Ward, sheet 3, line 21, NARA microfilm publication T9, roll 474; all census records accessed through www.ancestry.com. Announcements for performances by V. E. Macarty in *New Orleans Tribune*, September 17, 24, and 28, 1865, and "The Great Concert of the Day—Mr. V. E. Macarty," *New Orleans Tribune*, June 20, 1865. Thanks to Sonja MacCarthy, a descendant of Eugène Victor Macarty and Helöise Croy, for providing photocopies of these newspaper clippings.

56. Rousseve, *The Negro in Louisiana*, 104–8; Woodward, *The Strange Career of Jim Crow*, 67–71, 209–14; Taylor, *Louisiana Reconstructed*, 114–55, 162, 173–74, 279–96, 281–96, 437; Blassingame, *Black New Orleans*, 206–10; Logsdon and Bell, "Americanization of Black New Orleans"; Tregle, "Creoles and Americans," 171–72, 250–51; Domínguez, *White by Definition*, 27–29, 57.

57. "Social Equality—Excitement at the Opera," *Daily Crescent*, January 20, 1869, p. 1, col. 3; *Daily Crescent*, January 21, 1869, p. 1, col. 4, and p. 2, col. 2; "The McCarthy Ejection Case," *Daily Crescent*, January 28, 1869, p. 1, col. 4. Thanks to Jack Belsom and Sonja MacCarthy for calling my attention to these articles.

58. Eugène Victor Macarty v. E. Calabresi and Paul Albaiza, U.S. District Court for the Eastern District of Louisiana, 1869, docket no. 9,301, Record Group 21, National Archives, Regional Archives and Records Center, Fort Worth, Texas. This document is

worthless to the scholar; it includes no testimony and does not give the final decision of the court.

59. Desdunes, *Our People and Our History*, 83–84, 130–31 n. 6; Wyatt, "Six Composers of Nineteenth-Century New Orleans," 129–30; Sullivan, "Composers of Color in Antebellum New Orleans," 83–84, 91. City directories of the 1870s list V. E. (or E.V.) Macarty (or Macarthy) as a clerk, first at the Drainage Bureau, later at the Second Municipality Police Court.

60. Death record for Victor Eugène Macarty, June 25, 1881, Orleans Parish Deaths, vol. 79, p. 7, LSA; funeral announcement for E. V. Macarty-Croy, *Bee*, French edition, June 26, 1881, p. 1, col. 4; obituary for E. V. Macarty, *Weekly Louisianian*, July 2, 1881, p. 3, col. 2. Thanks to Sonja MacCarthy for providing these newspaper clippings and documents.

Chapter 9. The "Haunted House"

1. *Advertiser*, April 11, 1834; *Courier*, English edition, April 11, 1834; *Bee*, French edition, April 12, 1834; Boze to Ste-Gême, July 18, 1834, p. 6, folder 243, Ste-Gême Papers; Martineau, *Retrospect of Western Travel*, 267.

2. Sale of property by Placide Forstall, attorney in fact for Delphine Macarty, wife of Lalaurie, to Pierre Edouard Trastour for $14,000, Acts of Amédée Ducatel, March 24, 1837, vol. 4, act 132, p. 245; sale of property by Trastour to Charles Caffin for $14,000, Acts of Felix Grima, February 24, 1837, vol. 17, no. 578; mortgage by Charles Caffin and Claire Estelle Bello, his wife, in favor of the Consolidated Farmers Association of Louisiana, Acts of Amédée Ducatel, April 1, 1839, vol. 13, act 83, p, 245; all in NARC. Note that these sales were only for the house and service wing on the front lot.

3. Vieux Carré Survey, introductory notes for Square 50, THNOC.

4. Castellanos, *New Orleans as It Was*, 62.

5. Announcement for Franklin High School, *Courier*, January 6, 1848, p. 3, col. 2.

6. Sale of property by Charles Caffin to Amelia Zacherie Saul, wife of Horace Claiborne Cammack, for $17,000, Acts of Theodore Guyol, June 13, 1862, vol. 51, p. 253, NARC. Mrs. A. Z. Cammack, music teacher, 282 Royal Street, appeared in Gardner's *New Orleans Directory* for 1866 and 1867.

7. Notice for Palfrey and Hill, Auctioneers, *Daily Picayune*, May 28, 1867, p. 6, col. 5.

8. Sale of property by Amelia Z. Saul, Widow of Horace Cammack, to Joseph Barnes for $10,000, Acts of Amédée Ducatel, June 28, 1869, vol. 93, p. 455, NARC. "José" Barnes, a merchant of "leaf tobacco," is listed at 282 Royal Street in Edwards' *New Orleans Directory* for 1873.

9. Barthélémy Beobay v. Joseph Barnes, Sixth District Court, docket no. 4287, microfilm, NOPL; Barthélémy Beobay from sheriff's auction, April 4, 1873, Conveyance Office Book 100, p. 705. The price of $6,000 included the $4,000 owned to Beobay by Barnes, plus legal fees and $1,345 for unpaid city and state taxes and drainage assessment for 1871 and 1872. Barthélémy Beobay, butcher, Tremé Market, is listed in Soards' *New Orleans Directory* for 1874 and 1875.

10. For more on the controversy over integrated public schools, see Devore and Logsdon, *Crescent City Schools*, 64–81.

11. *New Orleans Times*: "The Color Line," December 15, 1874, p. 1, cols. 4–5; "Mixed Schools," December 16, 1974, p. 1, col. 4; "Forcible Reasoning," December 16, 1874, p. 1, col. 5; "Mixed Schools–Judge Dibble's Opinion," December 17, 1874, p. 1 col. 5; "A Promiscuous Row," December 18, 1874, p. 1, col. 5; "The Color Line in the Public Schools," December 18, 1874, p. 4, col. 1; "The Educational Problem," December 18, 1874, p. 8, col. 1; "The Regulators," December 19, 1874, p. 1, col. 4; "More of the School Trouble," December 19, 1874, p. 1, col. 5. *Daily Picayune*: "The School Imbroglio," December 16, 1874, p. 1, col. 7, and p. 2. col. 1; "The Public Schools," December 16, 1874, p. 4, cols. 2–3; "Negroes Invade the Boys' High School and Are Ejected," December 17, 1874, p. 2, col. 3; "Affray at the Keller Market—The Youthful Regulators," December 18, 1874, p. 1, col. 4; "The School Difficulty," December 19, 1874, p. 1, col. 6.

12. Cable, "Haunted House in Royal Street," 219–32.

13. Miller to Cable, "Scenes in an Old House in New Orleans" and other undated general notes, Cable Papers. The Lower Girls' High School was listed in Edwards' and Soards' city directories at Royal at the corner of Hospital between 1872 and 1877.

14. Soards' *New Orleans Directory* for 1878 shows that the name of the school was changed to the Lower Girls' Academic, and it was relocated to the Presbyterian Church opposite Washington Square in the Faubourg Marigny.

15. Cable's undated notes from his visit to the Lalaurie house, scribbled on slips of paper, are preserved in the Cable Papers.

16. Cable, "Haunted House in Royal Street," 192–99. Cable's description was repeated almost verbatim by Marie Points in her article "The Haunted House," *Daily Picayune*, March 13, 1892, p. 16, cols. 1–5.

17. *Picayune's Guide to New Orleans* (1896), p. 26; (1897), p. 20; (1900), pp. 36–37, THNOC. "A Miser's Snug Fortune," *Daily States*, February 28, 1892, p. 5, col. 1.

18. "The New Orleans Conservatory of Music—A Reception at the New Institution Last Night," *Daily Picayune*, January 11, 1883, p. 2, col. 6; Points, "The Haunted House," *Daily Picayune*, March 13, 1892.

19. Points, "The Haunted House," *Daily Picayune*, March 13, 1892.

20. Delavigne, "Haunted House of the Rue Royale," 254.

21. "New Orleans Paranormal Research Society Ghostly Gallery—The Haunted Mansion," www.neworleansghosts.com/haunted_new_orleans.htm, accessed November 30, 2005.

22. Death record for Joseph E. Vigne, age 71, February 3, 1892, Orleans Parish Deaths, vol. 101, p. 156, LSA; "A Miser's Snug Fortune," *Daily States*, February 28, 1892.

23. Sale of property by Barthelemy Beobay to Fortunato Greco for $5,800, Acts of J. R. Legier, June 16, 1893, vol. 149, p. 556, NARC. Fortunato Greco, Soards' *New Orleans Directory* for 1893.

24. "Ghosts Put to a Practical Use," *Times-Democrat*, June 4, 1893.

25. Soards' *New Orleans Directory* for 1895–1908 lists the Haunted Exchange, F. Greco, proprietor, V. Greco and F. Swan, managers, 1140 Royal corner Hospital.

26. Castellanos, *New Orleans as It Was*, 62. For more on prejudice against Italian immigrants, who were considered more akin to Negroes than to "respectable" white

people, see Gauthreaux, "An Inhospitable Land: Anti-Italian Sentiment and Violence in Louisiana, 1891-1924."

27. Delavigne, "Haunted House of the Rue Royale," 253.

28. Sale of property by Fortunato Greco to Lafayette Realty Company for $5,000, Acts of W. F. Milling, October 23, 1916, Conveyance Office Book 285, p. 472.

29. Sale of property by Lafayette Realty to Marcel Krauss [president of Krauss Brothers Lumber Company] for $8,000, Acts of R. H. Saal, May 21, 1920, Conveyance Office Book 318, p. 373; sale by Krauss to Thrift Homestead Association for $12,500, Acts of H. P. Stern, January 20, 1923, Conveyance Office Book 356, p. 513; sale by Thrift Homestead Association to Israel Jeffer [real estate agent] for $10,000, Acts of P. H. Stern, January 30, 1923, Conveyance Office Book 356, p. 513.

30. Gay, "Ghosts Quit Old Haunted Residence in Royal Street," *New Orleans States*, January 18, 1920, section 3, p. 1. Thanks to Greg Osborne for alerting me to this source.

31. Mary Len Costa, personal communications, February 4 and March 31, 2009, referring to her former coworker Ethyl Clesi, now deceased, whose family lived in the Lalaurie house.

32. Sale of property by Israel Jeffer to Warrington House, Acts of A. D. Danziger, February 16, 1923, Conveyance Office Book 356, p. 577. William J. Warrington, lunch house, 1140 Royal, Soards' *New Orleans Directory* for 1922-1923; Warrington House, Soards' directories for 1924-1942. H. Carter and B. Carter, *So Great a Good*, 178-79.

33. J. P. Coleman, "The Famous Haunted House in Royal Street," *Daily States*, November 2, 1924.

34. Richards, "Madame Lalurie Legend Just Fiction," photocopied newspaper clipping incorrectly labeled August 10, 1936, DeBuys Family Papers.

35. Sale of property by Warrington House to Grand Consistory of Louisiana for $4,950, Acts of Benjamin Wolf, April 2, 1932, Conveyance Office Book 465, p. 687. The headquarters of the Grand Consistory was at 619 Carondelet.

36. Sale of property by Grand Consistory of Louisiana to Guarantee Savings and Homestead Association for $9,000, Acts of Jerome Meunier, December 16, 1942, Conveyance Office Book 526, p. 144; sale of property by Guarantee Savings and Homestead Association to Mary H. Laycock for $5,500, Acts of Jerome Meunier, December 16, 1942, Conveyance Office Book 526, p. 144; sale of property by Catherine Mary Howell, divorced wife of Samuel G. Laycock Jr., to M. and E. de la Houssaye for $35,000, Acts of Theodore McGeiham, October 18, 1946, Conveyance Office Book 547, p. 613. The Cross Index to Streets in Soards' *New Orleans Directory* for 1942-1960 shows twenty apartments at 1140 Royal.

37. Sale of property by Malcolm L. and Roy E. de la Houssaye to Frank Occhipinti for $85,000, Acts of Anthony Occhipinti, July 24, 1964, Conveyance Office Book 660, p. 333. "New Owner to Restore Haunted House," *Times-Picayune*, August 9, 1964, Real Estate Section, p. 13, cols. 1-4. Cross Index to Streets for 1140 Royal Street, Haines' *New Orleans Directory*, 1967-1968.

38. Mortgage by Frank Occhipinti to Security Homestead Association for $140,000, Acts of Edmond Mironne, April 1, 1965, Conveyance Office Book 683, p. 366; mortgage

by Frank Occhipinti to Security Homestead Association for $152,000, Acts of Edmond Mironne, December 13, 1968, Conveyance Office Book 686, p. 662; sale of property by Frank Occhipinti to Harry Russell Albright for $230,000, Acts of Edmond Mironne, January 28, 1969, Conveyance Office Book 690, p. 57.

39. Schneider, "Sale Typifies French Quarter Values—Delphine's Old Mansion Sold," *Times-Picayune*, February 9, 1969, Real Estate section, p. 7, cols. 1–5.

40. Patrick Ahern, interview by the author April 2, 2009.

41. Plume, "Mansion with a Ghostly Reputation for Sale in Quarter for $1.9 Million," *Times-Picayune*, November 12, 1988, Real Estate section, p. 3, cols. 1–3.

42. Sale of property by Harry Russell Albright to James Monroe III through his agent and attorney in fact, Dorian Bennett of Sotheby's International Realty, for $1,700,000, September 1, 2000, Notarial Archives 2000-38154. In addition to the sale price for the house, the buyer paid an additional $500,000 for the fixtures. Transfer of ownership by James Monroe III, resident of Summit, Colorado, to his company 1140 Royal Street LLC of Denver, Colorado, July 18, 2002, Notarial Archives 2002-49778. Note that acts of sale from 1970 to the present are not housed in the NARC but in the main office of the Notarial Archives, and their system of citation differs from earlier acts.

43. Jensen, "Galatoire's Diner Recalls 'Awful Display'—Battery Suspect, Party Blasé after Retired Doctor Is Injured," *Times-Picayune*, January 06, 2005, pp. A-1 and A-11; Jordan, "Hillwood Marketing Manager Arrested in New Orleans," *Dallas Business Journal*, January 7, 2005, www.dallas.bizjournals.com/dallas/stories/2005/01/03/daily54.html; Giddens, "Hillwood Marketing Manager Charged with Battery," *Dallas Business Journal*, May 18, 2005, www.dallas.bizjournals.com/dallas/stories/2005/05/16/daily21.html; Steve Ritea, "Charges Dropped in Assault Outside Galatoire's after Settlement Arranged, *Times-Picayune*, December 19, 2006, pp. A-1 and A-6.

44. Sale of property by Regions Bank to Nicolas Cage/Hancock Park Real Estate Co. LLC for $3,450,000, December 12, 2006, Notarial Archives 2006-52582. "A Nicolas Cage New Orleans Double Whammy," *The Real Estalker*, April 20, 2009, www.realestalker. blogspot.com/2009/04/nicolas-cage-new-orleans-double-whammy.html. This article includes a humorous commentary on Cage's taste in interior decoration.

45. Tommy Williams, property manager for Nicolas Cage, interview by the author, March 24, April 2, October 31, and November 12, 2009. For unexplained reasons, Cage and his family stayed next door at 1134 Royal Street.

46. Listing for 1140 Royal Street by Dorian Bennett Sothebys International Realty, www.sothebysrealty.com/PropertyDetails, accessed December 19, 2008.

47. Judicial Sales for November 12, 2009, Paul R. Valteau Jr., Orleans Parish Civil Sheriff, no. 10, 2009-8494, Regions Bank v. Hancock Park Real Estate Company LLC, 1140 Royal Street, writ amount $5,548,260.78; Rebecca Mowbray, "Actor Nicolas Cage Can No Longer Call New Orleans Home after Property Auction," *Times-Picayune*, November 13, 2009, Real Estate section, pp. C6 and C7.

48. Sale of property by Regions Bank to Michael Whalen/WhaleNOLA LLC, for $2,100,000, July 30, 2010, Notarial Archives 2010-2174.

Conclusion

1. Grymes receipt dated June 22, 1829, attached to Delphine Macarty, wife of Lalaurie v. John R. Grymes, Parish Court, June 28, 1830, docket no. 5673.

2. *Courier*, April 10, 11, 12, 1834; *Bee*, April 11, 12, 15, 1834; *Advertiser*, April 11, 12, 14, 1834.

3. Deposition of Judge Jacques François Canonge before Judge Gallien Préval, *Bee*, April 12, 1834.

4. Boze to Ste-Gême, December 1, 1828, folder 134, pp. 8–9; Boze to Ste-Gême, July 20, 1829, folder 143, p. 10; Boze to Ste-Gême, May 31, 1832, folder 204, pp. 3–4; Boze to Ste-Gême, March 25–May 4, 1834, folder 238, p. 5–6; Boze to Ste-Gême, July 18–August 10, folder 243, p. 6; all in Ste-Gême Papers.

5. Saillard, *Les Aventures du Consul de France*, 101–3.

6. Interview with Amédée Ducatel by J.W. Guthrie, Cable Papers.

7. Gayarré's recollections were told to Grace King sometime in the late 1800s; Heidari, *To Find My Own Peace: Grace King in Her Journals*, 10.

8. Martineau, *Retrospect of Western Travel*, 263–67.

9. Bremer, *Homes of the New World*, 244.

10. Paulin Blanque, Paris, to Auguste DeLassus, New Orleans, August 15, 1842, DeLassus–St. Vrain Collection.

11. Boze to Ste-Gême, March 25–May 4, 1834, folder 238, p. 5, Ste-Gême Papers; *Advertiser*, April 14, 1834; Martineau, *Retrospect of Western Travel*, 265–66.

12. Saxon, *Fabulous New Orleans*, 202–17; Asbury, *The French Quarter*, 247–52; Delavigne, "Haunted House of the Rue Royale."

13. King gave a laudatory description of Delphine and the Macarty family in her 1921 *Creole Families of New Orleans*, 359–60, 368–82. The primary defenders of Madame Lalaurie in the 1930s and 1940s were Frost ("Was Madame Lalaurie . . . Victim of Foul Plot?" *Times-Picayune*, February 4, 1934); Arthur (*Old New Orleans*, 147); Richards ("Madame Lalurie Legend Just Fiction," photocopy incorrectly labeled *New Orleans Morning Tribune*, August 10, 1936, DeBuys Papers); and Brown ("Proof That Madame Lalaurie . . . Rests Here," *New Orleans States*, January 27, 1941). Much of their material was supplied by the wives of Rathbone DeBuys and Lawrence Richard DeBuys, descendants of Delphine Macarty Lalaurie, and by DeBuys family friend William Warrington.

14. Present-day theories and opinions come from many conversations with New Orleanians, including descendants of Madame Lalaurie, as well as scholarly and journalistic sources that have already been cited. Darkis, in his article "Madame Lalaurie of New Orleans," inclines toward the opinion that Delphine was innocent or that her deeds were not as horrific as they have been made out to be. See also Roehl, "Royal Street Mystery with No Solution," *Times-Picayune*, December 2, 1984, p. C8, cols. 1–4.

15. The habitual cruelty of Creole women to their slaves was stated in Robin, *Voyages to Louisiana*, 238–41; Stoddard, *Sketches . . . of Louisiana*, 324; Latrobe, *Impressions Respecting New Orleans*, 53; and Bremer, *Homes of the New World*, 244.

16. Martineau identified the coachman as Madame Lalaurie's spy (*Retrospect of*

Western Travel, 265), as did Cable ("The Haunted House in Royal Street," 207). Asbury first theorized that the coachman assisted Madame Lalaurie in her crimes (*The French Quarter,* 247, 250), and later writers elaborated on this idea (Loggins, *Where the Word Ends,* 28; Nash, *Look for the Woman,* 248; Benfey, *Degas in New Orleans,* 42–43).

17. Benfey, *Degas in New Orleans,* 45; Web sites *Famous Haunted Crime Scenes, New Orleans Paranormal Research Society Ghostly Gallery—The Haunted Mansion,* and *New Orleans and Its Ghosts;* Valentino, *Nightmares and Fairytales: 1140 Rue Royale.*

18. Saillard, *Les Aventures du Consul de France,* 102; Cable, "Haunted House in Royal Street," 207.

19. J. P. Coleman, "The Famous Haunted House in Royal Street," *Daily States,* November 2, 1924.

20. Paulin Blanque, Paris, to Auguste DeLassus, New Orleans, August 15, 1842, DeLassus–St. Vrain Collection.

21. Boze to Ste-Gême, December 1, 1828, folder 134, pp. 8–9, Ste-Gême Papers.

22. Interview with Amédée Ducatel by J.W. Guthrie, Cable Papers; Heidari, *To Find My Own Peace: Grace King in Her Journals,* 10.

23. Martineau, *Retrospect of Western Travel,* 264; Cable, "Haunted House in Royal Street," 206; Points, "The Haunted House," *Daily Picayune,* March 13, 1892.

24. Castellanos, *New Orleans as It Was,* 60–61.

25. Lalaurie neé Macarty, Paris, to Céleste Forstall, New Orleans, October 29, 1835, and January 12, 1835, DeBuys Family Papers. Jeanne Blanque DeLassus, Paris, to Charles DeHault DeLassus, New Orleans, July 26, 1836; Lalaurie neé Macarty, Paris, to Auguste DeLassus, New Orleans, May 31, 1842; Paulin Blanque, Paris, to Auguste DeLassus, New Orleans, June 15, 1838; Paulin Blanque, Paris, to Auguste DeLassus, New Orleans, August 15, 1842; and Pauline Blanque, Paris, to Auguste DeLassus, New Orleans, December 1, 1842, DeLassus–St. Vrain Collection.

26. Martineau, *Retrospect of Western Travel,* 263; Bremer, *Homes of the New World,* 246; Cable, "Haunted House in Royal Street," 202.

Epilogue

1. The Lalaurie mansion is referred to as the "most haunted house in America" on the Web sites *Haunted America Tours* (www.hauntedamericatours.com/lalaurie) and *Gina Lanier, Paranormal Investigator* (www.ginalanier.com/hauntedplaces.php), accessed July 28, 2009.

2. Mary Millan, Karen Jeffries, and Juliet Pazera, visit to Lalaurie mansion, April 10, 2009. Millan is a psychic and Voudou priestess who gives tours under the name "Bloody Mary." She has appeared on the *Travel Channel* and the *History Channel;* see www.bloodymarystours.com. Jeffries is a psychic, a tour guide, and owner of a guest house in the Faubourg Marigny. Pazera is a psychic who presently works at the NARC. I also thank Cari Roy, a professional psychic researcher who accompanied me to the Lalaurie mansion on March 27, 2008; Roy has appeared on the *Discovery Channel,* the *Travel Channel, Arts and Entertainment,* and the *Today Show;* see www.paranormalnew orleans.com.

BIBLIOGRAPHY

Primary Sources

Acts and Deliberations of the Cabildo, typed translation by the Works Projects Administration Louisiana Writers' Project, Louisiana Division, New Orleans Public Library.

Acts of the New Orleans notaries, Notarial Archives Research Center, New Orleans.

Acts of the Paris notaries, Minutier Central des Notaires Parisiens, Archives Nationales, Paris, France.

Acts Passed at the First Session of the First Legislature of the Territory of Orleans, begun and held on the 25th day of January in the year of our Lord one thousand eight hundred and six, and of the independence of the United States of America the thirtieth. New Orleans: Bradford and Anderson, Printers to the Territory, 1807.

Audiencia de Santo Domingo, Archivo General de Indias, microfilm, The Historic New Orleans Collection, New Orleans.

Ayrinhac, Henry Amans. *Marriage Legislation on the New Code of Canon Law.* New York: Benziger Brothers, 1919.

Barron, Bill, comp. *The Vaudreuil Papers: A Calendar and Index of the Personal and Private Records of Pierre de Rigaud de Vaudreuil, Royal Governor of the French Province of Louisiana, 1743–1753.* New Orleans: Polyanthos, 1975.

Bertin, P. M., comp. *General Index of All Successions Opened in the Parish of Orleans from the Year 1805 to the Year 1846.* New Orleans: Yeomans and Fitch, 1849.

Bossu, Jean-Bertrand. *New Travels in North America 1770–1771.* Translated, edited, and annotated by Samuel Dorris Dickinson. Natchitoches, La.: Northwestern State University Press, 1982.

Cable, George Washington, Papers, research notes, and correspondence between Cable and his assistants Dora Richards Miller and J. W. Guthrie, Special Collections, Howard-Tilton Memorial Library, Jones Hall, Tulane University, New Orleans, Louisiana.

Carter, Edwin Clarence, ed. and comp. *The Territorial Papers of the United States*, vol. 9, *Territory of Orleans, 1803–1812*. Washington, D.C.: Government Printing Office, 1940.

Christian, Marcus, Collection, Louisiana and Special Collections, Earl K. Long Library, University of New Orleans, New Orleans.

City directories: Matthew Flannery, *A Directory and Census Together with Resolutions Authorizing Same* (1805); B. Lafon, *Annuaire Louisianais* (1807, 1809); Whitney, *Directoire de la Nouvelle-Orleans* (1811); John Adem Paxton, *New Orleans Directory and Register* (1822–24); S. E. Percy & Co., *New-Orleans Directory of the City and Suburbs* (1832); Michel & Co., *New Orleans Annual and Commercial Register of the City and Suburbs* (1834, 1841, 1843, 1846); Gibson, *Guide and Directory of the Cities of New Orleans and Lafayette* (1838); Pitts and Clark, *Guide and Directory, New Orleans, Lafayette, and Gretna* (1841, 1842); Cohen, *New Orleans and Lafayette Directory, Including Algiers, Gretna, and McDonoghville* (1849–56); Mygatt, *New Orleans Directory* (1857); Charles Gardner, *New Orleans Directory* (1858–59, 1861–69); Graham's *New Orleans Directory* (1870); Edwards' *New Orleans Directory* (1871–73); Soards' *New Orleans Directory* (1874–1935); Haines' *New Orleans Directory*, 1967–1968.

Civil birth, marriage, and death records for Orleans Parish, Louisiana State Archives, Baton Rouge; marriage and death records available at Louisiana Division, New Orleans Public Library.

Civil birth, marriage, and death records for Paris, Prefecture du Department de la Seine, 2nd arrondissement de Paris, Archives de Paris, France.

Civil birth, marriage, and death records, notarial acts, wills, and successions for Villeneuve, Archives Départementales du Lot-et-Garonne, Agen, France.

Civil Code of the State of Louisiana. New Orleans: J. C. de St. Rome, 1825.

Conrad, Glenn R., ed. *First Families of Louisiana*. Vol 1. Baton Rouge: Claitors, 1970.

Conveyance Office Index to Purchasers and Vendors and Conveyance Office Books, Conveyance Office, New Orleans.

Cruzat, Heloise, trans. "Index to the Records of the Superior Council." *Louisiana Historical Quarterly* 12, no. 1 (1929): 143–44.

DeBuys Family Papers, Special Collections, Howard-Tilton Memorial Library, Jones Hall, Tulane University, New Orleans.

Decennial Censuses of the United States, population schedules 1830–1930. National Archives and Records Administration microfilm publications.

DeLassus–St. Vrain Collection, Missouri History Museum, St. Louis, Missouri.

De Laussat, Pierre Clément. *Memoirs of My Life, to My Son during the Years 1803 and After, Which I Spent in Public Service in Louisiana as Commissioner of the French Government for the Retrocession of That Colony and for Its Transfer to the United States*. Translated with an introduction by Agnes-Josephine Pastwa. Baton Rouge: Louisiana State University Press, 1978.

Digest of the Civil Laws Now in Force in the Territory of Orleans with Alterations and Amendments Adapted to Its Present System of Government. New Orleans: Bradford and Anderson, Printers to the Territory, 1808.

Forsyth, Alice Daly, ed. and trans. *Louisiana Marriages: A Collection of Marriage Records in New Orleans during the Spanish Regime and Early American Period 1784–1806*. New Orleans: Polyanthus, 1977.

Forsyth, Alice Daly, and Ghislaine Pleasonton, eds. and trans. *Louisiana Marriage Contracts: A Compilation of Abstracts from Records of the Superior Council of Louisiana during the French Regime, 1728–1769*. New Orleans: Polyanthos, 1980.

Hall, Gwendolyn Midlo, ed. *Databases for the Study of Afro-Louisiana History and Genealogy, 1699–1860*. (Includes *Louisiana Slave Database*.) CD-ROM. Baton Rouge: Louisiana State University Press, 2000.

Hill, Roscoe R. *Descriptive Catalogue of the Documents Relating to the History of the United States in the Papeles Procedentes de Cuba Deposited in the Archivo General de Indias at Seville*. Washington, D.C.: Carnegie Institution, 1916.

Libro Primero de Confirmaciones de esta Parroquia de San Luis de la Neuva Orleans, 1789–1841 [First Book of Confirmations of the Parish of Saint Louis of New Orleans, 1789–1841]. New Orleans: Genealogical Research Society, 1967.

Lislet, Louis Moreau. *Digeste General des Acts de la Legislature de la Louisiane*. Vol. 1. New Orleans: Benjamin Levy, 1828.

Nolan, Charles E., ed. *Sacramental Records of the Roman Catholic Church of the Archdiocese of New Orleans*. Vols. 1–18. New Orleans: Archives of the Archdiocese of New Orleans, 1987–2006.

Papeles Procedentes de Cuba, Archivo General de Indias, microfilm, The Historic New Orleans Collection, New Orleans, Louisiana; photostats, Manuscript Division, Library of Congress, Washington, D.C.

Peters, Richard, ed. *Public Statutes at Large of the United States of America*. Vol. 2. Boston: Charles C. Little and James Brown, 1845.

Pontalba Letters, typed translation by the Works Projects Administration Louisiana Writers' Project, Louisiana State Museum Historical Center, New Orleans.

Records of the French Superior Council and Judicial Records of the Spanish Cabildo, Louisiana State Museum History Center, New Orleans, Louisiana, available on microfilm at the Historic New Orleans Collection.

Records of the Parish Court, Court of Probates, First Judicial District Court, Second District Court, Third District Court, Fourth District Court, Fifth District Court, Sixth District Court, Criminal Court of the First District, Orleans Parish, City Archives, Louisiana Division, New Orleans Public Library.

Rowland, Dunbar, ed. *Official Letter Books of W. C. C. Claiborne, 1801–1816*. 6 vols. 1917. Reprint, New York: AMC Press, 1972.

Sacramental Registers of the Roman Catholic Archdiocese of New Orleans, Archives of the Archdiocese of New Orleans.

Saillard, Armand. *Les Aventures du Consul de France de New Orleans à Carthagene*. Edited by Max Dorian and Dixie Reynolds. Archives d'une vieille maison rochelaise series. La Rochelle, France: Editions Navarre, 1981.

Ste-Gême Family Papers, microfilm, The Historic New Orleans Collection, New Orleans.

Supreme Court of Louisiana. *Annual Reports of Cases Argued and Determined in the Supreme Court of Louisiana*. Vol. 3. St. Paul, Minn.: West Publishing Co., 1848.

Supreme Court of Louisiana Historical Archives, Collection 106, New Orleans 1846–1861, Louisiana and Special Collections, Earl K. Long Library, University of New Orleans, New Orleans.

Vieux Carré Survey, The Historic New Orleans Collection, New Orleans.

Voorhies, Jacqueline K., ed. *Some Late Eighteenth-Century Louisianians, Census Records, 1758–1796.* Lafayette: University of Southwestern Louisiana History Series, 1973.

Newspaper Articles

Daily National Intelligencer (Washington, D.C.)

"Shocking Brutality." April 29, 1834, p. 3, col. 4.

Dallas Business Journal

Jordan, Jaime S. "Hillwood Marketing Manager Arrested in New Orleans." January 7, 2005, http://dallas.bizjournals.com/dallas/stories/2005/01/03/daily54.html.

Giddens, David. "Hillwood Marketing Manager Charged with Battery." May 16, 2005, http://dallas.bizjournals.com/dallas/stories/2005/05/16/daily21.html.

Louisiana Advertiser

"A fire broke out this morning . . ." (reprint from the *Courier*). April 11, 1834.

"The mob assembled again . . ." April 14, 1834.

Louisiana Courier

"Ship *Fanny*, Bordeaux, Cargo and Recipients." February 17, 1825.

"To the Editor" (from Dr. Lalaurie). March 19, 1825.

"Notice" (from Dr. Lalaurie). May 23, 1832.

"A fire broke out this morning . . ." April 10, 1834.

"Application of the Lynch Law." April 11, 1834.

"Franklin High School." January 6, 1848.

New Orleans Bee

"The negro-wench named Phoebe . . ." June 20, 1829.

"The conflagration at the house . . ." April 11, 1834.

"The popular fury . . ." April 12, 1834.

"Authentic Particulars" (testimony of Judge Canonge before Judge Préval). April 12, 1834.

"Our contemporary is misinformed . . ." April 15, 1834.

"Judicial Sales—Estate of the late Louis Barthélémy Macarty." May 14, 1847.

"Auction of the Estate of Mrs. Lalaurie." March 5, 1853.

"Another Duel." April 24, 1870.

New Orleans Daily Crescent

"The Dismemberment of the Macarty Plantation." August 11, 1859.
"Expulsion of V. E. Macarty." January 20, 1869.

New Orleans Daily Picayune

"The School Imbroglio." December 16, 1874.
"The Public Schools." December 16, 1874.
"Negroes Invade the Boys' High School and Are Ejected." December 17, 1874.
"Affray at the Keller Market—The Youthful Regulators." December 18, 1874.
"The School Difficulty." December 19, 1874.
"The New Orleans Conservatory of Music." January 11, 1883.
Points, Marie. "The Haunted House—Its Interesting History and Strange Romance—Events in the Life of Madame Lalaurie Called to Mind—Cable's Fiction and a Few Facts." March 13, 1892.

New Orleans Daily States

"A Miser's Snug Fortune Revives Interest in the Famous Haunted House." February 28, 1892.

New Orleans States

Gay, Frances. "Ghosts Quit Old Haunted Residence in Royal Street." January 18, 1920.
Coleman, John P. "Historic New Orleans Mansions—The Famous Haunted House in Royal Street—Tragedy Led to Its Reputation." November 2, 1924.
Brown, Bob. "Proof that Madame Lalaurie, Haunted House Mistress, Rests Here—Copper Plate Bares Facts Sought by Historians—Reveals Mystery-Shrouded Woman Died in Paris, Body Brought to New Orleans." January 27, 1941.

New Orleans States-Item

"Ask A. Labas—History of the Warrington House." May 6, 1975, Lagniappe section.

New Orleans Times

"Duels on the Tapis." April 23, 1870.
"The Color Line." December 15, 1874.
"Mixed Schools." December 16, 1874.
"Forcible Reasoning." December 16, 1874.
"Mixed Schools—Judge Dibble's Opinion." December 17, 1874.
"A Promiscuous Row." December 18, 1874.
"The Color Line in the Public Schools." December 18, 1874.
"The Educational Problem." December 18, 1874.
"The Regulators." December 19, 1874.
"More of the School Trouble." December 19, 1874.

New Orleans Times-Democrat

"Ghosts Put to a Practical Use—New Owner of the Haunted House Charges to See It."
June 4, 1893.

New Orleans Times-Picayune

Frost, Meigs. "Was Madame Lalaurie of Haunted House Victim of Foul Plot?" February
4, 1934.

"Epitaph-Plate of 'Haunted' House Owner Found Here—Marble Cutter's Discovery
Starts New Talk of Madame Lalaurie." January 28, 1941.

"Last Rites Set for Dr. DeBuys—N.O. Pediatrician Dies of Heart Attack at Home." June
21, 1957.

"N.O. Architect Taken by Death—DeBuys Funeral Will Be Conducted Today." June 28,
1960.

"New Owner to Restore Haunted House." August 9, 1964.

Schneider, Frank. "Sale Typifies French Quarter Values—Delphine's Old Mansion Sold."
February 9, 1969.

Pitts, Stella. "New Paint, Old Stories Stir Interest in 'Haunted House.'" August 11, 1974.

Plume, Janet. "Mansion with a Ghostly Reputation for Sale in Quarter for $1.9 Million."
November 12, 1988.

Roehl, Marjorie. "Royal Street Mystery with No Solution." December 2, 1984.

———. "Paul Tulane Remained a Mystery to the End." January 29, 1989.

Jensen, Lynne. "Galatoire's Diner Recalls 'Awful Display'—Battery Suspect, Party Blasé
after Retired Doctor Is Injured." January 6, 2005.

Ritea, Steve. "Charges Dropped in Assault Outside Galatoire's after Settlement Arranged." December 18, 2006.

Mowbray, Rebecca. "Actor Nicolas Cage Can No Longer Call New Orleans Home after
Property Auction." November 13, 2009.

New York Times

"A Beauty of Former Days." August 11, 1881.

Niles Weekly Register (Baltimore)

"A Horrible Affair." May 3, 1834.

St. Tammany Farmer

"The New Hotel at Claiborne-Covington." February 19, 1890.

Weekly Louisianian

Obituary for E. V. Macarty, July 2, 1881.

Secondary Sources

Alexander, Elizabeth Urban. *Notorious Woman: The Celebrated Case of Myra Clark Gaines.* Baton Rouge: Louisiana State University Press, 2001.

Arthur, Stanley C. *Old Families of Louisiana.* 1831. Reprint, Gretna, La.: Pelican, 1998.

———. *Old New Orleans: A History of the Vieux Carré, Its Ancient and Historical Buildings.* New Orleans: Harmanson, 1936.

Asbury, Herbert. *The French Quarter: An Informal History of the New Orleans Underworld.* 1936. Reprint, New York: Garden City Publishing, 1938.

Baily, John. *The Lost German Slave Girl: The Extraordinary True Story of Sally Miller and Her Fight for Freedom in Old New Orleans.* New York: Grove Press, 2003.

Belsom, Jack. *Celebrating 200 Years of Opera in New Orleans.* New Orleans: Jack Belsom, 1998.

Benfey, Christopher. *Degas in New Orleans: Encounters in the Creole World of Kate Chopin and George Washington Cable.* Berkeley: University of California Press, 1997.

Bigg, Henry Heather. *Orthopraxy: The Mechanical Treatment of Deformities, Debilities, and Deficiencies of the Human Frame.* London: John Churchill and Sons, 1865.

Biographical and Historical Memoirs of Louisiana. 2 vols. Chicago: Goodspeed, 1892.

Blassingame, John. *Black New Orleans, 1860–1880.* Chicago: University of Chicago Press, 1973.

Bradley, Lloyd. *The Book of Secrets.* Kansas City: Andrews McMeel, 2005.

Brasseaux, Carl. *The "Foreign French": Nineteenth-Century French Immigration into Louisiana*, vol. 1, *1820–1839.* Lafayette: Center for Louisiana Studies, University of Southwestern Louisiana, 1990.

Brasseaux, Carl, and Glenn Conrad, eds. *Road to Louisiana: The Saint-Domingue Refugees, 1792–1809.* Lafayette: Center for Louisiana Studies, University of Southwestern Louisiana, 1992.

Bremer, Fredrika. *Homes of the New World: Impressions of America.* Vol. 2. New York: Harper and Bros., 1853.

Bryant, William Cullen, II, and Thomas G. Voss, eds. *The Letters of William Cullen Bryant*, vol. 1, *1809–1836.* New York: Fordham University Press, 1992.

Cable, George Washington. *The Creoles of Louisiana.* 1884. Reprint, Gretna, La.: Pelican, 2000.

———. "The Haunted House in Royal Street." In *Strange True Stories of Louisiana*, 192–232. 1889. Reprint, Gretna, La.: Pelican, 1994.

Carter, Hodding, and Betty Werlein Carter. *So Great a Good: A History of the Episcopal Church in Louisiana and of Christ Church Cathedral, 1805–1955.* Sewanee, Tennessee: University Press, 1955.

Castellanos, Henry C. *New Orleans as It Was: Episodes of Louisiana Life.* 1895. Reprint, Gretna, La.: Pelican, 1990.

Clapp, Theodore. *Autobiographical Sketches and Recollections during a Thirty-five Years' Residence in New Orleans.* 1857. Reprint, Freeport, N.Y.: Books for Libraries Press, 1972.

Coleman, Rick. *Blue Monday: Fats Domino and the Lost Dawn of Rock'n'Roll.* Cambridge, Mass.: Da Capo, 2006.

Darkis, Fred R. "Madame Lalaurie of New Orleans." *Louisiana History* 23 (Fall 1982): 383–99.

Davis, William C. *The Pirates Laffite: The Treacherous World of the Corsairs of the Gulf.* New York: Harcourt, 2005.

Debien, Gabriel, and René Le Gardeur. "The Saint-Domingue Refugees in Louisiana." In *Road to Louisiana: The Saint-Domingue Refugees 1792–1809,* ed. Carl Brasseaux and Glenn Conrad, 113-243. Lafayette: Center for Louisiana Studies, University of Southwestern Louisiana, 1992.

Delavigne, Jeanne. "The Haunted House of the of the Rue Royale." In *Ghost Stories of Old New Orleans,*248–58. New York: Rinehart, 1946.

Desdunes, Rodolphe Lucien. *Nos Hommes et Notre Histoire.* 1911. Translated by Dorothea Olga McCants as *Our People and Our History.* Baton Rouge: Louisiana State University Press, 1973.

Dessens, Nathalie. "De Jean Boze á Henri de Ste Gême, La Nouvelle Orléans, 1818–1839." http://www.ehess.fr/cena/colloques/2006/lettres/dessens-texte.pdf.

Devore, Donald, and Joseph Logsdon. *Crescent City Schools: Public Education in New Orleans 1841–1991.* Lafayette: Center for Louisiana Studies and Orleans Parish Schools, 1991.

Deyle, Steven. *Carry Me Back: The Domestic Slave Trade in American Life.* New York: Oxford University Press, 2005.

Din, Gilbert C. *Spaniards, Planters, and Slaves: The Spanish Regulation of Slavery in Louisiana 1763–1803.* College Station: Texas A&M University Press, 1999.

Din, Gilbert C., and John E. Harkins. *The New Orleans Cabildo: Colonial Louisiana's First City Government 1769–1803.* Baton Rouge: Louisiana State University Press, 1996.

Domínguez, Virginia. *White by Definition: Social Classification in Creole Louisiana.* New Brunswick, N.J.: Rutgers University Press, 1997.

Dormon, James H. Jr. "The Persistent Specter: Slave Rebellion in Territorial Louisiana." In *The African American Experience in Louisiana: From Africa to the Civil War,* ed. Charles Vincent, 285-97. Lafayette: Center for Louisiana Studies, 1999.

Duffy, John, ed. *The Rudolph Matas History of Medicine in Louisiana.* 2 vols. Baton Rouge: Louisiana State University Press, 1958.

Early, Eleanor. *New Orleans Holiday.* New York: Rinehart, 1947.

Ebeyer, Pierre Paul. *Paramours of the Creoles: A Story of New Orleans and the Method of Promiscuous Mating between White Creole Men and Negro and Colored Slaves and Freewomen.* New Orleans: Windmill, 1944.

Faye, Stanley. "Louis de Clouet's Memorial to the Spanish Government, December 7, 1814." *Louisiana Historical Quarterly* 22 (July 1939): 795–818.

Fick, Carolyn E. *The Making of Haiti: The Saint Domingue Revolution from Below.* Knoxville: University of Tennessee Press, 1990.

Floyd, E. Randall, comp. *More Great Southern Mysteries.* 1990. Reprint, New York: Barnes and Noble, 2000.

Fortier, Alcée, ed. *Louisiana: Comprising Sketches of Parishes, Towns, Events, Institutions, and Persons Arranged in Cyclopedic Form.* Vol. 1. Madison, Wisc.: Century Historical Association, 1914.

French, Benjamin Franklin. *Historical Memoirs of Louisiana, from the First Settlement of the Colony to the Departure of Governor O'Reilly in 1770.* New York: Blakeman and Law, 1853.

Gauthreaux, Alan. "An Inhospitable Land: Anti-Italian Sentiment and Violence in Louisiana, 1891–1924." *Louisiana History* 51 (Winter 2010): 41–68.

Gayarré, Charles Etienne Arthur. "Barthélémy de Macarty's Revenge." *Harper's New Monthly Magazine*, January 1890, 278–82.

———. *The Creoles of History and the Creoles of Romance: A Lecture Delivered in the Hall of the Tulane University, New Orleans, by Hon. Charles Gayarré, on the 25th of April, 1885.* New Orleans: C. E. Hopkins, 1885.

———. *History of Louisiana: The American Domination.* 1866. Reprint, Ann Arbor: University of Michigan Scholarly Publishing Office, 2006.

———. *Louisiana: Its Colonial History and Romance.* Vol. 1. New York: Harper, 1852.

———. "The New Orleans Bench and Bar in 1823." In *An Uncommon Experience: Law and Judicial Institutions in Louisiana 1803–2003*, ed. Warren Billings and Judith K. Schafer, 643–56. Lafayette: Center for Louisiana Studies, 1997.

Gehman, Mary. "Madame Lalaurie: Fantasy of the Haunted House." In *Women and New Orleans*, 35–38. New Orleans: Margaret Media, 2005.

———. "Visible Means of Support: Business, Professions, and Trades of Free People of Color." In *Creole: The History and Legacy of Louisiana's Free People of Color*, ed. Sybil Kein, 208–22. Baton Rouge: Louisiana State University Press, 2000.

Godwin, Parke. *A Biography of William Cullen Bryant, with Extracts from his Private Correspondence.* Vol. 1. New York: D. Appleton and Company, 1883.

Gordon, Christopher. "Finding Madame Lalaurie." *Le Journal*, Fall 2006, 6–11.

Gould, Virginia Meacham. "In Full Enjoyment of Their Liberty: The Free Women of Color of the Gulf Ports of New Orleans, Mobile, and Pensacola, 1769–1860." Ph.D. diss., Emory University, 1991.

Greene, Glen Lee. *Masonry in Louisiana: A Sesquicentennial History, 1812–1962.* New York: Exposition Press, 1962.

Hall, Gwendolyn Midlo. *Africans in Colonial Louisiana: The Development of Afro-Creole Culture in the Eighteenth Century.* Baton Rouge: Louisiana State University Press, 1992.

———. "The Franco-African Peoples of Haiti and Louisiana: Population, Language, Culture, Religion, and Revolution." In *Revolutionary Freedoms: A History of Survival, Strength, and Imagination in Haiti*, ed. Cécile Accilien, 41–47. Coconut Creek, Fla.: Caribbean Studies Press, 2006.

Hambly, Barbara. *Fever Season.* New York: Bantam, 1998.

Harwood, Thomas F. "The Abolitionist Image of Louisiana and Mississippi." *Louisiana History* 7 (1966): 281–308.

Heard, Malcolm. *French Quarter Manual: An Architectural Guide to New Orleans' Vieux Carré.* Jackson: University Press of Mississippi, 1997.

Heidari, Melissa Walker, ed. *To Find My Own Peace: Grace King in Her Journals, 1886–1910*. Athens: University of Georgia Press, 2004.

Hirsch, Arnold, and Joseph Logsdon, eds., *Creole New Orleans: Race and Americanization*. Baton Rouge: Louisiana State University Press, 1992.

Holmes, Jack D. L. "Do It! Don't Do It! Spanish Laws on Sex and Marriage." In *Louisiana's Legal Heritage*, ed. Edward Haas, 19–42. New Orleans: Louisiana State Museum, 1983.

———. *Gayoso: The Life of a Spanish Governor in the Mississippi Valley*. Gloucester, Mass.: Peter Smith, 1968.

Ingersoll, Thomas N. "Free Blacks in a Slave Society: New Orleans 1718–1812." In *The African American Experience in Louisiana: From Africa to the Civil War*, ed. Charles Vincent, 154–80. Lafayette: Center for Louisiana Studies, 1999.

———. *Mammon and Manon in Early New Orleans: The First Slave Society in the Deep South, 1718–1819*. Knoxville: University of Tennessee Press, 1999.

———. "Slave Codes and Judicial Practice in New Orleans, 1718–1807." *Law and History Review* 13, no. 1 (1995): 23–62.

James, C. L. R. *The Black Jacobins: Toussaint L'Ouverture and the San Domingo Revolution*. 1938. Reprint, New York: Vintage Books, 1989.

Johnson, Jerah. "Colonial New Orleans: A Fragment of the Eighteenth-Century French Ethos." In *Creole New Orleans: Race and Americanization*, ed. Arnold Hirsch and Joseph Logsdon, 12–57. Baton Rouge: Louisiana State University Press, 1992.

Kendall, John S. *History of New Orleans*. Chicago: Lewis, 1922.

———. "Old New Orleans Houses." *Louisiana Historical Quarterly* 17 (1934): 680–85.

———. "Shadow over the City." *Louisiana Historical Quarterly* 22 (1939): 142–65.

King, Grace. *Creole Families of New Orleans*. New York: Macmillan, 1921.

———. *New Orleans, the Place and the People*. New York: Macmillan, 1895.

King, Grace, and John Rose Ficklen. *A History of Louisiana*. New Orleans: L. Graham, 1905.

Lachance, Paul. "The 1809 Immigration of Saint-Domingue Refugees." In *Road to Louisiana: The Saint-Domingue Refugees 1792–1809*, ed. Carl Brasseaux and Glenn Conrad, 165–80. Lafayette: Center for Louisiana Studies, University of Southwestern Louisiana, 1992.

———. "The 1809 Immigration of Saint-Domingue Refugees to New Orleans: Reception, Integration, and Impact." *Louisiana History* 29 (Spring 1988): 110–42.

———. "The Foreign French." In *Creole New Orleans: Race and Americanization*, ed. Arnold Hirsch and Joseph Logsdon, 103–30. Baton Rouge: Louisiana State University Press, 1992.

———. "The Politics of Fear: French Louisianians and the Slave Trade, 1706–1809." In *The African American Experience in Louisiana: From Africa to the Civil War*, ed. Charles Vincent, 123–53. Lafayette: Center for Louisiana Studies, 1999.

Latour, Arsène Lacarrière. *Historical Memoir of the War in West Florida and Louisiana in 1814–1815*. Philadelphia: John Conrad and Co., 1816.

Latrobe, Benjamin Henry Boneval. *Impressions Respecting New Orleans, Diary and Sketches 1818–1820*. Ed. Samuel Wilson Jr. New York: Columbia University Press, 1951.

Lawrence, John. "Picture Perfect: The New Orleans of Pierre Clément Laussat, 1803–4." *Louisiana Cultural Vistas* (Summer 2003): 42–45.

Lea, Henry Charles. *A History of the Inquisition in Spain.* New York: Macmillan, 1906.

Leglaunec, Jean-Pierre. "Slave Migrations in Spanish and Early American Louisiana: New Sources and New Estimates" and "A Directory of Ships with Slave Cargoes, Louisiana, 1772–1808." *Louisiana History* 66, no. 2 (2005): 185–209.

Lemmon, Alfred E., John T. Magill, Jason Weiss, and John R. Hébert, eds. *Charting Louisiana: Five Hundred Years of Maps.* New Orleans: Historic New Orleans Collection, 2003.

Leng, Charles William. *Staten Island and Its People: A History, 1609–1929.* New York: Lewis Historical Publishing Co., 1930.

Loggins, Vernon. *Where the Word Ends: The Life of Louis Moreau Gottschalk.* Baton Rouge: Louisiana State University Press, 1958.

Logsdon, Joseph, and Caryn Cossé Bell, "The Americanization of Black New Orleans, 1850–1900." In *Creole New Orleans: Race and Americanization*, ed. Arnold Hirsch and Joseph Logsdon, 201–261. Baton Rouge: Louisiana State University Press, 1992.

Love, Victoria Cosner, and Lorelei Shannon. *Mad Madame Lalaurie: New Orleans' Most Famous Murderess Revealed.* Charleston: History Press, 2011.

Martin, François Xavier. *History of Louisiana, from the Earliest Period.* 1827. Reprint, New Orleans: Pelican, 1963.

Martineau, Harriet. *Retrospect of Western Travel.* Vol. 1. London: Saunders and Otley, 1838.

Morlas, Katy Frances. "La Madame et la Mademoiselle: Creole Women in Louisiana 1718–1865." Master's thesis, Department of History, Louisiana State University, 2005.

Nash, Jay Robert. *Look for the Woman: A Narrative Encyclopedia of Female Poisoners, Kidnappers, Thieves, Extortionists, Terrorists, Swindlers, and Spies, from Elizabethan Times to the Present.* New York: M. Evans, 1981.

Navard, Andrew Jackson ("Andre Cajun"). *Stories of New Orleans.* New Orleans: Cajun Publishing, 1945.

Officer, Lawrence H., and Samuel H. Williamson. "Purchasing Power of Money in the United States from 1774 to 2007." http://www.measuringworth.com/ppowerus.

Palmer, Vernon V. "The Origins and Authors of the *Code Noir.*" In *An Uncommon Experience: Law and Judicial Institutions in Louisiana 1803–2003*, ed. Warren M. Billings and Judith K. Schafer, 331–59. Lafayette: Center for Louisiana Studies, 1997.

Paquette, Robert L. "'A Horde of Brigands?' The Great Louisiana Slave Revolt of 1811 Reconsidered." *Historical Reflections* 35, no. 1 (2009): 72–96.

———. "Slave Insurrection of 1811." In *KnowLA Encyclopedia of Louisiana*, ed. Joyce Miller. Louisiana Endowment for the Humanities. http://www.knowla.org.

Phillips, Faye. "Writing Louisiana Colonial History in the Mid-Nineteenth Century: Charles Gayarré, Benjamin Franklin French, and the Louisiana Historical Society." *Louisiana History* 49 (Spring 2008): 163–90.

Picayune's Guide to New Orleans. New Orleans: The Picayune, 1896, 1897, 1900.

Porteous, Laura. "Torture in Spanish Criminal Proceedings." *Louisiana Historical Quarterly* 8 (January 1925): 6–22.

Post, Marie Caroline de Trobriand. *The Post Family.* New York: Sterling Potter, 1905.

Rasmussen, Daniel. *American Uprising: The Untold Story of America's Largest Slave Revolt.* New York: HarperCollins, 2011.

Reeves, Sally K. "Cruising Contractual Waters: Searching for Laffite in the Records of the New Orleans Notarial Archives." *Provenance* 16 (1998): 1–21.

Robertson, James Alexander, ed., *Louisiana under the Rule of Spain, France, and the United States, 1785–1807,* 2 vols. 1910. Reprint, Freeport, N.Y.: Books for Libraries Press, 1969.

Robin, Claude-Cézar. *Voyages dans l'interieur de la Louisiane, de la Floride Occidentale, et dans les Isles de las Martinique et de Saint-Domingue, 1802–1806.* 1807. Translated as *Voyages to Louisiana* by Stuart Landry. Gretna, La.: Pelican, 2000.

Rousssève, Charles Barthélémy. *The Negro in Louisiana: Aspects of His History and His Literature.* New Orleans: Xavier University Press, 1937.

Russell, Liz. "Cast Iron and New Orleans." *Preservation in Print* 37 (February 2010): 10–11.

Savitt, Todd L. "The Use of Blacks for Medical Experimentation and Demonstration in the Old South." *Journal of Southern History* 48, no. 3 (1982): 331–48.

Saxon, Lyle. *Fabulous New Orleans.* 1928. Reprint, Gretna, La.: Pelican, 1988.

———. "The Haunted House of Old New Orleans." *Southern Architectural Review* 1, no. 1 (1936): 13–15, 20.

Schafer, Judith Kelleher. *Brothels, Depravity, and Abandoned Women: Illegal Sex in Antebellum New Orleans.* Baton Rouge: Louisiana State University Press, 2009.

———. *Slavery, the Civil Law, and the Supreme Court of Louisiana.* Baton Rouge: Louisiana State University Press, 1994.

"Secret and Benevolent Associations." In *Biographical and Historical Memoirs of Louisiana,* 2:170–78. Chicago: Goodspeed, 1892.

Seebold, Herman De Bachellé. *Old Louisiana Plantation Homes and Family Trees.* Vol. 2. New Orleans: Pelican, 1941.

Silliman, Benjamin, ed. *Statistics of the Class of 1837, with a Notice of Their Meeting Held at Yale College, August 19, 1847.* New Haven, Conn.: Byington & Adams, 1847.

Souvestre, L. *Le Courrier des États-Unis,* December 8, 1838. Reprinted as "Madame Lalaurie: A Contemporary French Account." Translated by Harriet Molenaer. *Louisiana Studies* 7 (Winter 1968): 378–90.

Sparks, William Henry. *Memories of Fifty Years, Containing Brief Biographical Notes of Distinguished Americans and Anecdotes of Remarkable Men.* Philadelphia: Claxton, Remsen & Haffelfinger, 1870.

Stanley, George F. G. *New France: The Last Phase, 1744–1760.* Toronto: McClelland and Stewart, 1968.

Starr, S. Frederick. *Bamboula: The Life and Times of Louis Moreau Gottschalk.* New York: Oxford University Press, 1995.

Stoddard, Amos. *Sketches, Historical and Descriptive, of Louisiana.* Philadelphia: Matthew Carey, 1812.

Stone, Ferdinand. "The Law with a Difference and How It Came About." In *An Uncommon Experience: Law and Judicial Institutions in Louisiana 1803–2003,* ed. Warren M. Billings and Judith K. Schafer, 20–38. Lafayette: Center for Louisiana Studies, 1997.

Sublette, Ned. *The World That Made New Orleans: From Spanish Silver to Congo Square.* Chicago: Lawrence Hill Books, 2008.

Sullivan, Lester. "Composers of Color in Antebellum New Orleans: The History Behind the Music." In *Creole: The History and Legacy of Louisiana's Free People of Color,* ed. Sybil Kein, 71–100. Baton Rouge: Louisiana State University Press, 2000.

Tallant, Robert. *The Romantic New Orleanians.* New York: Dutton, 1950.

Taylor, Joe Gray. *Louisiana Reconstructed, 1863–1877.* Baton Rouge: Louisiana State University Press, 1974.

Thompson, Thomas Marshall. "National Newspaper and Legislative Reactions to Louisiana's Deslondes Slave Revolt of 1811." *Louisiana History* 33 (Winter 1992): 5–29.

Thrall, Homer S. *A Pictorial History of Texas, from the Earliest Visits of European Adventurers, to A.D. 1879.* St. Louis: N. D. Thompson, 1879.

Thrasher, Albert. *On to New Orleans! Louisiana's Heroic 1811 Slave Revolt.* New Orleans: Cypress Press (Afro-American Historical Society of New Orleans), 1996.

Tinker, Edward Larocque. "Cable and the Creoles." *American Literature* 5, no. 4 (1934): 313–26.

Toledano, Roulhac, and Mary Louise Christovich, eds., *New Orleans Architecture: Faubourg Tremé and the Bayou Road.* Vol. 6. Gretna, La.: Pelican, 1980.

Toledano, Roulhac, Sally Kittredge Evans, and Mary Louise Christovich, eds. *New Orleans Architecture: The Creole Faubourgs.* Vol. 4. New Orleans: Friends of the Cabildo, 1974.

Trask, Benjamin H. *Yellow Fever in New Orleans, 1796–1905.* Lafayette: Center for Louisiana Studies, 2005.

Tregle, Joseph. "Creoles and Americans." In *Creole New Orleans: Race and Americanization,* ed. Arnold Hirsch and Joseph Logsdon, 131–85. Baton Rouge: Louisiana State University Press, 1992.

Turner, Arlin. *George W. Cable: A Biography.* Durham, N.C.: Duke University Press, 1956.

Valentino, Serena. *Nightmares and Fairytales: 1140 Rue Royale.* San Jose, Calif.: SLG Publishing, 2007.

Vella, Christina. *Intimate Enemies: The Two Worlds of the Baroness de Pontalba.* Baton Rouge: Louisiana State University Press, 1997.

Vogt, Lloyd. *Historic Buildings of the French Quarter.* Gretna, La.: Pelican, 2002.

Wallace, Joseph. *The History of Illinois and Louisiana under the French Rule, Embracing a General View of the French Dominion in North America with Some Account of the English Occupation of Illinois.* Cincinnati: Robert Clarke & Co., 1893.

Wardill, Frank H. "The Scene of the Le Breton Murder." *Louisiana Historical Quarterly* 8 (April 1925): 266–67.

Washington, Harriet A. *Medical Apartheid: The Dark History of Medical Experimentation on Black Americans from Colonial Times to the Present.* New York: Doubleday, 2006.

Whitaker, Arthur Preston. *The Mississippi Question, 1795–1803; A Study in Trade, Politics, and Diplomacy.* New York: Appleton-Century, 1934.

Whitaker, Daniel Kimball. "Some Stories of Bench and Bar." *New Orleans Monthly Review,* February 1875, 68–73.

Williams, Diana Irene. "They Call It Marriage: The Interracial Louisiana Family and the Making of American Legitimacy." Ph.D. diss., Harvard University, 2007.

Wilson, Carol. *The Two Lives of Sally Miller: A Case of Mistaken Racial Identity in Antebellum New Orleans*. New Brunswick, N.J.: Rutgers University Press, 2007.

Wilson, Mary Ann. "Grace King, New Orleans Literary Historian." In *Louisiana Women: Their Lives and Times*, ed. Janet Allured and Judith Gentry, 137–54. Athens: University of Georgia Press, 2009.

Woodward, C. Vann. *The Strange Career of Jim Crow: A Brief Account of Segregation*. New York: Oxford University Press, 1955.

WPA Louisiana Writers' Project. *Guide to New Orleans*. Boston: Houghton-Mifflin, 1938.

———. *Louisiana: A Guide to the State*. New York: Hastings House, 1941.

Wyatt, Lucius R. "Six Composers of Nineteenth-Century New Orleans." *Black Music Research Journal* 10 (Spring 1990): 125–40.

INDEX

Page numbers in italics refer to figures.

Carolyn Morrow Long began visiting New Orleans in 1978, when she became fascinated by the city's history and culture. She is the author of *Spiritual Merchants: Religion, Magic, and Commerce*, and *A New Orleans Voudou Priestess: The Legend and Reality of Marie Laveau*. Now retired from the Smithsonian Institution's Museum of American History, she devotes her time to writing articles and giving presentations about New Orleans. Also an artist, Long created the cover illustrations for *A New Orleans Voudou Priestess* and this book.